Restructuring Schools

Restructuring Schools:

An International Perspective on the Movement to Transform the Control and Performance of Schools

Edited by

H. Beare and W. Lowe Boyd

 The Falmer Press

(A member of the Taylor & Francis Group)
Washington D.C. • London

USA   The Falmer Press, Taylor & Francis Inc., 1900 Frost Road, 101, Bristol, PA 19007

UK   The Falmer Press, 4 John St., London, WC1N 2ET

First published 1993

Library of Congress Cataloging-in-Publication data are available on request

A catalogue record for this book is available from the British Library

ISBN 0 75070 121 8 cased
ISBN 0 75070 122 6 paper

Cover design by Caroline Archer

Set in 9.5/11pt Times
Graphicraft Typesetters Ltd., Hong Kong

Printed in Great Britain by Burgess Science Press, Basingstoke on paper which has a specified pH value on final paper manufacture of not less that 7.5 and is therefore 'acid free'.

Contents

Contents

Part 3: Issues in the School-reform Movement

List of Figures and Tables

List of Acronyms

ACT	Australian Capital Territory (Australia)
AERA	American Education Research Association (US)
AFT	American Federation of Teachers (US)
ASEP	Australian Science Education Project (Australia)
CEO	Chief Executive Officer (Australia, UK, US)
CPRE	Center for Policy Research in Education (US)
CSEC	Cabinet Social Equity Committee (New Zealand)
DE	Department of Employment (UK)
DES	Department of Education and Science (UK)
DOGS	Defense of Government Schools (Australia)
ECS	Education Commission of the States (US)
ESEA	Elementary and Secondary Education Act (US)
ET	Employment Training (UK)
GST	Goods and Services Tax (Canada and Australia)
IEA	Institute of Economic Affairs (UK)
LEA	Local Education Authority (UK)
LMC	Local Management of Colleges (UK)
LMS	Local Management of Schools (UK)
MSC	Manpower Services Commission (UK)
NAEP	National Assessment of Educational Progress (US)
NAFE	Non-advanced Further Education (UK)
NASSP	National Association of Secondary School Principals (Australia)
NCER	National Council of the Educational Reform (Japan)
NCVQ	National Council for Vocational Qualifications (UK)
NDEA	National Defense Education Act (US)
NEA	National Education Association (US)
NGA	National Governors Association (US)
NVQ	National Vocational Qualification (UK)
OECD	Organization for Economic Cooperation and Development
PCFC	Polytechnics and Colleges Funding Council (UK)
PSI	Policy Studies Institute (UK)
QERC	Quality of Education Review Committee (UK)
SAT	Standard Attainment Task (UK)
SES	Senior Executive Service (Australia)

SIMS	Second International Mathematics Study (Canada)
TA	Training Agency (UK)
TAFE	Technical and Further Education (Australia)
TEC	Training and Enterprise Council (UK)
TVEI	Technical and Vocational Education Initiative (UK)
TREA	Taskforce to Review Education Administration (New Zealand)
UFC	University Funding Council (UK)
UGC	University Grants Council (UK)
UGC	University Grants Committee (New Zealand)
YTS	Youth Training Scheme (UK)

Part 1

A Comparative Perspective

Chapter 1

Introduction

H. Beare and W.L. Boyd

The decade 1980–90 saw a spate of educational reconstruction occurring simultaneously in many countries around the world. Although there appear to have been multiple borrowings from each other, those involved with the reforms have not always been aware of the activity in neighbouring countries or even in neighbouring states and provinces, and certainly not of the detail. So there is a tendency for local reformers to believe that they are attempting something new, when the changes are in fact only new for them. It is therefore an opportune time to look at the commonalities emerging from the restructuring movement, if only to ensure that we learn from each other's efforts. The fact that school restructuring is an *international* trend should also excite our curiosity. What is driving this movement, why is there such a consistent concern across the globe to improve schooling outcomes and school performance, and who typically are the prime policy actors?

The school restructuring of the past ten years has been called the 'education-reform movement', but that term is somewhat misleading. School reform of one kind or another has been going on continuously for decades. We are struck by the fact, however, that the reforms of the 1980s and those proposed for the 1990s are being called 'restructuring', even though that word carries different meanings in different countries and states. Clearly, these reforms are of a particular kind. While they may affect curricula and may indeed use school programs and student performances as their justification, they do not seem to begin as curricular reforms, as was the case, for example, in the United States after Sputnik in 1957. Nor, it seems, do they begin with teachers and educators; they appear to have been imposed from outside, at least initially. Furthermore, the current efforts seem to aim primarily at the control and governance of both schools and school systems, at who makes the decisions, and especially those relating to what is taught in schools. In short, they target the management of education. Why?

To address these issues, this book[1] concentrates on the way in which schools and school systems are being reorganized, on the way they are con-figured, how their resources are allocated or deployed, how the functions are parcelled out and what kinds of people are assigned those functions. We are also concerned with who holds the purse strings, where the power points are, who controls and governs these institutions, who are pushing for the reforms and why they are doing so now. We are curious about the fact that the same obsessions seem to be surfacing almost simultaneously in several countries across the world, and that education has become 'high politics' (to use the term coined by Koppich and Guthrie in Chapter 2). It is big on the political agenda in many countries. There are quite different manifestations of these concerns; they lead to an array of reform strategies, and they have developed different answers to what are perceived as the problems. But why is it that so many people in so many countries have woken up this morning with the same stomach pains? Is there a common epidemic abroad? What are the experts and policy makers prescribing as antidotes to heal the pains? And do the medicines contain similar chemicals?

We have chosen six countries (the United States of America, the United Kingdom, Canada, New Zealand, Australia, and Japan) to provide us with the tangible evidence with which to make comparisons and from which to generalize. We could of course have chosen other countries, but these six provide us with a rich texture of parallels and contrasts. Four of them are federations and therefore supply us with the conflicts of national and state or provincial interests. Canada, New Zealand, and Australia were colonies of Great Britain and their schooling patterns were derived from those in the mother country; in the same way, the post-war Japanese system derives a great deal from the United States. So it will be evident that each of the six countries looks over the shoulder, as it were, to check what is happening in the other five, and that the UK and US patterns are likely to be pace-setters. The set also represents European, North American, and Asian/Pacific orientations; all six are 'developed' economies. Indeed, economic and political interactions abound among the six, but above everything else, all of them have experienced the infatuation with educational reform throughout the 1980s.

In the **United States of America** the watershed year appears to have been 1980, the year Ronald Reagan first acceded to the White House. Two countervailing forces were then operating on schools in the United States. From the time of the publication of the Coleman report in 1966 and of the Jencks study in 1972, both dealing with equality of educational opportunity, there was a strong body of public opinion that a child's progress at school was affected only marginally by the school itself and that it depended overwhelmingly on the child's home background. The 1970s saw the generation of many programs aimed at social justice, at minorities, at disadvantaged children and the schools they attended, at innovation in both the curriculum and the way it was taught, at alternative modes of delivery, and at teacher preparation for these tasks. These programs grew up in other countries too, not only in the US, but they were based upon the same research findings and policy imperatives.

Simultaneously, and almost as a counter-revolution to balance the radicalism of the 1970s, the 'effective schools movement' appeared, with a panoply of measures to sponsor excellence, to assess outcomes, to build 'school-improvement plans', to make 'efficiency' and 'effectiveness' popular, and to emphasize that the instructional program of the school is its highest priority. The effect was to reassert the primacy of schools, the validity of the traditional forms of schooling, and the centrality of common features to the curriculum like literacy and numeracy. Researchers into school effectiveness tended to use as their performance indicators those which were extant among educators at the time, namely standardized test scores gathered by national testing of competencies in mathematics and verbal ability (i.e., reading).

By the early 1980s it had been demonstrated to many people outside of education that those test-score averages appeared to have been declining consistently, year by year, for about two decades (see, for example, Hanushek, 1986). Yet this was the same period when new funding had been injected into schools, when teacher qualifications had risen and class sizes had fallen, when school buildings and equipment had made quantum leaps in quality and sophistication. What had gone wrong? Had the money been wisely spent? There followed a period of major public reports on education arguing that education was now in crisis. The 'bible of the reform movement', the result of a taskforce set up by the President, appeared in 1983 titled *A Nation at Risk*.

Strangely, however, it was a time when the President was following a consistent policy of pulling back from massive funding in the areas in which the states had legislative authority. So welfare programs were cut, and among them education. There was a deliberately fostered slippage of power and responsibility from the federal to the state authorities. The governors and the chief state-school officers became very active in setting educational priorities; the Education Commission of the States (ECS) became a powerful arena for generating ideas about the nature of the reforms which should be visited upon education. It was clear, too, that new economic rivalries were emerging among the several states, and that the existence of a well-educated workforce was a strong determinant of whether international and national business houses would locate part of their operation in a particular city or state.

By the turn of the decade, several recurrent themes were evident. The large education bureaucracies were too ineffective and too unwieldy to meet the challenges of the 1990s. Schools should be freed from many of the centrally imposed regulations which constricted their ability to provide the kind of educational services which their client populations were demanding. The governance patterns for schools should be altered to allow for a school-site council of parents, teachers, and students. The management, organization, structures, and the managerial personnel needed to be upgraded and developed. School-based management was in favour.

In the **United Kingdom** a parallel development had been taking place. Following the publication in 1977 of the Taylor report, the result of a national inquiry into the way elementary and secondary schools were governed, action was taken to revise the membership, functions, and legal authorities of the boards of governors and the boards of managers which had governed schools in Britain for decades. The United Kingdom had had school-site councils for many years, but the Education Act of 1980 revised their powers and responsibilities.

The Conservative government of Margaret Thatcher dominated the educational-policy arena for the decade of the 1980s. Bringing a strong right-wing, free-market and economically driven ideology to the education portfolio, Secretary of State for Education Sir Keith Joseph and then Kenneth Baker proceeded to redraw the map of British education, with interventionist policies from the centre. For example, the Manpower Services Commission was given money to sponsor initiatives in technical and vocational education in local authorities and schools. New certification processes were introduced. The examining authorities were persuaded to experiment with new assessment formats. A series of youth policies were aimed at making available to every school-leaver who did not proceed to higher education a place in a training program. Employment or, more accurately, youth unemployment was a pervasive motivator for many of the reforms.

The Thatcher government moved to break up a number of the power blocs which appeared to be dominant in education. The Schools Council, on which the national teacher unions were heavily represented, was abolished and replaced with two lean bodies, one to run the national examination system, the other to advise on a national curriculum. The move symbolized a more general shift towards conservatism in education. The primacy of traditional subjects was confirmed; the importance of science and mathematics was underlined; and the return to a regime of hard-nosed scholarship in basic disciplines was signalled in the favour shown to private and elite or selective schools.

The schools systems in large metropolitan areas, particularly in the former smokestack cities in the industrial North, had been an annoyance to the Thatcher government because they were controlled by unions and they solidly supported Labour. Indeed Labour-party members were in the voting majority on their councils (and education authorities), and they challenged many of the Conservative initiatives. There was, for example, a celebrated clash between the Liverpool council and the national government in 1985, in which the city threatened to spend its way into bankruptcy in defiance of the rate-capping imposed by Westminster. So the national government moved to disband the recalcitrant metropolitan boroughs. Thatcher's most spectacular act in this respect was to do away with the Greater London Council (the GLC), and then to wipe out probably the most conspicuous school system in Great Britain, the Inner London Education Authority (ILEA), which for decades had been a Labour stronghold.

In an attempt to empower local schools, and at the same time defuse the power of local education authorities which had not taken willingly to the Thatcher reforms, the government enacted provisions to allow local schools to opt out of their local authorities and to operate as free-standing entities within a national framework. The government also targeted the management of schools, sponsoring and funding schemes to train heads of schools in effective management techniques. Reform followed reform in rapid succession, culminating in the Education Reform Act of 1988, a bill whose consequences may turn out to be as far-reaching as those which flowed from the 1944 Education Act.

The changes in Great Britain and the United States, analysed in the respective chapters by Thomas and by Koppich and Guthrie, have been the unofficial yardsticks for the reforms in other places. At the least, the writings and policy initiatives in those countries have been well perused and drawn on by educators, policy analysts and policy makers around the world. The changes in the four other countries in our set of six therefore throw up parallels which are provocative.

In **Australia** one must note, in the reforms which went on unabated for the whole of the 1980s, the collective impact of the spate of 'better schools' reports in the Australian states in the 1980s, the growth of the non-government sector (especially the Catholic-schools sector), the restructuring of the state Departments of Education and the public-school systems, and the strongly interventionist activities of the federal government (especially since 1987). The latter manifestations included the creation of a federal 'mega-Ministry of Education' (the national Department for Employment, Education and Training); the consequential abolition of the free-standing Australian Schools Commission and Commonwealth Tertiary Education Commission (CTEC) and their metamorphosis into a National Board for Employment, Education and Training directly answerable to the national minister; the development of a 'unified national system' in higher education; and triggered the growing power and influence of the national council of Ministers of Education (the Australian Education Council). During the decade, every state and territory school system underwent some kind of substantial restructuring, including in 1989 the huge New South Wales system which exceeds in enrolment size the largest system in the US, the New York system.

Our chapter on Australia could have taken several perspectives, the three most obvious being: the impact on Australian schools of the universal restructuring of the state and territory school systems; the federal initiative, zealously followed through, of wiping out the binary system in higher education and replacing it, through widespread amalgamations of institutions, with a nationally controlled system consisting of larger, fewer, multipurpose, multicampus universities; or the strongly dominant interventionist role played by the national government, which has turned federal–state relations on its head. The chapter concentrates on this last aspect, and has been written by two insiders to the process, Louden, who was the chief executive of one of the state systems (Western Australia) and Browne, who for the decade was the executive director of the council of education ministers.

The reconstruction of the **New Zealand** national school system was a model for the New South Wales action and is spectacular in several respects, not least in the way it has led to an astonishing degree of decentralization. The taskforce to review education administration (known as the Picot committee — the name derived from its chairperson Brian Picot) spoke of 'excessive ministerial involvement', 'sectoral fragmentation', and a 'lack of priorities at the centre'. It therefore proposed turning the system on its head. Whereas schools had discretion over a mere 1.9 per cent of the education vote, the Picot recommendation was that 94.5 per cent of the money should now be placed directly in the hands of schools. To push through the reforms, the government brought in on short-term contract a non-educator from another portfolio to head the Education Department. The chapter by Macpherson considers the reasons why political intervention in the management of schools in New Zealand occurred as dramatically as it did in 1988. He analyses the reasons for the Picot report of 1988, and the consequential changes to the local and national management of schools.

The education reforms in **Canada** in the 1980s are considered by Lawton in Chapter 6. Canada has always been acutely conscious of its powerful neighbour to the south, but the exploding economic market-place in Asia and particularly the North Pacific during the last decade has had a profound impact on the country in somewhat the same way as it has on Australia and New Zealand. The educational reforms in Canada appear to have placed heavy emphasis on the multicultural nature of the country and in particular on the effort to make Canada bilingual. A similar kind of dynamic operates in New Zealand with its Maori population, and also in Australia where recent immigration has transformed its demographic make-up. While these obsessions with ethnic minorities may appear inward-looking, they in fact reflect a growing uneasiness about the world community and the need to make new accommodations with it. The proximity to Asia has had a telling impact, as Lawton points out, and it has produced a new kind of political, social, and racial melting-pot. Lawton also shows in the case of Canada that the economic pressure because of its closeness to the United States, the political and economic developments in Asia and the Pacific, and the racial mix within the Canadian population have produced a politicized context for school reform.

Finally, it is chastening to read Takeshi Sasamori's account of the attempted educational reforms in **Japan** since 1984, for many will be unaware how closely they parallel the thinking in Europe and North America, even though Japan has such a buoyant economy that it might seem to be a country to be copied rather than to be changed. Koppich and Guthrie refer to American apprehension that the Japanese were outstripping the Americans in terms of education, and yet at the very same time the Japanese were attempting to change their schools. One could have been forgiven for concluding that here was one country which had got things right. Why then did Prime Minister Nakasone set up in 1984 a national commission to reform Japanese education, and why was it presumably of such high priority that the action was taken at prime-ministerial level and not by the national Ministry for Education? What has been the impact of the four major reports produced by the commission between 1984 and 1987? Sasamori's chapter also explores why the reform movement came from the national government level and not from the prefectures, why the commission appears to have used little expert input from educators, and why the reforms have had so little impact on the way individual schools operate. Indeed, it is surely of interest that educators, repeatedly and in several countries, have been left out of the policy process which is the antecedent of the reforms. And when they have been included, those with right-wing, conservative, and business-compatible orientations have been chosen, almost regardless of which political party is in power.

When all these countries are viewed synoptically, then, it becomes apparent that there are several common themes inviting investigation. How are we to disentangle the threads and to explore the warp and woof of the fabric? We need a framework within which we can analyse the developments, allowing for comparisons across state and national boundaries. Guthrie and Koppich, using their insights honed from many years of experience with public policy, have built up in Chapter 2 a 'policy paradigm' which could form the base from which to interrogate and formally research the education-reform phenomenon. They pose questions like the following. When is a 'reform' really a reform? How are we to recognize a reform when we see one? What political imperatives push the reform (they have an illuminating discussion of reform as 'high politics')? And what propositions have emerged from the education-reform movement?

This framework, spelt out in Chapter 2, is a valuable and provocative contribution for it serves as a mental organizer while the reader considers the reforms in particular countries. Macpherson (with the case of New Zealand), Thomas (with Great Britain), and Koppich and Guthrie (in their own chapter dealing with the United States) make direct reference to the model. It has important resonances with the final chapter in Part 3, where Swanson adds another perspective on how to explain why the reform movement has taken the shape it has.

No book could hope to be exhaustive about the patterns and themes which have emerged from our multi-nation study, but several of the major ones are addressed in the chapters of Part 3. A common vocabulary has now emerged in the educational reform movement; the same words keep recurring to explain what the reform agenda is about — ubiquitous terms like excellence, quality, school effectiveness, equity, efficiency, accountability, centralization, and decentralization. The chapter by Caldwell takes a synoptic view of the terminology and education restructuring, pointing out the paradoxes and uncertainties which are developing over the way schools are governed and controlled. He discusses the almost universal trend towards school-based management, with the common features in the US, Great Britain, Canada, Australia, and New Zealand considered.

To understand the education-reform manoeuvres in any country, one is forced to confront the concepts of centralization and decentralization, which seem to underlie so much of the discussion and writings about restructuring of schools. The issue has arisen in all the countries considered in this book. The words themselves present us with difficulties, of course, for they have their own paradigm implicit in the imagery which gave them their derivation. 'Decentralization' (meaning 'down from the centre') implies that the centre has the power in the first place, but condescends to share it with others of lower status. 'Devolution' has the same implication. Thus in many respects if the terms are not offensive, then they ought to be, for they imply a view about education and its management which ought to be challenged. Furthermore, educational planning is bound to be confused and contradictory unless these concepts are first clarified, and then the implications in accepting the concepts are explored. In particular, problems about accountability cannot be dealt with unless the definitions of these terms are clear. Slater has attempted such an analysis in Chapter 10, and then has shown the educational consequences implicit in the definitions.

It will be obvious from the six chapters dealing with the country case-studies that 'restructuring' can focus on national systems (as in Japan and Great Britain) or state–provincial–district systems (as in Australia and Canada) or on schools themselves (as in the US and New Zealand). But whatever the entry point, in the end the intention is to change schools. Thus in the United States, restructuring has concentrated on the way schools are organized and governed rather than on school systems or on state and national bodies which allocate the resources to schools and which set political priorities for them. Restructuring is associated therefore with curriculum redesign, with school-based management, and with the institution of school-site councils on which parents and public members are represented. This approach has been particularly evident in the 'second wave' of reforms.

In Australia and the United Kingdom, on the other hand, restructuring usually means devising a new administrative format to govern the ways state and federal departments and school systems are configured, the way their functions are distributed, and how their resources are managed. In short, there is a heavier emphasis on what is systemic. One of the abiding problems is that schools and school systems are being remodelled according to a managerial pattern found in business firms operating in the private sector of the economy, and with an orientation to the conditions of the post-industrial economy. As a result, two quite profound dilemmas underlie the restructuring of schools, and the first of these is taken up by Anderson in Chapter 11.

Much of the education reform, especially that which is taking place in Great Britain, Australia, and Europe, and to a lesser degree in the United States, is driven by the politics of privatization, and it has thrown into sharp confrontation the differences between private (or independent) schools and public schools, those provided at government or public expense. It is a matter with far-reaching consequences when government itself helps to finance those private schools from the public purse, yet both the major political parties in Australia are committed to state aid for private schools.

The privatization syndrome has other effects too. Education has also become part of the movement to sell off government assets, to force public institutions to operate in a kind of free market, to force on to public institutions the patterns favoured by the private sector of business, and to advocate excellence at the expense of equity. There are some devastating consequences, especially in sociological terms and particularly to public schools, when a sharp dichotomy between public and private, between government and non-government schooling, is allowed to develop.

A second dilemma arises from the setting up of school-site councils, usually to govern or manage the local school. But it is not always clear why these councils are being created, who wants them, and what political purpose, either overt or covert, they fulfil. Who should sit on those councils? What is the justification for the pattern of membership and the balance of voting powers? Why have teacher unions tried to ensure a voting majority for teachers? Should the principal be a full voting member, an adviser to the council, or its executive officer without a seat on the council? Does it matter if the principal is also the council's chair? And what functions should the council be allowed to discharge? It is obvious that how one answers these questions depends upon how one conceives the council in the first place. There are underlying assumptions which need to be brought out into the open. Indeed, the paradigms at work could be quite incompatible with each other, and members of the same council may be carrying in their heads radically different views about what the council is and what it is empowered to do. These issues and their consequences we have tried to tease out in Chapter 12.

Swanson rounds out our canon in what we consider to be an important last chapter. In asking why the 1980s and 1990s have produced such turbulence over educational governance, he suggests that for two centuries democracies have tried to maintain a balance among the three respective goods of liberty, equality, and fraternity. Koppich and Guthrie raised the same point in Chapter 2, except that they substituted 'efficiency' for 'fraternity'. The terms have of course been given new names now; thus we speak of parental choice and the deregulation of schools (freedom), equity (instead of equality), and the development of community, enculturation, socialization, and shared social values (instead of fraternity). But experience over several decades seems to suggest that political parties tend to favour one of these values above the other two in the policies they enunciate for education, and, as Koppich and Guthrie point out, they produce periods of 'value disequilibrium' which leads to reforms. Thus, at any one time, we can predict the trend in educational reform by asking whether freedom and choice (liberty), or equity and social justice (equality), or community and national priorities (fraternity) are being given priority. Swanson looks at some of the consequences in the countries considered in this book.

When the fundamental assumptions about the school restructuring movement are made explicit like this, we are in a position to derive a framework within which both to understand and to predict what is happening to education, and why the reforms are really being imposed. So what are our hunches? We began this project with some fairly clear-cut impressions about the international reform movement in education. To conclude this introduction, then, we think it is prudent to lay out what we thought we would discover, judged from what we already knew, albeit in a less systematic way than this book provides, taken as a whole. There were seven trends which we thought would be confirmed.

Firstly, we thought, the reconstruction generally is driven by political forces, and it is important for educators to come to terms with this reality. The reforms do not originate with educators or with the schools or systems to which they are attached; they are mandated from outside by political actors.

Secondly, economic factors not only determine but also pattern the nature of the restructuring. In a post-industrial economy the workforce is employed predominantly in the services sector; indeed, it has been estimated that about four jobs in every five will soon be found in services or information industries. It is these sectors where both the established and the emerging professions are found; and to hold employment in them, in fact to gain a license to practise, it is necessary to hold a formal qualification gained through post-school study. A post-industrial economy is therefore directly dependent on education.

Thirdly, and largely because of that second factor, national governments are now powerful actors in education even though in the federal systems like those found in the United States, Canada, and Australia the national government has no constitutional authority to intervene in education. In Great Britain, which for so long has had a 'national system locally administered', the pattern of national intervention is also changing. National governments are becoming involved because the health of national economies depend on how well-educated the workforce is.

Fourthly, restructuring has aimed at a specific target, namely the way schools and school systems are run. There is a consistent thread in the reforms which has removed the policy-making about education from the grip of educators, largely because other actors want to use education for instrumental purposes. Economic gain is about productivity, about how public and private enterprises are run. So business is tending to impose upon education the kinds of structures which allow firms in the private sector of the economy to be resilient and to survive in post-industrial conditions.

Fifthly, it is obvious that countries are learning from each other, adopting ideas and models from elsewhere with a speed which has never been seen before. Telecommunications, international travel, the interlocking international economy, and the fact that a large number of workers in influential positions now behave like citizens of the world ensure that ideas travel quickly. In many respects, education itself is an international industry now, and educators — whether in classrooms, administration, or in field positions — have to be international in their credentialling, in their modes of operation, in their curriculum programming, and in the acceptability of the services they give. Education now operates in an internationally competitive setting.

Sixthly, the economic imperative is also providing a new rationale for education and, more narrowly, for schooling. Schools are expected to compete

for customers. They are being asked to manage their resources as though they
are private firms. They are being required to give an account of themselves in a
sophisticated way, by means of formal reporting of outcomes. They are being
asked to show their managerial maturity by demonstrating their productivity
through negotiated performance measures. The free-market analogy is being
used to explain how schools should operate.

And seventhly, the restructuring is not over yet, and does not look as though
it will be for the duration of the 1990s, simply because the forces which produced
the current spate — economic competitiveness, the interdependent international
economy, the realigning of political forces, the emergence of new national
groupings, and values disequilibrium — will produce policy turbulence for some
time to come. Only the resilient, adaptable, quick, and creative will thrive.

Perhaps it is provocative to suggest these 'conclusions' at the start of the
investigation. We do so to encourage you to look for themes and trends as you
negotiate your way through the material we have assembled here. Whether we
read the signs correctly should be known by the time you have reached the last
chapter. In the process, it will have become obvious that the education-reform
movement is certainly not a parochial affair, and that those involved in it or
affected by it need an expanded and more comprehensive vision if they are to
influence the flow of events or to survive the flood. If we can see the picture
synoptically and as a whole, we may find ourselves better able to read the trends,
to intervene at the critical times, and to ensure that good educational outcomes
do in fact emerge from the spate of reforms.

Note

1 Material from this chapter also appears as chapter 1 of a parallel volume:
  HARMAN, G.S., BEARE, H. and BERKELEY, G. (1991) *Restructuring School Manage-
  ment: Administrative Reorganization of Public School Governance in Australia*,
  Deakin, ACT: Australian College of Education. Used with permission.

References

COLEMAN, J.S. *et al.* (1966) *Equality of Educational Opportunity*, Washington, DC, US
  Government Printing Office.
HANUSHEK, E.A. (1986) 'The Economics of Schooling: Production and Efficiency in
  Public Schools', *Journal of Economic Literature*, September 1986, 24, pp. 1141–
  77.
JENCKS, C.S. *et al.* (1972) *Inequality: A Reassessment of the Effect of Family and
  Schooling in America*, New York, Basic Books.
NATIONAL COMMISSION ON EXCELLENCE IN EDUCATION (1983) *A Nation at Risk: The
  Imperative for Educational Reform*, Washington, DC.
SALLIS, J. (1977) *School Managers and Governors: Taylor and After*, London, Ward
  Lock Educational.
SALLIS, J. (1988) *Schools, Parents and Governors: A New Approach to Accountability*,
  London, Routledge.
(TAYLOR REPORT) COMMITTEE OF ENQUIRY INTO THE MANAGEMENT AND GOVERNMENT OF
  SCHOOLS (Chair: Councillor T. Taylor) (1977) *A New Partnership for our Schools*,
  London, Her Majesty's Printing Office.

Chapter 2

Ready, A.I.M., Reform: Building a Model of Education Reform and 'High Politics'

J.W. Guthrie and J.E. Koppich

There have been times and places in the past where education and big-time politics did not, or at least were not supposed to mix. Such conditions, if they ever really did exist, are certainly no longer the mode. Sometimes in contemporary settings, education is mostly politics, and, sometimes, though more rarely, politics is mostly education. In an earlier essay, we explored the economic correlates of national education reform.[1] This chapter assumes a new *realpolitik* of education and posits a theoretical explanation of national education-reform politics. The intent is to explore how and why education issues periodically gain prominence on the political agenda, escalate beyond the constraints of conventional special-interest group-dominated dynamics, and enter the larger realm of 'high politics'.

We present a tripartite paradigm of 'high politics' and educational reform. The model specifies that reform is crucially contingent upon the presence of three preconditions: Alignment, Initiative, and Mobilization (AIM). In order for significant political system changes, including education reform, to occur, a number of politically related phenomena must exist and must be appropriately aligned. This critical alignment is itself contingent upon an initiating event, or series of events, which inject uncertainty or disequilibrium into a political system. These irritating or unsettling conditions or set of provocations initiate political alignment. Finally, enactment of a reform agenda depends crucially upon the existence of a political 'champion'. A motivating individual or catalytic group is necessary to take advantage of enabling conditions and predisposing events. This policy entrepreneur provides intention, direction, and sustains reform momentum.

Expanding hopes of worldwide democratization, East–West *détente*, efforts to defuse religious conflict, and intense global economic competition dominate the late twentieth-century popular political landscape. These strikingly visible issues and conditions currently constitute the sum and substance of press head-lines and stimulate near-saturation coverage on television news. These are the issue dimensions that most occupy government and corporate leaders and around which nations orient much of their strategic planning, both foreign and domestic. In short, these issues usually constitute today's 'high politics'.[2] Decisions taken around these issues often have major, and sometimes long-lasting policy consequences.

The politics of education is usually much less visible. It generally is conducted in a microcosm of the overall political system. It typically is concentrated on issues of an incremental nature and is dominated by the historic 'iron triangle' of interest-group representatives, executive-branch education officials, and a narrow band of legislators who specialize in education. Conventional education issues seldom penetrate the rarefied air of 'high politics' or command the same degree of media attention as issues such as international disarmament, technological spectacles or global environmental threats. If education issues reach the political agenda at all, they typically fall within the province of 'routine politics', normal day-to-day decision-making.

Periodically, however, education bursts beyond the bubble of its subordinate and self-contained political arena and becomes 'high politics'. A series of proposals or events, when accompanied by a political champion who takes advantage of a triggering event and set of appropriate background conditions, can galvanize a polity into concentrated and dramatic action regarding geographic scope. This appears to be occurring with increasing frequency and expanding geographic scope. Almost every modern nation, and many developing ones as well, are engaged in sustained and extensive programs to transform their education systems.

This chapter represents an effort to develop a hypothesis about education reform. What prompts and drives education-reform movements? What causes them to ebb and flow? Specifically, what forces or conditions create the climate necessary to launch and sustain an education-reform movement? The ultimate objective is to build a theoretical explanation of school-reform movements that can be tested in a variety of national settings. This chapter concentrates upon these three central questions:

- How why, and under what conditions does an education issue escalate into the domain of high politics?
- What are the policy dynamics behind national education reform?
- Why are these international reforms emerging now?

These are the major topics upon which this chapter concentrates. The essay ends with a set of theoretical propositions regarding school-reform political dynamics that can be tested, and refined, in a variety of national settings. Before turning to these tasks, however, it first is necessary to clear away several dimensions of definitional undergrowth. In that this essay is about the politics of education reform, it is appropriate to digress for a brief discussion of these two ideas.

How Do You Know a 'Reform' When You See One?

This is a difficult question. Most changes by individuals and organizations, including governments, are incremental. They involve only minor alterations in the manner in which something is done. Periodically, however, a polity will substantially alter one or a set of its decision rules or policies. It may, for example, abolish slavery, dramatically change the conditions under which individuals participate in government or run for public office, collect a whole lot more in taxes, redefine who is a citizen or who can vote, conscript for military service, redistribute material wealth or privilege.

These substantial alterations may be defined as 'reforms'. However, when is substantial really *substantial*? How does one know if a reform is occurring? When is a change simply an incremental alteration and when is it a reform? Must an effort at change leave a policy 'residue' before it qualifies as a reform? Answers to these questions inevitably involve personal judgments, and almost always hindsight will prove more precise than prediction. Nevertheless, described below are threshold criteria that can be employed to determine if a governmental change qualifies as a 'reform'.

When Is a Governmental Change a Reform?

The abstract decision rule is as follows. A government reform has occurred when one or a combination of the following conditions has been met:

- A significant public office or agency, or group of private individuals, gains possession of, or access to, a material item, activity, or decision which previously either did not exist or from which it was excluded.

This, of course, is emphasizing the positive — somebody gaining something. Examples of government reform by this definition would be the abolition of slavery, giving women and 18-year-olds the right to vote, providing schooling for handicapped students, devolving administrative decisions to school sites, acknowledging teachers' right to bargain collectively, or equalizing school revenues across operating units.

The above definitional rule can also be framed in the negative: A reform has occurred when:

- A significant public office or agency, or group of private individuals, loses all or partial possession of, or is denied access to, a material item, activity, or decision.

This rule is illustrated by reforms such as the imposition of taxes, criminal penalties, residential restriction clauses, jurisdictional decisions, immigration quotas, exclusionary clauses, imposition of a centrally determined curriculum, or college-admission standards.

Finally, a government reform has occurred when:

- A significant public office or agency, or group of private individuals, is required to perform, or is prohibited from performing, an act.

This rule is illustrated by regulations prohibiting sale of contraband items, advertising cigarettes, or racial or gender discrimination.

Cutting across these threshold definitional criteria are operational and temporal dimensions. What if a 'reform' is only proposed? Does that qualify as substantial change? What if it is enacted, but never implemented? What if it is implemented, but subsequently reversed and an *ex ante* condition restored? How long does a change have to exist before it is sufficient to qualify as a reform, and does the change have to have had a lasting effect? These questions suggest the need for two additional minimal criteria.

- The new decision-rule must become operational and be implemented for a period sufficient to determine its primary effect.

These criteria, operation and time, preclude consideration of proposals that never become reality. Anyone or any government can propose sweeping changes but unless they are at least partially implemented, they cannot reasonably qualify as reforms. Failed proposals may be crucial for rhetorical purposes or influence politics dramatically. Indeed, unaccepted proposals frequently establish the groundwork upon which operational reforms are subsequently constructed. Nevertheless, no matter how popular, widely discussed, wise, visionary, bold, or potentially far-reaching in its consequences, unless it becomes operational, a proposed change is not a 'reform'.

Secondly, specifying existence sufficient to determine primary effects does not mean that the changes must be permanent, or even long-standing. If a Labour-party sweep occurred in the 1990s and all 1980s' efforts at privatization were completely reversed, e.g., Jaguar, British Air, and the telephones were again state-owned, would that mean that a 'Thatcher revolution' had never occurred in England? Hardly! A reform thus need not leave a long-lasting residue, either material or procedural, positive or negative. However, it must have been implemented sufficiently to have had at least a primary effect. Some individual or agency must have taken a decision from which there were consequences. Somebody, or group must have built a structure, been licensed, taxed, denied a request, attended a new school, moved, been born or died as a result of the change. If so, assuming it met one or more of the above-listed change criteria as well, then the action could be considered a 'reform'.

Once beyond a set of minimum or threshold decision-rules, what are other indicators of reform? It will sometimes be the case that what appears on the political horizon as a full-fledged reform will have its edges so dulled by compromise as to emerge subsequently from the policy-making process as only incremental change. Conversely, with the advantage of retrospection, a continuum of incremental changes may come to be seen as a full-fledged reform. There is no escaping, the conclusion that 'reform' is a relative term.

How to Recognize a Reform

Be that as it may, it is possible to issue several guidelines to reform. If one were sitting on the sidelines watching policy change parade by, here is how one might differentiate 'reform' from incremental alterations. The big policy parade banners to which those measuring the magnitude of change should be alert are dramatic alterations in distribution and ideology. Some significant individual, office holders, or group will be able to do, or possess, something that previously was impossible or did not exist and a publicly acceptable reason will be given for the change. Here are a few more detailed yardsticks.

Decision Shifts

Governmental reforms frequently entail a transformation in decision-making power. This can be of three kinds: binary, transactional, or inclusory. In the first instance, decision authority is fixed. It either exists or it does not exist. The President has the power to impound funds appropriated by Congress. No other official has such authority. Then Congress enacts a budget-reform act and determines that the President no longer has the right to impound. The President lost a power. Local school boards in California once had property-taxing authority, but that has now been removed from them. The binary switch was 'on' and it was turned 'off'.

In a 'transactional' shift decision authority is moved from one office or agency to another. The licensing of teacher candidates was previously a function performed by the State Education Department. However, under a recently enacted statute, this function is now performed by a newly created, independent, professionally dominated commission on 'teacher credentialling'.

The expansion of voting rights illustrates the third category of decision transformations. Giving women, slaves, or younger persons the right to vote is to include them in government decision-making. This need not be a zero-sum situation in which one group foregoes a power completely in order that another has it. Decision-making simply is now more widely shared.

Resource Shifts
Reforms frequently involve the distribution or redistribution of resources. Prior Labour-party governments nationalized various English industries and vastly expanded public housing. The Thatcher government subsequently reprivatized the industries and transferred public-housing ownership to tenants. Government tuition payments to households or students, financial subsidies to educational institutions, school-meal programs, and equalizing grants to local educational agencies illustrate resource shifts.

Regulatory Shifts: Mandates and Prohibitions
Government reforms frequently involve regulations demanding that an agency or individuals conduct or cease a particular activity. New rules requiring that schools serve handicapped or non-English-speaking students or that districts disband dual-school systems for children of different races are examples.

Value Shifts
A government reform will frequently be triggered or accompanied by a shift in value emphasis. A subsequent section of this essay describes the three value streams which undergird public policy: equality, efficiency, and liberty. Suffice it to specify here that these three values shape much of public policy and the debate surrounding it. A democratic society is engaged in a never-ending effort to achieve a dynamic equilibrium among the three.

Periodically, events external to government, generally demographic, technologic, and economic in nature, will stimulate among the populace the ascendance of one value stream over the others. Political decision may substantially alter policies, and government reforms may result. When this occurs, a publicly acceptable ideology or value rationale will be provided for the reform.

The elections of the Reagan and Thatcher administrations represented the subsidence of equality as a dominant value stream and the re-emergence of concerns for efficiency and liberty, or choice. Government rhetoric regarding education reform mirrored this shift. Empowerment of consumers, attacks on government bureaucracies, devolution of authority, deregulation, free-market remedies, privatization, and competition came to be labels attached not only to economic reforms but also to school-change proposals.

Creation of a New Constituency or Coalition
Reforms that develop and ultimately take hold, however temporally, must respond to some perceived need among a particular segment of society. Sometimes those who desire reform represent a rather narrow, self-contained band of society. Access of handicapped children to public-school educations, for example, was sought in the 1970s primarily by the parents and teachers of those children. At other times, supporters of change reflect the desires of a much broader, though not all-encompassing, sweep of the populace. The goal of the civil-rights movement of the 1960s was to bring at least statutory equality to black Americans. Yet this reform movement attracted a broad-based national constituency.

Reform, then, involves the development of a constituency for change. Moreover, this new constituency, which may actually be a coalition of previously formed constituencies, becomes identified with the reform effort and monitors its implementation.

What Is Meant by Politics?

For many who are narrowly informed, the term 'politics' has long conjured images of evil cabals, corrupt machines, big-city bosses, back-room conspiracies, and overly partisan, short-sighted selfishness. This is an unfortunate view, one coloured by misperception. Such a dismal description may apply to politics of a kind one dislikes, but it does not apply to politics in general. Political dynamics determine who gets what, when, and in what circumstances. Thus, in principle, politics is good. At worst, it is a necessity. At best, it may be noble. Politics, when looked at from this perspective, is an absolute necessity. A society that denigrates politics, or eschews politicians, risks receiving ignoble political decisions.

Aside from frequent misperceptions, what is politics? There is nothing definitionally complicated here. Politics is the set of processes by which a social group allocates valued resources. Once this is stated, however, matters immediately lose their simplicity. What is it that is 'valued' by a society? What 'processes' are to be included? Where are the boundaries around these processes? What is 'politics' and what is something else?

David Easton's political-systems model provides preliminary answers to these questions. This model maps the major elements of a political system and displays their relationship to each other. It does not, nor was it intended to, explain causation. That is, while providing a useful political 'map', it is not a theory of politics or an explanation of policy dynamics. Its major assumptions and components are as follows.

Easton constructs a model of the social universe to convey his 'systems approach' to politics. He describes political life as a 'system of behavior' (Easton 1965). In Easton's construct a natural boundary exists between the political world and the environment, which consists of everything that is not politics. Exchanges, or transactions, occur between a political system and its environment.

Potential political issues first emerge as wants, hopes, or desires. These issues make their way to the political agenda by way of the interactions that occur through demands made on the political system and supports for that system. Demands provide the incentive for the system to act. Institutional 'gatekeepers' determine which demands are 'heard' by the system. The political system, Easton maintains, is an open system. Boundaries move as the political system attempts to cope with problems generated by its exposure to the larger world. Outputs — policy decisions — serve to link occurrences within the political system to the environment.

Why Widespread Attention to Reform Now?

'Modern economics' is the easy answer to this question. Powerful armed forces, possession of strategically significant geographic locations, access to valuable raw materials, and widespread capacity in basic industries were once the mainstays of national power and international hegemony. Such is less the case today. Conventional military power is declining in economic significance, as is geography. The new strategic raw material, upon which economic productivity is now crucially dependent, is human capital.

Throughout history, technological innovations have redistributed power, enabled a tribe, a people, or a nation to vie for and gain dominance. Fire, ferrous metal, and farming are historic discoveries which transformed nations and transferred power. Modern examples include internal combustion engines, interchangeable parts, electrical energy, and electronic components. The list is longer but the point is the same. Significant technological revolutions formerly were founded upon episodic discoveries. Increasingly, such shifts are crucially dependent upon conscious invention.

Rapid communication, expanding information, and modern organization are transforming national economies. Nations are now global in their competitive outlook, internationally interdependent, insatiable in their quest for technological innovation, and crucially dependent upon the availability of talent. Reliance upon an intellectual elite appears increasingly outmoded. Modern manufacturing and service-industry techniques demand a workforce capable of making informed decisions. Highly developed human intelligence is increasingly viewed as a nation's primary economic resource, and it is needed in large amounts.

It is the human-capital imperative that is driving widespread national education-reform efforts. Everywhere the objective is the same: expand the supply of human capital such that a nation is capable of technological innovation and modern workforce implementation. Specific reform tactics may differ from nation to nation, depending upon history, contemporary politics, resource levels, and current educational structures. For example, in national systems founded on an elitist schooling model such as France, England, and members of the British Commonwealth, the clear long-run education-reform goal is to expand the numbers of individuals eligible for, and interested in, seeking higher levels of schooling. In egalitarian-dominated systems such as the United States, the long-run goal of education reform is to elevate achievement standards such that there are larger numbers of well-educated workers. Regardless of the variety of national tactics, the strategic objective is the same. The long-run goal is to utilize trained intellect as a means for a nation to gain or retain an economically competitive position in the global market place. Pursuit of this objective explains current widespread national efforts at education reform.

The question remains, within a nation, what are the political dynamics that permit or promote education reform? From where do reform proposals come, and how do they become part of the political process? How do the demands of the human-capital imperative cross the permeable membrane between economics and politics? How does education reform become the invisible thread binding economic competitiveness, political action, and schools? What political conditions or dynamics must be present to permit or facilitate education reform? This is the focus of the next section of this essay.

Education-reform Political Dynamics: A Theoretical Perspective

The complex social world of human interactions constitutes a vast and swirling primordial-value ooze out of which technical, cultural, and political conditions periodically coalesce to create policy predispositions. Actual policy change, however, may await the spark of a particular event and the leadership, or at least advocacy, of a particular individual or cohesive group.

This essay posits that three conditions must coincide in order for a major policy reform to take place. These conditions — alignment, initiative, and mobilization — comprise a policy reform paradigm. Components of the reform paradigm, while not lending themselves to precise prediction, nevertheless alert one to the broader patterns and dynamics of policy emergence and influence. Each section of the paradigm and its respective components is explained below.

Alignment

Among the necessary preconditions of reform is the alignment of four politically related phenomena: (1) a culture's deep-seated public-policy preferences, (2) a societal condition defined as a 'political problem', (3) an alternative policy or set of alternative policies, and (4) favourable politics.

Public-Policy Preferences
Most cultures embrace three strongly preferred values that significantly influence public policy: equality, efficiency, and liberty. National government decisions regarding defense, housing, taxation, antitrust regulation, racial desegregation, and hundreds of other social dimensions, including education, are molded by one or more of these three values.[3] During any given period, one value will hold greater sway over policy outcomes than will the others. Shifting political-economic tides will cause different values to gain new policy precedence. Not every culture holds each value stream on a par with the emphasis that may be given in other cultures on the other two values in the set. Nevertheless, the dynamic interplay between proponents of value streams influences public policy across cultures.

Equality, liberty, and efficiency are viewed by many citizens as conditions that government should maximize. Each of these values serves for individuals as a deep-seated intellectual substratum from which stem many practical ideas. The values are not ends in themselves but criteria against which policy processes and products are judged. These three values are considered good, just, and right. Belief in them has historical roots that are deeply embedded in the cultural heritage of most western nations. This belief permeates the ideologies promulgated by political parties, religions, schools, and other social institutions. Thus, in democratic situations, popular pressure will be exerted to fulfil these preferences. Despite widespread popular devotion to these values as abstract goals, their simultaneous fulfilment is well nigh impossible. Tension exists among the values as they are, on their face, antithetical. Exclusive pursuit of one obviates fulfilment of another.

Liberty connotes freedom of choice. Equality signifies parity of opportunity, outcome, or treatment. Proponents of efficiency strive for tools and techniques capable of producing greater output. Whereas citizens may hold these values in common in the abstract, practical expressions may provoke conflict. Any particular individual's perception of the practical means for maximizing a value may conflict with another person's perception for obtaining either that value or achieving one of the other two values.

For example, imagine that government, in an effort to increase equality, nationalized the construction industry and mandated standardized production of housing. Presumably all citizens above a specified age would be guaranteed a government-produced home. Only one or a limited number of building types, perhaps with minor variations, would be manufactured. Consequently, all eligible housing consumers would be provided with identical products and would, by definition, have equal housing. Added technical efficiency might be achieved, at least in the short run, through high-volume manufacturing of uniform products.[4] Unit cost of houses might be reduced. However attractive the goals of equality and efficiency, in this instance liberty would be sacrificed. A limited variety of housing would severely restrict or totally prevent choice. In the absence of choice, there is no liberty. Moreover, in time, lack of competition might discourage the search for new production techniques and thus impair economic efficiency. Reasonable people might disagree about whether the absence of slums would be worth the presumed loss of freedom and efficiency. Policy makers constantly must face trade-offs such as these, most of which are far more subtle and many of which are more controversial that this hypothetical example.

Pursuit of equality exclusively will restrict or eliminate liberty and efficiency. Conversely, complete attention to either liberty or efficiency will diminish other values. Efforts to rearrange society so as to maximize one of the three values are constrained by forces for preserving the *status quo*. This dynamic equilibrium among the three values constantly shifts, with the balance at any particular point being fixed as a consequence of a complicated series of political and economic compromises and cultural perceptions.

A reform is unlikely to occur unless either one of the following conditions is in effect. Either (1) the value stream with which a prospective reform is most closely aligned must be dominant or ascending, or (2) a society must be in a period of substantial uncertainty regarding its value preferences. When a society is saturated with, or strongly dominated by, popular concern for policy preferences aligned with equality, practical proposals to enhance efficiency and liberty are unlikely to receive a full hearing, much less complete policy-system adoption. Conversely, when efficiency or liberty are ascendant, it is difficult to gain an agenda opening for egalitarian policy issues. Timing, alignment, is critical.

A second precondition that provides a window of opportunity for a reform is when a society is unsure regarding its value preferences. In a period of substantial value ambiguity or uncertainty, or in a period of significant cultural transition, when no one of the three values dominates, it may be possible for advocates of reform to gain a place on the political agenda for their particular proposal. This assumes that the other politically oriented preconditions, to be described subsequently, are also aligned appropriately. Education is one of the prime instruments through which society attempts to promote all three values. Hence education is a policy sector that most assuredly is subject to the test of public-policy preference coincidence. If a policy-reform proposal is out of value alignment, it is likely to be out of consideration.

A Problem Defined as Political

Reform is also critically dependent upon the societal 'problem' crossing over into the political domain. In effect, reform is impossible if the 'intolerable condition' to be eliminated or corrected is outside of the realm of politics, or more likely has not yet been defined as a part of the political agenda. Anthony Downs proposes a series of stages by which problems move onto, and frequently all the way through, the political agenda.[5]

Downs proposes an 'issue-attention cycle'. His proposition is that in a modern media-oriented society any given issue or problem can gain the public's attention only briefly, sometimes influencing public behaviours and attitudes for a short time, but then fades into the background largely unresolved. If the issue remains in focus sufficiently through events and attitudes, popular political pressure will build to produce effective change. Problems themselves do not change as much as alternating heightened awareness and boredom with a problem. Nevertheless, heightened popular awareness can serve to propel a problem into the political arena, to make it a 'political problem'.

Downs proposes five stages to the issue-attention ascendance. These are (1) the pre-problem stage; (2) alarmed discovery and euphoric enthusiasm; (3) realizing the cost of significant progress; (4) gradual decline of intense public interest; and (5) the post-problem stage.

In the pre-problem stage, a 'highly undesirable social condition' is yet to be noticed by the public. However, it has the attention of experts and interest groups. The actual conditions have worsened by the time the public takes notice (examples are racism, poverty, toxic-wastes risks, and malnutrition). In the alarmed discovery and euphoric-enthusiasm stage, dramatic events such as riots bring the problem's evils to public attention. With modern society's optimistic predisposition that every problem can be solved, 'euphoric enthusiasm' to do something is generated in a short time. Technologically sophisticated societies approach problems with the idea that with sufficient effort 'every obstacle can be eliminated and every problem solved without any fundamental reordering of society itself' (Downs, 1972, pp. 39–50). The third issue-ascendance stage is realizing the cost of progress and further realizing that solving the problem may mean significant sacrifices by major segments of society. If a technical means of solving the problem is not available, major restructuring will have to be considered. Enthusiasm diminishes if the solution requires substantial restructuring of society or loss of popular benefits. There is a gradual decline of intense public interest as people realize the difficulty and cost of implementing a solution. Interest wanes as new issues present themselves. In the final post-problem stage, the problem moves 'into prolonged limbo — a twilight realm of lesser attention or spasmodic recurrence of interest'. New institutions, programs, and policies have been developed to help solve the problem. Yet policy participants have come to believe that while the problem is real, there are no available immediate solutions and they turn their attention to other issues.

Downs maintains that problems that go through the 'issue-attention cycle' will have special characteristics. First, only a minority (less than 15 per cent of the population) will be affected by the problem. Second, suffering created by the problem is caused by social arrangements that provide significant benefits to the majority of the population of powerful people. Third, the problem has no 'intrinsically exciting qualities'. Today's mass media, with its ability to 'consume' news and entertain the public, must find dramatic and exciting issues to maintain the public's attention. When Downs' three conditions are met and the issue is able to compete for television viewing time as a crisis, the 'issue-attention cycle' will progress.

Downs' description provides an understanding of the dynamics by which a societal problem becomes defined as a political problem. However, problem definition is, by itself, insufficient. In addition, problem solutions must also exist.

Available Alternative Policies
Reform also hinges critically upon the availability of alternative policies. In fact, there is seldom a lack of alternative proposals. There is almost always a substantial set of proposals circling in a policy-holding pattern, waiting for somebody to pay attention to them. Cynics claim that there are always many policy solutions searching for a problem to solve.

In the policy stream, policy proposals are formulated, refined, and wait for a problem to appear. There are numerous specialists who serve in agencies, bureaus, on staffs, work for interest groups, or are scholars who have solutions, theories, ideas, and criticisms that float in and out of the policy stream. These individuals wait for problems to come by to which they can attach their solutions. Kingdon aptly describes the policy stream as the 'policy primeval soup composed of communities of specialists'.

> Within the policy communities ... many, many ideas are considered at some stage and in some way. Many people have proposals they would like to see considered seriously, alternatives they would like to see become part of the set from which choices are eventually made. They try out their ideas on others in the policy community. Some proposals are rather rapidly discarded as being somehow kooky; others are taken more seriously and survive, perhaps in some altered form. But in the policy primeval soup, quite a wide range of ideas is possible and is considered to some extent. The range at this stage is considerably more

inclusive than the set of alternatives that is actually weighted during a shorter period of final decision making. Many, many things are possible here. (Kingdon, 1984, p. 128)

Predisposing Politics

The final politically related alignment necessary for reform success is the availability of a set of favourable politically predisposing conditions. Kingdon lists among these conditions phenomena such as mood shifts in public opinion, public surveys, election results, partisan stances, changes in executive branch administrations, and partisan attitudes.[6]

An historic political event nicely illustrates this final predisposing condition. In the United States proponents of extensive federal-government financial assistance to public schools had attempted to gain enactment of a major school-aid bill for more than a century. Repeatedly proposals appeared popular with education interest groups and were supported by the President. Nevertheless, they always suffered defeat because of the absence of sufficient alignment among predisposing conditions. However, starting in the second half of the twentieth century, public preferences, educational problems, and alternative policies began to fall into an unprecedented synchrony. The clincher came with the 1964 presidential election. The landslide victory of Lyndon Baines Johnson over Barry Goldwater brought into office an overwhelming Democratic-party majority in the House and Senate. The outcome was a voting block capable of guaranteeing enactment of virtually any Johnson-administration social-reform proposal. His 1965 Elementary and Secondary Education Act was passed through Congress at such a rate that Republican opponents frequently referred to it on the floor as the 'National Railroad Act'. What had previously been practically impossible — enactment of a major education-reform bill — became an easy reality because of Johnson's sweeping political victory.[7]

The coincidence of public preferences, a politically defined problem, policy alternatives, and a predisposed political environment creates what Kingdon labels a 'window of opportunity'. However, the existence of such favourable co-incidences itself raises a question. What creates a window of opportunity? What triggers or galvanizes these disparate conditions into a state of alignment? What initiates the broad social movements that constitute the fortuitous coincidence? This leads to an explanation of the next major paradigmatic component: Initiative. Here is mapping of the forces generally responsible for macro-societal trends, for galvanizing broad, secular movements in society.

Initiative

The previously described political alignments and realignments are themselves initiated by an unsettling series of conditions or irritating stream of events perceived popularly as disconcerting or threatening. This distressing condition provokes dissatisfaction with the *status quo*, begins to move the populace toward a value disequilibrium, and initiates shifts in deep-seated value preferences and popular opinion. Eventually, if the unsettling or threatening conditions persist or are perceived as sufficiently dangerous, alterations in public moods create a disposition toward policy action. The principal contemporary sources of such value uncertainty or popular distress are economic, including technological lag, and demographic dynamics.

Economic and Demographic Dynamics

Throughout the world contemporary, educational policy reform, and its eventual expression in schooling, is propelled by two variable conditions in external environment: demography and economics. These conditions are themselves related, though the nature of the relationship at any point in time depends upon many additional conditions, such as a society's level of technical development and its climate. For example, in a technologically undeveloped society an explosion in the birthrate may trigger famine, poverty, and great human hardship. Conversely, in a technologically sophisticated, commercially oriented society a dramatic upsurge in births may spur economic expansion and an increase in living standards.

Two economic dimensions exert important influences upon policy: level of overall economic development and rate of economic growth. Obviously, a technologically sophisticated industrialized or information-oriented economy will have different policy concerns and predispositions from an agricultural or pre-industrial society. Similarly, low productivity and the absence of economic growth may create conflict between elites and the poor and, depending upon a society's political dynamics, may focus policy discussions obsessively on issues of economic redistribution.

Demography also has a two-dimensional influence. A society's policy predispositions are influenced not only by overall population size, but also by the geographic, ethnic, and age distribution of the population. A society in which the median age is relatively low might invest a disproportionate share of its social resources in children and youth. Conversely, when the median age rises, as is currently the case in the United States, senior citizens may begin to attract a disproportionate share of social resources. Also, a geographically compact and racially heterogeneous society may have different domestic-policy concerns from a sparsely settled or racially homogeneous people.

Regardless of the particular attributes of any given economic, technological, or demographic condition, it is these sorts of alterations that stimulate a disequilibrium in a policy's value preferences and various other politically related conditions. However, here again, alignment, of itself, is insufficient to explain reform. Another element must be present. A mobilizing force is necessary to take advantage of policy windows.

Mobilization

Alignment is crucial, but, by itself, insufficient as a predictor of policy reform. A second condition is critical: intentionality. Some individual or group of individuals must mobilize existing resources to take advantage of the window of opportunity. The previously described, coinciding, political conditions, while important, are somewhat subject to caprice. It is difficult to know when alignment will take place. When it does, however, some individual, or group, has to be in a position to take advantage of it. In short, reform begs for 'policy entrepreneurs'. These are mobilizing individuals, or cohesive groups, who have at least two qualities. First, they want reform — in some manner they are advocates for change. In addition, they must be sufficiently savvy politically to recognize a window of opportunity when it presents itself.

Kingdon asserts that policy decisions or reforms can only take place when 'policy windows' open. Policy windows open when the three separate and independent streams — problems, policies, and politics — join and present opportunities for action. Behind the scene are 'policy entrepreneurs' who wait and are ready when the window opens to promote their solution or a favoured alternative.

> These entrepreneurs are not necessarily found in any one location in the policy community. They could be in or out of government, in elected or appointed positions, in interest groups or research organizations. But their defining characteristic, much as in the case of business entrepreneurs, is their willingness to invest their resources — time, energy, reputation, and sometimes money — in the hope of a future return. That return might come to them in the form of policies of which they approve, satisfaction from participation, or even personal aggrandizement in the form of job security or career promotion. (Kingdon, 1984, p. 129)

When the policy entrepreneur sees the possibility of a window opening, he or she leaps to play a central role in 'coupling' the three streams to the window. Timing is all-important. Kingdon asserts that the policy window remains open for only a short time, and if no action is taken, the opportunity for change is lost. He also states that there are 'predictable windows' that open on a schedule and are cyclic in nature. These predictable windows not only include programs that expire, need reauthorization or a budget review, but also include issues and problems that reassert themselves on cyclical bases. Moreover, Kingdon believes there is evidence to support the notion of 'reform cycles'.

> There are also larger cycles, less precisely scheduled but still noticeable in their occurrence and their regularity. Various scholars have written about reform cycles in American politics in which a burst of reform energy is followed by a period during which the system rests, followed anew by another burst. The rest period provides a time for reassessment and consolidation, but during this time pressure builds for another period of intense activity directed toward substantial change. (Kingdon, 1984, p. 181)

Figure 2.1 graphically illustrates these three reform predispositions: alignment, initiative, and mobilization. The following section poses a set of propositions that flow from the educational-reform paradigm.

Propositions to Be Tested

The following research propositions have been deduced from the preceding paradigmatic discussions. Each proposition is capable of being operationalized for a

Figure 2.1: Preliminary Policy Paradigm

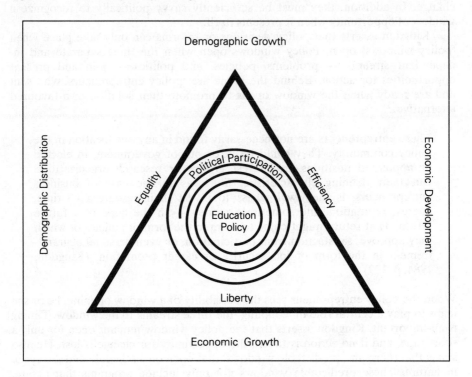

particular national political setting and tested with empirical information. The overall explanation, obviously, should be altered or expanded in keeping with research findings.

- Social reform, education reform included, is a lagged political-system response to social disequilibrium. (This condition is more likely to be evident in retrospect than in the present.) The period preceding a reform movement will be one characterized by significant societal disharmony. In the late twentieth century this societal dissonance is the result of demographically or economically induced tensions. In earlier historical periods international, military tensions precipitated disequilibrium;
- Reform is likely to occur during periods of value disequilibrium, not during periods of value dominance. Reform movements are likely to occur during periods of public value ambiguity, uncertainty, or shift. Conversely, reform is unlikely during periods of clear popular value preference;
- Reform is likely to be a response to a 'politically' recognized problem. Conversely, decision makers are unlikely to place an issue on the policy-making agenda which has not first cycled into a position of media prominence;

- Proposed reforms are likely to possess the following two qualities. First, they will have previously been proposed, though not successfully enacted or implemented. Reforms expressed as policy options will have been circulating in the environment and the initial groundwork will have been laid for acceptance. Second, the probability of a proposed reform being enacted is positively related to the degree to which proponents can shape its particulars to appear consistent with ascending public value preferences. In the case of education reform, advocates for change must also justify education as instrumental to the solution of the politically defined problem;
- Reform enactment is likely to occur as a consequence of, or at least to coincide with, a significant political shift, e.g., executive-branch transition, political-party ascendance, legislative turnover, major public-opinion shift, or a significant judicial decision;
- Reform movements are not self-propelling. Reform is likely to depend crucially upon the existence of a 'policy entrepreneur', an individual or set of individuals who champion the change and attempt to maintain reform momentum.

Notes

1 See James W. Guthrie and Julia E. Koppich (1988) Chapter 3.
2 With the benefit of historical perspective, today's highly visible political issues may some day themselves be seen as consequences of larger secular developments such as accelerated communication capacity, vastly expanded information availability, the fluid flow of capital, and biotechnology.
3 An explanation for the manner in which individuals' political preferences are influenced by their culture is offered by Aaron Wildavsky (1987) and Thomas Sowell (1987).
4 For a distinction between technical and allocative efficiency, see James W. Guthrie, Walter I. Garms, and Lawrence C. Pierce (1988) Chapter 14.
5 The authors are grateful to Ralph Brott for his synthesis of Downs' and Kingdon's positions. See Ralph Brott (1989), Anthony Downs (1972) and John Kingdon (1984).
6 These latter ideological shifts are far more specific than the alterations in public-policy preferences described above. The latter are far more fundamental than views about political ideology. Public-policy preferences can be illustrated by a question such as 'Do you believe parents should be able to choose their child's school?' The answers to a question such as this, while certainly subject to influence by contemporary events and change over time, are far less fluid than popular responses to a political-opinion inquiry such as 'How would you rate Prime Minister Thatcher's job performance?' The underlying position reflected in a response to this latter query is far more likely to shift according to current events than is a parent's response to the first illustrative question.
7 For added detail, see James W. Guthrie (1968).

References

BROTT, R. (1989) 'The Political Cycles Involved in Certification', Unpublished doctoral dissertation, University of California, Berkeley, CA.

DOWNS, A. (1972) 'Up and Down with Ecology: The Issue-Attention Cycle', *The Public Interest*, pp. 39–50.

EASTON, D. (1965) *A Systems Analysis of Political Life*, New York, Wiley.

GUTHRIE, J.W. (1968) 'A Political Case History: Passage of the ESEA', *Phi Delta Kappan*, 49, 6, pp. 302–6.

GUTHRIE, J.W. and KOPPICH, J.E. (1988) 'Exploring the Political Economy of National Education Reform, in BOYD, W.L. and KERCHNER, C.T. (Eds) *The Politics of Excellence and Choice in Education*, New York, The Falmer Press, pp. 25–47.

GUTHRIE, J.W., GARMS, W.I. and PIERCE, L.C. (1988) *School Finance and Education Policy*, Englewood Cliffs, NJ.

KINGDON, J.W. (1984) *Agendas, Alternatives, and Public Policies*, Boston, Little Brown.

SOWELL, T. (1987) *A Conflict of Visions*, New York, Morrow.

WILDAVSKY, A. (1987) *Choosing Preferences by Constructing Institutions: A Cultural Theory of Preference Formation*, Survey Research Center Working Paper Series, Berkeley, CA.

Part 2

Case Studies from Six Countries

Chapter 3

The Education-reform Movement in England and Wales

H. Thomas

Introduction

Commenting on the origins of the 1988 Education Reform Act, a deputy secretary at the Department of Education and Science (DES) noted the convergence of a number of concerns in the thinking of the government. These were concerns about standards of achievement; a growing conviction that economic well-being 'was being adversely affected by the performance of an education service that was neither as good as it could be or as good as it needed to be'; and finally, a need 'to reduce and control public expenditure in proportion to GDP in the aftermath of the inflationary hike caused by the oil crisis of the mid-1970s and to be more sure about getting value for money'. (Stuart, 1990)

These largely economic factors can be cited as causal variables underlying the reform initiatives in England and Wales and constituted in large part, although not exclusively, in the 1988 Education Reform Act. Yet concern about economic performance is of long-standing and it is possible to argue that education reforms over many decades have been, at least to some extent, a response to that endemic problem. Thus economic as well as demographic factors may be necessary conditions for reform, but they do not explain their specific form or answer questions like: Why this reform and why now? Why was it, for example, that in 1985 the government published an authoritative statement on education in which it declared that it did not envisage altering the distribution of legal responsibilities for the curriculum (DES, 1985) yet, only two years later, the same government proposed the most radical change for at least forty years in the distribution of those legal responsibilities?

In their earlier discussion of the dynamics of education reform, Guthrie and Koppich propose three conditions which have to be met if we are to answer and explain questions such as: Why this reform now? The conditions of their policy-reform paradigm are: alignment, initiative, and mobilization from which they derive six research propositions as a means of testing their policy paradigm. A later section of this chapter will apply those six propositions to the reforms in England and Wales but only after two preceding sections intended to provide the information necessary for testing the Guthrie and Koppich model. The first of these concentrates upon the main features of the reforms and is followed by an examination of the economic, demographic, and ideological conditions which gave rise to them.

Education Reform Described

Challenging the Producer Interest

The education service in England and Wales has been subject to change at almost all levels as a result of legislative and regulatory reform by the central government, more detailed descriptions of which are provided elsewhere (Flude and Hammer, 1990; Lawton, 1989; Maclure, 1989). The common strand to these reforms is that they challenge the role of educationists in key aspects of education policy-making as well as in its subsequent definition in the practice of education. This challenge to the 'producer interest' has led to a set of reforms which contain the apparent contradiction of simultaneously seeking to centralize and decentralize control of policy and practice. Viewed as a challenge to the producer interest, however, this contradiction assumes a greater coherence. By centralizing control over some aspects of policy, such as for the school curriculum, the reforms attempt to reduce the control of professional educators in this area. By decentralizing control over human and physical resources to the governing bodies of schools and colleges the reforms reduce the power of education administrators in local government and require head teachers and principals to work more closely with their governors. Moreover, since the particular form of decentralization selected introduces more competition into a market-place where clients will have more opportunity to choose between the quality and type of service apparently on offer in different schools and colleges, the power of the client is enhanced in relation to that of the producer.

Centred upon the principle of challenging the producer interest through centralization, decentralization and competition, education reform in England and Wales assumes a coherence which can be identified in all the main sectors of state-funded provision — schools, colleges, and higher education — and these are outlined below. We do well to note now, however, both that policy-making is seldom as neat as it appears and that policy outcomes are rarely as predictable as policy makers desire. Consequently, the discussion on 'explaining reform' will consider some of the contradictions underlying the making of these educational reforms as well as posing some preliminary questions about the uncertainties attendant upon their outcomes.

Reform in Schools

For schools the reforms have four main features. The first is the introduction of a national curriculum and a national system of assessment for children from 5 to 16 years. The Education Reform Act (1988) defines mathematics, English, and science as core subjects with a second group as foundation subjects; these are history, geography, technology, music, art, and physical education. A modern foreign language must also be included as a foundation subject for all year groups in secondary schools. For all subjects there are to be attainment targets which identify the knowledge, skills, and understanding pupils are expected to have, and these must be specified in relation to four key stages relating to ages 5–7, 7–11, 11–14 and 14–16. Accompanying the attainment targets are programs of study which define 'the matters, skills and processes which must be taught to pupils during each key stage'. Finally, there are *assessment arrangements* 'for assessing pupils at or near the end of each key stage, for the purpose of ascertaining what they have achieved in relation to the attainment targets for that stage'. (DES, 1989)

The national curriculum is to be introduced over a number of years. From September 1989 there was an obligation on all schools to take account of the subject definition of the curriculum in their curriculum planning but for most there were no programs of study providing detailed guidance on subject content. The leading role in the introduction of programs of study has fallen to the teachers of reception classes in infant and junior schools, for whom programs of study in English, maths, and science had already been published. It is these schools who will also be in the first phase of national assessment. The testing of 7-year-olds, using the nationally prepared Standard Attainment Tasks (SATs) was planned for Summer 1991. Its results were not, however, reported to parents and it was not until 1992 that they received information on the performance of their children on the national assessment program.

Significant changes were occurring to these reforms as they were being implemented. Concern that too much time would be devoted to testing led the Secretary of State to abandon plans for the national testing of 7-year-olds in all national-curriculum subjects. The SATs for 7-year-olds is now to be used only in the core subjects of English, maths, and science. Whilst this change was welcomed, because of concerns about time spent administering the SATs — as evidenced from the pilot projects commissioned to develop the Tasks — it does create a new problem, that teachers are more likely to concentrate their time on teaching the core subjects.

The second change pre-dates the 1988 Education Reform Act and is concerned with strengthening the vocational emphasis of the upper-secondary school curriculum. The Technical and Vocational Education Initiative (TVEI) was launched in 1982 with the official intention of opening a 'technical and vocational route to recognized national qualifications' (DE/DES, 1984). Whilst there was disagreement among ministers as to the 'target group' of children and its role as means of differentiating children (Chitty, 1989) its purpose was also to strengthen government control over the curriculum as a means of ensuring a better match between education provision and the needs of the economy, as perceived by the government. Launched at a time when the DES was a department with no constitutional powers to direct the school curriculum, this change was sponsored by the Manpower Services Commission (MSC), the training agency of the Department of Employment. The MSC negotiated contracts with the Local Education Authorities (LEAs), the terms of which provided additional funds to LEAs in return for specified cohorts of 14 to 18-year-olds receiving a curriculum with a more vocational emphasis, the terms of which were agreed between the MSC and each LEA. More recently the scheme has been extended so that all 14 to 16-year-olds will have an explicit vocational emphasis in their curriculum. How this will be reconciled with the demands of the national curriculum is yet to be satisfactorily resolved.

TVEI and TVE (Extension) illustrate the uncertainties attendant upon the outcomes of policy initiatives. When TVEI was first announced, mainstream educational opinion was deeply hostile to the proposals, yet during its implementation it became clear that teachers were able to develop the content and process of the curriculum in ways which were compatible with their professional preferences. Indeed, there is a generally positive view concerning the extension of TVE to all maintained secondary schools and colleges. As Hickox and Moore (1990) observe of those originally opposed to TVEI:

> It is probably true to say that today many of those same liberal teachers are expressing considerable support for TVEI and fear the possible consequences which the National Curriculum and the GCSE might pose for it.

As the policies enshrined in the Education Reform Act are translated into practice there must be some likelihood that the practice of a reformed education system will generate some outcomes significantly different from those intended.

The third major change for schools is the introduction of a system of school management known as the Local Management of Schools (LMS) (DES, 1988a). It is a change which has many of the features of an educational voucher scheme. From April 1990 school budgets for staffing, premises, and services were to be delegated to schools where they were to be under the final control of governing bodies with a lay majority. The delegated budget is funded by a formula largely determined by the number of pupils attending a school and the tenure of staff will depend upon the ability of the school budget to meet anticipated expenditure. If there is an expected budget deficit, staff can be dismissed with their continued employment dependent only upon the readiness of other governing bodies to offer an appointment; it is not possible for the Local Education Authority to require a governing body to make an appointment against their wish. This change in the tenure of staff can be expected to lead to greater competition between schools over the enrolment of pupils, an expectation reinforced by a change in admissions' regulations which reduce the powers of LEAs to limit admissions to schools: schools in future will have to admit pupils to their capacity (DES, 1988b). The inter-school competition for recruitment is further supported by a growing emphasis on the development of performance indicators which are intended, in part, to give parents more information when they — and their children — are choosing a school (Coopers and Lybrand, 1988). The published profile of a school's pupils on the national assessment is one example of the kind of performance information available. In exercising their local-management powers governors and head teachers must take account of their prior duty to provide the national curriculum. In order to do this they are required to prepare a management plan (DES, 1989a) which must show how they allocate resources to meet national-curriculum requirements.

These changes together constitute a 'pupil-as-voucher' scheme (Thomas, 1988). Schools which are successful will attract more pupils and more funds and will, as a result, be able to appoint staff of their choice. Those schools which are unsuccessful (or simply in areas of declining enrolment) will have fewer pupils, less money, and will need to dismiss staff. LMS is an integrated package, introducing more competition as a way of strengthening accountability and, according to its supporters, raising standards. As with earlier observations on the impact in practice of curriculum reform, it is only with time that the real effect of LMS will become apparent. What is evident, however, is that LMS is not the only device by which competition is being used to make the education service more accountable.

The fourth strand of change for schools is the introduction of grant-maintained schools (DES, 1988c). The Education Reform Act allows the governors of all secondary schools, and primary schools with more than 300 registered pupils, to apply to the Secretary of State for maintenance by grant from the central government and to cease to be maintained by the LEA. This change and the associated creation of twenty-four city technology colleges, also independent of LEAs, was designed to increase the range and diversity of schools from which parents and children can choose. In effect, while the organization for the 'local management of schools' was intended to make schools more responsive to parents, the organization for 'grant-maintained schools', in threatening the viability of LEAs, put pressure upon them to be more responsive, both to schools-as-clients and to parents-as-clients. Like LMS, competition is seen as a crucial means for improving the responsiveness and performance of the public-education system. The same characteristics are to be found in changes in the management of colleges serving principally the 16 to 19 age range.

Reform in Colleges

Local Management of Colleges (LMC) creates a funding and management arrangement for colleges which has similar features to the scheme for schools (DES, 1988d).[1] There was to be delegation of control over the budget and funding by a student-led formula. Governors would also have responsibility for appointing and dismissing staff. Colleges have for some time been required to produce more information on performance, data which can be used to inform the choices of clients, whether they are students or employers negotiating course packages. The Act also altered the legal composition of college governing bodies so that at least half the places could by taken by representatives of local employers and no more than 20 per cent of their membership may be LEA appointees (DES, 1988e).

In reconstructing the management relationship between LEAs and their colleges, the DES may have enhanced the relative position of LEAs, a change quite opposite to the general trend of reducing their powers. LMC requires each LEA to prepare a strategic plan within which individual colleges work and one part of the plan involves setting each college target student-admission numbers, which then determine levels of funding. However, for many LEAs the preparation of a strategic plan for their colleges is a departure from existing practice where, in its absence, colleges have had a large measure of autonomy and been in the market, competing for students. Given that this change may reduce the earlier freedoms of colleges, how it will work in practice is uncertain, particularly as it threatens to run counter to the pressures towards competition.

Colleges do not receive all their funding through the LEA formula. As in the past, some activities are funded through contracts between colleges and local employers but there is also separate and substantial funding from the

Department of Employment's training agencies. Since 1986/87 approximately one-quarter of the funds for what is termed Non-Advanced Further Education (NAFE) has been channelled to colleges through the MSC (and its successor organization, the Training Agency). Colleges receive the money in return for contracts which specify their contribution to employment-training programs, principally the Youth Training Scheme (YTS) and Employment Training (ET). As a result of proposals first announced in 1988 (DE, 1988), however, the management of these funds and the administration of YTS and ET are to be done on behalf of the Training Agency by newly created regional organizations known as Training and Enterprise Councils (TECs). Local employers must constitute two-thirds of the membership of each Council, the programs of which have budgets ranging between £15m and £50m. The employer influence was set out by Norman Fowler, the Secretary of State for Employment: 'Never before has government been willing to hand executive responsibility to employers [in this area, for] never before has government afforded employers at government expense the financial wherewithal' (quoted in Benn, 1990). Some writers have described this policy as a major step in the privatization of the government's training budget (Benn, 1990; Unwin, 1990) and it can be understood as such, both in terms of the control of training funds and the delivery of training. There is no requirement for the NAFE budget channelled through the Training Agency and the TECs to be spent in colleges, as private colleges and other agencies can seek contracts for the delivery of YTS and Employment Training.

Through control of one-quarter of the NAFE budget, MSC and latterly the Training Agency have negotiated the curriculum of trainees on YTS and ET programmes. Another agency of the Department of Employment, the National Council for Vocational Qualifications (NCVQ), is interpreting its role in course accreditation to shape other parts of the vocational curriculum. This body was set up in 1986 by the Secretary of State for Employment with the aim of rationalizing the awards provided in this area and accrediting all vocational qualifications. Its function has been interpreted as an opportunity for a wholesale review of the pattern of provision in ways which 'place a clear emphasis on competence criteria for the award of such qualifications' (Bash and Coulby, 1989); in other words, courses and methods of assessment are reviewed as part of the process of accreditation and subject, therefore, to revision.

Significant implications follow from this process in a training system that is already geared towards a mixed-economy model of private and public provision. Unwin (1990) observes that because National Vocational Qualifications (NVQs) 'demand a shift from courses to competences and, because they are assessment driven, they can be delivered via any agency that registers with a relevant awarding body'. She notes that a number of large and small firms are already approved to deliver NVQs.

The combination of employer-dominated TECs and competency-based training challenges the traditional role of colleges as major providers of vocational education. These new funding and accreditation arrangements have revised the market conditions within which vocational training takes place and colleges must become part of the 'enterprise culture' if they are to maintain their market share in vocational training.

What is notable about these reforms in vocational education is the limited significance of the 1988 Education Reform Act and, indeed, of the Department of Education and Science. Policy in this area still appears to be driven by the Department of Employment. It is interesting to observe, however, that the Act takes reserve powers over the curriculum in relation to 16 to 19-year-olds whether attending school or college (Section 24). In Section 19 it also states that courses leading to external qualifications may have to be approved by the Secretary of State. Is this an opportunity being taken by the DES to gain access, through the legitimizing role of statute, into an area from which, in practice, it has been largely excluded in recent years? Tension over policy control among central departments should not obscure the coherence of the reform movement in England and Wales as a means of reducing the influence of the producer interest. The role of the Training Agency, its TECs and the NCVQ further illustrates the ways in which central government, and its agencies, are taking a lead in the specification of the curriculum whilst simultaneously enhancing the influence of clients over choice of provider. Similar processes can be identified in the reform of higher education.

Reform of Higher Education

Higher education in Britain is provided mainly by universities, polytechnics, and colleges of higher education. The management of all are changed by the Education Reform Act. The Act ends local-authority control of the polytechnics in England and Wales and fifty other colleges, all of which become independent statutory corporations. Public funds are channelled through a new body known as the Polytechnics and Colleges Funding Council (PCFC) which complements a Universities Funding Council (UFC) set up to replace the University Grants Council. These councils have stronger industrial representation than their predecessors but this is a less significant change than the enhanced power of the Secretary of State who can 'by order confer or impose on either of the Funding Councils such supplementary functions as he thinks fit [and] in exercising their functions under this Part of this Act each of the Funding Councils shall comply with any directions given to them by the Secretary of State' (Section 134).

The Act also abolished life-time tenure for university appointments and promotions made after November 1987, a change which can be viewed as affecting their governance insofar as it was designed to enable universities to modify their staffing profile as their pattern of work alters. Williams (1990) argues that the changes in the government of higher education represent the logical culmination of policies for higher education for many years and that, in themselves, they are much less significant than the demographic pressures which arise from a sharp fall in the age group which form their traditional clientele. Competition will arise from these demographic pressures alone with government policy being significant in shaping 'the form the competition takes and the determination of likely winners and losers' (p. 260). These pressures are reinforced by changes in the funding of teaching and students, which increase the proportion of income received from tuition fees and shift the funding of student support from grants to loans, both designed to increase the power of the client over providers.

As with other parts of the education system the government is intent on shaping the nature of the work of higher education. For schools and colleges this has focussed upon the curriculum, whereas for higher education the focus is also upon its research activity. From the mid-1980s the funding of research in the universities became increasingly selective, recent directions from the Secretary of State essentially giving added emphasis to that policy (UFC, 1989). For the institutions funded by the PCFC the guidance of the Secretary of State may indicate a further sharpening in the distinction between their role and that of the universities. They are advised that their research funding must come largely from industry and other end-users, the government having no intention of providing funds for the support of basic research. Far from recent changes indicating a closing of the gap between universities and PCFC institutions, Williams argues that 'the distinct role of the universities and the PCFC institutions in research is made more explicit than in any previous official pronouncement [and] in many ways the 1988 Education Act and the Letters of Guidance to the Funding Councils are the clearest expressions of a binary policy'.

The Training Agency has also intervened in higher education. In 1987 it announced an 'enterprise in higher education' program. The intention was 'to encourage the development of qualities of enterprise among those seeking higher education qualifications' in a project whereby funding is given on the basis that the program be 'integrated into the education provision of the institution with the aim of providing opportunities for all students within an agreed timetable' (MSC, 1987). Together with the emphasis on competition for research funds and the introduction of tendering arrangements for numbers of student places, Bash and Coulby (1989) see the development of policy for higher education as reflecting the government's intention of extending the enterprise culture to all parts of education. As will be argued in the next section there is symmetry between the development of policy in education and in other public services.

Explaining Reform

Markets, Competition, and Accountability

Influential in the construction of much government policy over the past decade has been a belief in the benefits of market-oriented solutions for the provision of goods and services in the public and private sectors of social and economic activity. The view that competitive markets meet needs automatically can be cited in the speeches of many leading members of the government over the past decade. When he was still Chief Secretary to the Treasury, John Major (1989) set out the virtues of privatization as 'quite simply the best way to ensure that service to the consumer naturally comes first'. Much earlier Keith Joseph recognized that private ownership was not a sufficient condition to protect the consumer interest: 'It is competition that harnesses the self-interest of the businessman to the interests of the consumer' (quoted by Chitty, 1989).

It is these ideas which have contributed to the definition of the programs of reform pursued by the Conservative government in office since 1979, policies which have drawn upon the work of several right-wing 'think tanks' such as the Institute of Economic Affairs (IEA), the Adam Smith Institute and the Policy Studies Institute (PSI). With a specific interest in education policy the Hillgate Group has also made a distinctive contribution.

Table 3.1: The Government's Reform Program: A Broad Perspective

	State enterprises	Central government departments and agencies	Local government	Private sector
Change of ownership	x		x	
Market regulation		x	x	x
Financial management	x	x	x	
Political accountability			x	

Understanding the nature and origin of the education reforms, therefore, requires some appreciation of the broader perspective of the government's reform program. These reforms have included: (1) change of ownership; (2) market regulation; (3) financial management, and (4) political accountability. These are listed on the vertical axis of Table 1 with the foci of reform shown on the horizontal axis. The occupied cells show where these reform measures have been applied.

Changing ownership has meant the transfer of enterprises from collective or social ownership to private and institutional shareholders, whether from the United Kingdom or overseas. Examples are gas and water utilities, steel, motor manufacturing, road transport, and telecommunications. In some respects this could be described as the ideal type of privatization where the government ceases altogether to own these assets. In some of these cases, however, the government has retained, for a fixed term, a 'golden share' giving it a right of veto over future change of ownership. A slightly different model of privatization has been the sale of the majority share of an enterprise, leaving the government in ownership of a residual share of the equity. Changing ownership in other forms has affected housing policy. This has included allowing tenants of municipal housing the right to buy the freehold and, more controversially, schemes transferring the ownership of municipal estates to private-sector companies (Spencer, 1989). Education and health provide a different form of change of ownership. Grant-maintained schools and self-managing hospitals are institutions which leave their former owners and become self-managing trusts. In the event of their closure, the assets of a grant-maintained school would revert to the local authority.

Market regulation includes the possibility of transferring the management of municipally owned housing to private-management companies; changes to reduce restrictive practices in the legal profession; and reforms in the financial sector designed to end traditional demarcations. In education the new rules for local management alter the market conditions in which schools and colleges function, giving parents, students, and employers more choice by linking funding and jobs to enrolment. The creation of an internal market not unlike LMS and LMC was also a feature of the health-service reforms planned for 1991.

Financial management has been a developing feature of the management of the public sector since before 1979. It was the Labour government 1976–9 which changed the controlling principle of public expenditure from a volume of service to a cash-limited basis, a change congruent with economic policies which stressed the need to maintain control of public sector debt because of its implications for money supply. The Conservative government has developed policies on financial management through a variety of initiatives. Cash-limiting has been extended from whole programs (e.g., education or defence) to cost-centre budgeting of increasingly smaller parts of programs. Public finance for the universities, for example, has been strongly cash-limited since 1981, which has meant the cash limiting of the budgets of individual universities. More recently, however, this has been extended to the definition of subject areas within individual universities as cost centres, whose performance on a system of triennial review shapes its subsequent level of funding from the Universities Funding Council. As a result of LMS and LMC schools and colleges also become cash-limited cost centres.

The role of the Audit Commission as an agency monitoring the spending of local government has been strengthened. Its appraisals of the performance of the education service include studies of further education (Audit Commission, 1985); non-teaching costs in schools (Audit Commission, 1984); the management of secondary education (Audit Commission, 1986) and the local inspectorate of schools (Audit Commission, 1989). For central government, the Prime Minister has used special advisers to report on the efficiency of departments and to propose systems which promote greater value for money. In education this included a study of the effectiveness of HMIs (Her Majesty's Inspectors) (DES, 1982). These developments have a common origin in the Prime Minister's initiative for greater economy, efficiency, and effectiveness in the spending of public money and has contributed to more emphasis on financial management, where performance criteria are set and funding is dependent upon achieving specified goals. John Major (1989) summarized the changes within the public services as 'nothing less than a revolution in progress. We are creating an environment in which everyone has clearly delegated authority and responsibility. Ministers and senior managers concentrate on setting policy objectives, performance targets, and the resources needed to meet them; and the individuals who deliver the services use their ability and skills to tackle problems'.

In its reform of financial management the government believed that spending by local government has been too high and not as efficient as it might be. In its search for efficiency it legislated for more competition; an ending of subsidies; separation of service responsibility from service provision; and a reduction in 'producer interests' (Stewart and Stoker, 1989). Since education is by far the largest single activity of local government, reforms to the system within which it operates cannot fail to have an impact upon the schools and colleges, transforming the network of working relationships within which they function. It means, for example, that those locally provided services which schools have used in the past (such as cleaning the premises and maintaining the grounds) will no longer be provided directly by the local authority but by a contracted agent. It also means that the pressures towards more competition and performance assessment, which are a characteristic of the LMS and LMC reforms in education, are replicated and reinforce in other areas of local-government service the competitive ethos, as does the monitoring of local government by agencies such as the Audit Commission.

In its attempts to control the level of local-government spending, central government has argued that high spending arises from too weak a relationship between spending and political accountability. A tax levied upon individuals has replaced a tax on the value of business and private property. Introduced in 1990 in England and Wales, the declared intention of the 'community charge' (popularly known as the 'Poll Tax') was to strengthen electoral accountability, so that those local authorities which planned to spend more than a target assessed by central government would have to fund the difference solely by adding to the charge levied upon the local electorate. Whether or not this works in the long term as a means of controlling the local-government part of public-sector spending was less significant in 1990 than the focus of political unpopularity for the levels set for the tax in its first year.

The Pursuits of Self-interest

A central assumption underlying many of these policies is that, for social and economic activities, forms of private exchanges, ownership, and control contribute more to the sum of welfare than structures of collective provision. The reasoning turns on a model of man associated with neo-classical economics, which assumes that individuals act to maximize their self-interest and that markets provide the means whereby individuals have the freedom to exchange goods and services in ways which promote their individual interests. Since the market allows individuals to maximize their self-interest, the sum of these exchanges maximizes social welfare. While there are exceptions to this rule, for example, natural monopolies, public goods such as national defence, and the need to protect minors, the general conclusion is that the provision of goods and services is best done through the market.

This philosophy has informed the publications of groups such as the IEA, which, in its work in education, has stressed the need for reducing government control of education (West, 1970), for the introduction of vouchers as a means of encouraging choice in schools (Seldon, 1986), and student loans as a means of strengthening client control over higher education. More recently it provided a means of publicizing work on magnet schools (Cooper, 1987) and decentralized funding (Humphrey, 1988). In March 1987 a pamphlet authored by the director of the IEA's education unit foreshadowed the proposals for LMS and grant-maintained schools contained in the Conservative election manifesto published in May (Sexton, 1987).

The assumption that individuals pursue their self-interest creates a double jeopardy for any collectively provided service, even including those providing public goods. Public-choice theorists argue that decision makers in non-market conditions are not 'economic eunuchs' who will be ruled by 'artificial criteria of choice', prepared to choose 'in accordance with the costs and benefits predicted for the whole community' (Buchanan, 1969). They reject 'any kind of organic theory of the state which superimposes higher "values" on those of individuals' (Wiseman, 1979). What emerges is a view of public servants as concerned with goals such as high salary, perquisites of office, power, and patronage rather than efficiency (Mueller, 1979). The logic is the need to explore decision-making in the political arena with the aim of enhancing consumer control of public decisions by introducing rules which seek to mimic market behaviour. The public-choice literature is, in large part, a product of a concern that without appropriate regulation public servants have little incentive to act in the collective interest (Mitchell, 1989). The double jeopardy is inherent to the assumptions of public-choice theorists. If their assumptions about the behaviour of public servants are correct, those same public servants have no incentive to advise their political 'masters' of policies which will effectively reduce the power of the 'bureaucrats'.

It can be argued that the education reforms in England and Wales are wholly consistent with the reasoning of public-choice theorists. They are reforms which have been introduced by central government and their net effect has been to strengthen the role and status of officials at the DES at the expense of other levels of government and tiers of public officials and professionals. Whether the consistency of these reforms with the expectations of public-choice economics means that these theories provide a sufficient explanation for the shape of the reform package should be neither accepted nor dismissed too hastily. Why market-oriented policy makers have been able to secure the implementation of polices designed to increase consumer control and choice of places in schools and higher education but appear, for example, to have been unsuccessful in giving consumers more control over the school curriculum, may have more to do with the complexity of factors surrounding the debate over the control of the curriculum than with the self-interest of DES officials seeking their personal aggrandizement. Let me now turn, therefore, to policy on the curriculum and its role in generating human capital.

Human Capital and Planned Growth

The belief that the level of a nation's educational achievement is a key component of economic growth is as pervasive as the lack of convincing evidence of the form of the relationship between particular types of educational activity, their implications for the quality of the labour force and levels of economic performance (Blaug, 1976; Mace, 1987). This absence of convincing evidence has not, however, prevented policy makers pursuing policies which have *inter alia* increased central influence and control over the curriculum while having their declared purpose the aim of strengthening the responsiveness of education to the needs of the economy.

As with governments elsewhere British governments remain committed to the positive nexus between education and economic growth. What has changed, however, is the specific form which this nexus now takes. Whilst in the 1960s there was a belief in the economic value of education spending *per se*, the continuing relative underperformance of the British economy led to questions being asked about how educationists were actually using their discretionary authority when deciding what and how children and students should learn. These concerns were deepened by the oil shock of 1973 and the years since then have been characterized by various initiatives designed to limit producer control over the curriculum. As set out earlier, they have included stronger specification of curriculum by statute and by contractual arrangements as well as the setting of performance criteria, which are intended to contribute both to controlling the direction of the service and its standard of performance.

Whilst policies on the curriculum may share this general direction, it should not be assumed that all policy initiatives have been entirely consistent with others. In his analysis of the politics of curriculum change from the mid-1970s, Chitty (1989) examines the conflict of views about the direction of policy. Different emphases on breadth and balance are seen in the views of, for example, HMI against those of officials in the DES. The TVEI announced in 1982 and sponsored by the MSC represents a more vocational orientation to the curriculum from those who were to advocate a national curriculum in 1987. Different again were the views of those who opposed prescription for the curriculum, insisting that it should be left to emerge from the more market-oriented system of governance introduced for schools. As Ranson (1988) observes, in the decision to legislate a national curriculum, the Hillgate Group's view that the curriculum provides a means of incorporating a statement of the nation's culture and values, and that central prescription was necessary, was to be more influential than the view of the Adam Smith Institute or the IEA that the content of the curriculum should be resolved by the choices of parents in the education marketplace.

These differences should not, however, ignore what is common to the views of all these groups, which is that the education service has failed to meet the needs of the economy and that reforms are required for correcting that perceived deficiency. Even as the national curriculum's programs of study were announced, the consensus that greater space should be accorded to science, technology, and modern languages went largely unnoticed as attention focused upon, for example, the debate over the nature of the history which should be taught. The new status accorded to science, a core subject alongside maths and English, was further reinforced by the decision to limit the national testing of 7-year-olds to these three subjects. The implications for the distribution of time in learning could be considerable. The influence of the science and engineering lobby on education policy in Britain was identified long ago by Gannicott and Blaug (1969) and discussed subsequently by Mace (1980). Its influence has moved from lobbying for a larger share of activity in higher education to the balance of time in the school curriculum. The evidence that this is the key to Britain's economic regeneration remains, however, as elusive as ever. With respect to the curriculum it is legitimate to ask: Whither the market?

Whither the Market?

What is apparent is that the school curriculum is too important to be left to the market, an irony given the general position of the government on the virtues of consumer freedom and choice. A department of state with few previous powers to direct activity in education has now taken upon itself statutory authority to determine the school curriculum. With its appointed agencies, the DES will define the programs of study for schools and the means of assessment, sharing a role with the Training Agency in the specification of a more vocational orientation for upper-secondary education. The direct implication of the remarks of Nick Stuart's with which this chapter began is that this will lead to defining the most economically appropriate curriculum which, with associated testing, will also raise standards in schools and lead to an improvement in our economic performance. The role of clients in the schools' market is largely limited to quality control, choosing between institutions, the product specification of which has been significantly predetermined.

Whether the curriculum of colleges will be more client-driven than that of schools depends upon who are defined as clients. It is clear that employers have a much enhanced role in product specification and quality control through their representation on governing bodies, the NCVQ and the TECs. By the curious logic of training policy, those who have in the past systematically underinvested their own resources in the training of human capital now have a much stronger say in spending public funds on training. The direction of this change is certainly towards a more client-controlled system but still in an administered market, where it is employers and not trainees who control public resources available for training.

For higher education, the DES-appointed UFC, PCFC and research Councils will have a tighter control over the distribution of numbers of students on degree programs and will selectively fund research on specified performance criteria. Meanwhile the Training Agency negotiates an enterprise emphasis to the curriculum of degree programs. The amount of client control over the curriculum depends both upon who are defined as clients but also upon which components of university work is being considered. A gradual shift to loans as a means of funding students increases their influence as clients, a factor given added emphasis by the declining numbers in the age cohort from which the student population is largely drawn. Their degree of influence on program content is significantly less in areas such as accountancy, law, medicine, and engineering where the requirements of the professional groups who control access must be recognized in the content of teaching programs. On research, the end-client view is represented insofar as performance criteria reflect their views. In a system where the level of research funds gained through competition is a major criteria for a high-performance rating, it could be argued that this serves as a reasonable indirect indicator of client views.

When the policies of centralization, decentralization and competition are analysed across the different sectors of education, what emerges is a complex and varied pattern, the final outcomes of which are largely unknown at this stage. There are, however, some particularly fascinating areas which require monitoring, not least the performance of the DES which, in Dunleavy's term, was a largely 'non-executant' department before the 1988 Education Reform Act. Until the 1988 Act its main executive responsibility was concerned with ensuring an appropriate level of teacher supply for schools, a policy area which has not been notable for a high level of success in the years since 1944 (Zabalza, 1979; Thomas, 1985; Smithers, 1990). Another area is the reform of the control of training into an employer-dominated administered market; this will test their capabilities for improving the skill levels of the workforce. Within the terms of the public-choice critique there is no obvious reason why employers should make better decisions than bureaucrats when the money they are spending is not their own. Overarching their work, however, as well as that of higher education is the declining cohort of school-leavers, a factor which alone may lead to the training system and higher education becoming more responsive to the perceived needs of trainees and students-as-clients. How these and other factors can be interpreted through the prism for understanding reform developed by Guthrie and Koppich is the focus of the next section.

Alignment, Initiative, and Mobilization

The introductory section of this chapter posed three questions about reform: *why* reform; why *this* reform and why this reform *now*? These are questions which have similarities with, respectively, the concepts of initiative, alignment, and mobilization from which Guthrie and Koppich derive six propositions for testing their policy paradigm. These propositions provide the structure for this section but, first, we do need to be clear as to which reform the discussion will concentrate upon. Whilst the earlier section describing the reforms referred to changes other than those contained in the 1988 Act, the Act itself is sufficiently innovative and, as a challenge to the producer interest, has a coherence that invites its examination and explanation as a single reform. Why in March 1985, in an authoritative statement on education policy, did the Conservative government declare 'that the action now necessary to raise standards in school education can in the main be taken within the existing legal framework' (DES, 1985) yet, in May 1987, publish an election manifesto proposing the radical reforms later incorporated into the 1988 Act? How does the Guthrie and Koppich model assist us in explaining: Why this reform now?

Education Reform as a Lagged Response

The economic and demographic factors which may provide the structural reasons for education reform in Britain are not new. Not only has our economic performance been a chronic problem since 1945 but demographic factors have contributed to disequilibrium since the later 1970s. In particular there has been declining school enrolment at a time of rapid growth in numbers of dependent aged, a large number of young unemployed and, during the 1990s, a declining cohort of young people entering the labour market. Since what is being described is a state of chronic disequilibrium in factors which have great significance for education policy, it will be no surprise that education has been subject to a series of reforms, giving rise to considerable complexity and consequent difficulty for any analysis concerned with establishing causal relationships between particular economic or demographic events and specific reforms. Nonetheless, that there is a relationship is one with which this writer concurs.

Whether or not the reforms embodied in the 1988 Act are a lagged response to economic and demographic factors is no less complex. The Conservative government elected in 1979 was committed to a wide-ranging reform agenda which included education and training. This led to some reforms which could be interpreted as a lagged response to perceived economic problems. Other policies, such as those for widening school choice for some parents, including supporting access to the private sector and effectively ending further moves towards non-selective secondary education, are more convincingly explained as reflecting the ideological commitment of the government. We should also not set aside the ideological aspect of policies for reducing the size of the public sector, as the British have a government which believes that private ownership and markets are normally not only more economically efficient but socially and politically superior to publicly provided services. Allied to the argument early in this chapter that the 1988 Act assumes coherence only when viewed as a challenge to the 'producer interest', we may need to recognize that the exogenous variables — explaining why there was a need for reform — arise as much from ideological as economic and demographic factors.

Reform and Value Disequilibrium

Guthrie and Koppich observe that equality, efficiency, and liberty are core societal values which inform much debate on public policy and that it is the state of their dynamic equilibrium which shapes the issues that gain ascendance on the political agenda. Of the recent reforms in Great Britain there is little doubt that equality has been eclipsed by demands for efficiency and liberty. However, while concern about efficiency has been rising since the 'great debate' of 1976, demand for liberty — understood here as allowing some parents and children to have a wider choice of schools — becomes more prominent after 1979. Yet extending this form of liberty faced public resistance. With a large parliamentary majority it was possible to legislate some reforms but when one Conservative-controlled LEA attempted to reintroduce selection for secondary schooling it was decisively rejected by local opinion.

Reforming education was, in the event, easier to legitimate on grounds of efficiency than liberty, so much so that the policies for enhancing liberty-through-choice (creation of city technology colleges and grant-maintained schools, altering regulations on control of admissions) were presented in efficiency terms: competition contributes to improvements in standards. They also became feasible either, as with city technology colleges, through bypassing the LEA or, as with grant-maintained schools, by allowing one school to make a decision on its own behalf without having to take account of the consequences for the larger community in the area. The difficulties encountered by the government in extending its own view of liberty adds weight to the argument that its ideological position should be placed on an equal footing with economic and demographic factors explaining recent British reforms.

Reform as a Response to a Political Problem

Notable by their absence from this chapter are the teachers, for which there is good reason. Because its purpose is to challenge the 'producer interest', the Education Reform Act was concerned with setting the agenda for teachers — and other professional educators — but not involving them in the process of setting that agenda. Education reform is a political issue because the interaction between government and teachers moved it into the political domain. In some respects this happened when Prime Minister Callaghan initiated a 'great debate' on education in 1976 but it was taken further in the 1979 election with Conservative slogans such as 'educashun isnt wurking' and still further by the erosion of the relative incomes of teachers in the middle and late 1980s.

With particular reference to the 1988 reforms and the further 'politicization' of education we cannot ignore almost two years of industrial action by teachers from 1985 to 1987. For a government which had rewritten so much labour-relations legislation it must have been particularly unhappy with action which took full advantage of teachers', relatively open, employment contract, allowing them to disrupt work in schools but to do so on full pay. For the government this must have provided further evidence of the negative effects of 'producer control' and the need for legislation such as LMS and LMC which makes staff tenure dependent upon cash-limited pupil or student-driven budgets.

Choice of Reform Measures

Is nothing new? In their fourth proposition Guthrie and Koppich suggest that reforms will have been previously proposed but that a condition of their acceptance is that they are shaped in ways which accord with the preferences of policy makers. This is true of much of the 1988 reforms. Proposals for a national curriculum had existed for some time as had proposals for regular testing to monitor standards. A variant of LMS had been operated by some LEAs for several years while the advocates of vouchers had long been influential with government. The idea of directly funded schools, the grant-maintained schools, recreated a form of centrally funded school which had ceased barely ten years before. Even the creation of city technology colleges could be traced back to the TVEI when, at one time, the MSC threatened to create its own schools.

Shaping proposals so that they were consistent with the values of ascendent policy makers was not difficult for a number of the reforms, not least because they were formulated by the policy makers themselves, who placed more emphasis on values such as pupil and student choice, loans and categorical funding for higher education. Curriculum control and national assessment are more complex because there were influential advisers, particularly from the IEA, who opposed a national curriculum on the grounds that the curriculum should arise from the coincidence of wants in the local-education market-place. In its final format, however, it does fit neatly with the idea (*vide* John Major) of government setting policy targets and monitoring performance but allowing units at the local level to work out the best way of achieving those targets.

A Mandate for Reform

The proposals contained in the 1988 Act were largely set out in the Conservative election manifesto of 1987 and were a central part of that document. In searching for a radical agenda for a third term, the government had identified education as an activity about which there was public concern and which remained largely untouched by the market-oriented policies shaping other areas of public policy.

The Entrepreneurs of Reform

At once the most interesting and problematic element in the Guthrie and Koppich model is that of the 'policy entrepreneur'. Defined as an individual or set of individuals who champion the change and attempt to maintain the momentum of reform, they are crucial in answering the question 'Why this reform *now*?' because it is they who take advantage of those 'windows of opportunity'

which present themselves for those seeking reform. The idea of policy entrepreneurs is not challenged in this chapter and neither is the existence of various
individuals and groups in shaping reform proposals. Guthrie and Koppich do
not, however, refer to interest and pressure groups or to the idea of a departmental interest — see Salter and Tapper's (1981) discussion of the role of the
educational state apparatus — which, in some ways, transcends the notion of
individualism embodied in the idea of the entrepreneur. In applying Dunleavy's
(1980) model of intergovernmental relationship to education, Slater (1985) adds
an influence flow between one central government agency on another, illustrat-
ing it with the relationship between the DES, the MSC (now Training Agency)
and the Department of Employment. It may well be that the approach of the
MSC to training policy caused the DES to become more proactive on education
policy, not only because the actions of the MSC threatened the DES but also
because it provided a model of how to take a greater role in shaping policy.

With respect to the 1988 Act, it may be that a significant contributory factor
to the introduction of a national curriculum with national assessment — in
Ranson's (1988) terms 'a victory for the Hillgate Group's neo-conservatism
against the IEA's neo-liberalism' — lies in a departmental interest in securing
more power and being able to do so in ways which were demonstrably consistent with the logic of the reform as a whole. In understanding the 1988 reforms,
then, the idea of the entrepreneur may need to be elaborated into one which
recognizes, at least, the place of the *departmental interest*. The individualism
associated with entrepreneurialism may also imply a degree of uncertainty with
respect to the outcomes of the policy-making process because they depend upon
how well individuals and groups are able to marshall arguments and support for
a particular policy position. It is an idea which can be extended into a speculative
and brief final discussion.

Conclusion: The Entrepreneurs of Outcomes

Reform had been legislated in England and Wales and is being implemented,
although whether final outcomes will match the intentions of reformers must
remain unknown at this stage. Despite the exclusion of education professionals
from the making of policy and the scope of their future role, they cannot be
excluded from implementation. Yet how professional educators interpret their
roles and responsibilities has a crucial bearing on, for example, the level of
competition between institutions, the nature of governor involvement in making
policy for schools and governors, the relationship between LEAs and their
institutions, and what that means for the political as against constitutional reality
of delegated management.

Notwithstanding the contribution of parents and pupils, governors, teachers
and LEA staff, it is suggested that, typically, it will be college principals and head
teachers who will have the crucial role in shaping the implementation of these
reforms (Thomas, 1989). Institutions have sufficient autonomy that they can, if
they choose, largely ignore their own LEA and, within institutions, it is the head
or principal who is at once its leading professional and chief executive (Hughes,
1985). How that leadership and executive office is exercized will shape the institution's internal effectiveness and, externally, the level of competition and

collaboration with others. They will be the entrepreneurs of outcomes. Much will depend upon whether they are able to construct a regulated market in which collaboration can coexist with fair levels of competition or whether a largely unregulated market develops where collaboration has largely ceased. Will heads and principals be entrepreneurs or pirates?

Note

1 Colleges of Further Education cater principally for the 16 to 19 age range although they also make provision for adult education and training. The focus of their work is predominantly vocational. In March 1991 the government announced proposals for transferring their control and funding away from local government to the Department of Education and Science.

References

AUDIT COMMISSION, THE (1984) *Obtaining Better Value in Education: Aspects of Non-Teaching Costs in Secondary Schools*, London, HMSO.

AUDIT COMMISSION, THE (1985) *Obtaining Better Value from Further Education*, London, HMSO.

AUDIT COMMISSION, THE (1986) *Towards Better Management of Secondary Education*, London, HMSO.

AUDIT COMMISSION, THE (1989) *Assuring Quality in Education. The Role Of Local Education Authority Inspectors and Advisers*, London, HMSO.

BASH, L. and COULBY, D. (1989) *The Education Reform Act: Competition and Control*, London, Cassell.

BENN, C. (1990) 'The Public Price of Private Education and Privatization', *Forum* 32. 3, Summer.

BLAUG, M. (1976) 'The empirical status of human capital theory: A slightly jaundiced survey', *Journal of Economic Literature*, 14, September.

BUCHANAN, J.M. (1969) *Cost and Choice: An Inquiry in Economic Theory*, Chicago, Markham.

CHITTY, C. (1989) *Towards a New Education System: The Victory of the New Right?* Lewes, The Falmer Press.

COOPER, B. (1987) *Magnet Schools*, London, IEA Education Unit.

COOPERS AND LYBRAND (1988) *Local Management of Schools*, A Report to the Department of Education and Science, London, HMSO.

DES (1982) *Study of HM Inspectorate in England and Wales*, London, HMSO.

DES (1985) *Better Schools*, Cmnd 9469, London, HMSO.

DES (1989) *Education Reform Act 1988: The School Curriculum and Assessment*, Circular 5/89, London, DES.

DES (1988a) *Education Reform Act: Local management of Schools*, Circular 7/88, London, DES.

DES (1988b) *Admissions of Pupils to Country and Voluntary Schools*, Circular 11/88, London, DES.

DES (1988c) *Education Reform Act: Grant Maintained Schools*, Circular 10/88, London, DES.

DES (1988d) *Education Reform Act 1988: Local Management of Further and Higher Education Colleges: Planning and Delegation Schemes and Articles of Government*, Circular 9/88, London, DES.

DES (1988e) *Education Reform Act 1988: Government of Maintained Further and Higher Education Colleges*, Circular 8/88, London, DES.

DE (1988) *Employment in the 1990s*, London, DES.

DE/DES (1984) *Training for Jobs*, Cmnd 9135, London, HMSO.

DUNLEAVY, P. (1980) *Urban Political Analysis*, London, Macmillan.

EDUCATION REFORM ACT, THE (1988) *The Education Reform Act, 1988*, (Chapter 40), London, HMSO.

FLUDE, M. and HAMMER, M. (Eds) (1990) *The Education Reform Act, Its origins and implications*, Lewes, The Falmer Press.

GANNICOTT, K. and BLAUG, M. (1969) 'Manpower Forecasting Since Robbins: A Science Lobby in Action', *Higher Education Review*, 2, 1.

HICKOX, M. and MOORE, R. (1990) 'TVEI, Vocationalism and the Crisis of Liberal Education', in FLUDE, M. and HAMMER, M. (Eds) *The Education Reform Act, Its Origins and Implications*, Lewes, The Falmer Press.

HUGHES, M. (1985) 'Leadership in Professionally Staffed Organisation', *Managing Education: The System and the Institution*, Eastbourne, Holt, Rinehart and Winston.

HUMPHREY, C. (1988) *Financial Autonomy in Solihull*, London, IEA Education Unit.

LAWTON, D. (1989) *The Education Reform Act: Choice and Control*, Sevenoaks, Hodder and Stoughton.

MACE, J. (1980) 'The Finniston Report: An Economist's View', *Education Policy Bulletin*, 8, 1, Spring.

MACE, J. (1987) 'Education, the Labour Market and Government Policy', in THOMAS, H. and SIMKINS, T. (Eds) *Economics and the Management of Education: Emerging Themes*, Lewes, The Falmer Press.

MACLURE, S. (1989) *Education Re-formed: A Guide to the Education Reform Act 1988*, Sevenoaks, Hodder and Stoughton.

MAJOR, J. (1989) 'Public Service Management: Revolution in Progress', Management Lecture organized by The Audit Commission, June.

MSC (1987) *Enterprise in Higher Education*, London, Department of Trade and Industry.

MITCHELL, W.C. (1989) *Government as it is*, London, IEA.

MUELLER, D.C. (1979) *Public Choice*, Cambridge, University Press.

RANSON, S. (1988) 'From 1944 to 1988: Education, Citizenship and democracy', *Local Government Studies*, 14, 1.

SALTER, B. and TAPPER, T. (1981) *Education, Politics and the State: The Theory and Practice of Educational Change*, London, Grant McIntyre.

SELDON, A. (1986) *The Riddle of the Voucher*, London, IEA.

SEXTON, S. (1987) *Our Schools — a Radical Policy*, London, IEA.

SLATER, D. (1985) 'The Education Sub-Government: Structure and context', in HUGHES, M. *et al.* (Eds) *Managing Education: the System and the Institution*, Eastbourne, Holt, Rinehart and Winston.

SMITHERS, A. (1990) *Teacher Loss*, Interim Report to the Leverhulme Trust, School of Education, University of Manchester.

SPENCER, K.M. (1989) 'Local Government and the Housing Reforms', in STEWART, J. and STOKER, G. (Eds) *The Future of Local Government*, London, Macmillan.

STEWART, J. and STOKER, G. (1989) (Eds) *The Future of Local Government*, London, Macmillan.

STUART, N. (1990) Lecture at the BEMAS Annual Conference, University of Leicester, September 1989, Quoted by THOMAS, H. and KIRKPATRICK, G. 'Managing Quality and Accountability', *Educational Management and Adminstration*, 18, 3.

THOMAS, H. (1985) 'Teacher Supply: Problems Practice and Possibilities', in HUGHES, M. *et al.* (Eds) *Managing Education: The System and the Institution*, Eastbourne, Holt, Rinehart and Winston.

THOMAS, H. (1988) 'Pupils as vouchers', *Times Educational Supplement*, 3779, 2 December.

THOMAS, H. (1989) 'Who will control the secondary school in the 1990s?', in LOWER, R. (Ed.) *The Changing Secondary School*, Lewes, The Falmer Press.

UFC (1989) *UFC Resource Allocation and Planning Arrangement*, Circular 39/89, London, University Funding Council.

UNWIN (1990) 'Learning to Live Under Water: The Education Reform Act and its Implications for Further and Adult Education', in FLUDE, M. and HAMMER, M. (Eds) *The Education Reform Act, Its Origins and Implications*, Lewes, The Falmer Press.

WEST, E.G. (1980) *Education and the State*, 2nd ed, London, IEA.

WILLIAMS, G. (1990) 'Higher Education', in FLUDE, M. and HAMMER, M. (Eds) *The Education Reform Act, Its, Origins and Implications*, Lewes, The Falmer Press.

WISEMAN, J. (1979) 'The Political Economy of Nationalised Industry', in IEA (1979) *The Economics of Politics*, IEA Readings 18, London, IEA.

ZABALZA, A., TURNBULL, P. and WILLIAMS, G. (1979) *The Economics of Teacher Supply*, Cambridge, University Press.

Chapter 4

Examining Contemporary Education-reform Efforts in the United States

J.E. Koppich and J.W. Guthie

Introduction

A Nation at Risk was published in 1983 with its, now famous, warning that a 'rising tide of mediocrity' threatened to engulf the nation's schools. This small book, issued by the National Commission on Excellence in Education, a prestigious *ad hoc* panel chaired by University of California's President David Gardner, sounded an education call to arms and unleashed a firestorm of reform activity. Written in language reminiscent of calls for national defense build-ups in times of foreign military threat, the report succeeded in capturing and holding the nation's attention.

Among the indicators of an education system gone soft which were cited by the National Commission were: American students' poor showing on international comparisons of academic achievement; a quarter-century-long decline in student scores on standardized tests; the twenty-years downward spiral in average SAT scores; and the American business community's increasingly vocal concern about the millions of dollars it was spending on remedial programs for new employees who had recently graduated from American high schools (Bell, T., 1990).

The reverberations produced by *A Nation at Risk* triggered a wave of reform activity in the states. Political rhetoric rapidly was translated into policy action as governors and state legislators became energetic advocates of school reform. Within a year of the publication of the National Commission's report, more than a hundred formal state commissions and taskforces, often composed largely of corporate chief executives, had been established to study public education and make recommendations for improvement.

The recommendations emanating from these state-level education commissions were often broad and sweeping. Many states initiated extensive education reform efforts. A fifty state survey conducted by the national education newspaper, *Education Week*, at the end of 1983 found that thirty-three states had enacted or were considering legislation to increase teachers' salaries and seven states had approved legislation to lengthen the instructional day or year or both. Many states increased high-school graduation requirements, instituted statewide student-assessment programs, and tightened teacher-certification procedures, including requiring teacher-competency tests. A follow-up fifty-state survey by

Education Week in 1986 found that 'the drive to improve the schools has generated an unprecedented level of legislative and policy-making activity'.

States were not the only players in the American education-reform arena in the early 1980s. The President exhorted action from his vantage point on the nation's highest bully pulpit. Moreover, the list of organizations which advocated reform read like a 'Who's Who' of the political, business, and education communities. Among the groups which issued prominent reform reports were the National Governors' Association, the Carnegie Forum on Education and the Economy, and the Committee for Economic Development. The media also hoisted the standard of reform, making education the subject of newspaper headlines and television documentaries. National magazines such as *Time, Newsweek*, and *The New Republic* featured lengthy articles on education reform. Schools were front-page news.

Setting the Stage for Reform

Before turning to an examination of some of the specifics of contemporary American education reform, it is important to understand the detonating mechanism for this explosive surge in interest in the schools. America has always had a love affair with education. From earliest colonial times, Americans have viewed education as the key to social mobility and economic opportunity. Education has served to transmit a common, pluralistic culture to a nation of immigrants and has been the prime vehicle to prepare individuals to participate as productive citizens in a democratic society. Moreover, Americans historically have turned to schools in times of national crisis. Education is viewed in American society as possessing enormous curative powers, often acting as a powerful and persuasive palliative for an otherwise ailing society.

When the Soviets launched Sputnik in 1957, the United States' failure to be first in space was popularly attributed to deficient education in the nation's public schools. President Dwight D. Eisenhower delivered a message to Congress in which he stressed the significance of education as key to national defense. Congress responded by enacting the National Defense Education Act (NDEA), which was intended to strengthen mathematics and science instruction in the nation's public schools as the first step toward producing scientists capable of surpassing the Russians.

The 1960s, when the nation found itself in the throes of the civil-rights movement, gave birth to the Elementary and Secondary Education Act (ESEA). Part of President Lyndon Baines Johnson's 'war on poverty', ESEA authorized federal financial support to school districts for education programs designed to meet the needs of educationally deprived and economically disadvantaged children. The federal government appropriated funds to broaden and strengthen the education of children of poverty with the expectation that improving education was instrumental to breaking poverty's vicious and cyclical grip and preventing the creation of a permanent American underclass.

What was the triggering mechanism in the early 1980s for the contemporary American education-reform movement? There seemed to be no imminent international military threat, nor threat of widespread internal domestic disorder. But there was a national crisis of confidence, a rising fear that the United States' ability to remain economically competitive in an ever more globally inter-dependent world was in increasing jeopardy. The link between education and the global economy was made explicit.

Forging the Link between Education and the Economy

A Nation at Risk called the public schools to task for contributing to America's flagging economic competitiveness. The ensuing national enthusiasm for reform has been fuelled by the nation's increasing anxiety about the possibility of becoming an economic junior partner to Japan. Contemporary reform dis-cussions thus centre on the need to increase educational productivity, enhance human capital, and prepare workers who, in the twenty-first century, will be required to 'think for a living'.

This is a new strategic position in which the United States finds itself. At the conclusion of World War II, the United States was the only advanced industrialized economy in the world. The basis of American economic prosperity of post-World War II could be found in the nation's industries. Americans made things: steel, automobiles, television sets. The nation's capacity as manufacturer of high-quality goods produced a living standard for Americans which was un-equaled anywhere in the world.

The United States was not selfish with its success. The nation used its own prosperity and economic security to rebuild the economies of western Europe and support the development of the Pacific Basin and third-world nations. As the decades advanced, however, the world began to change. Slowly but inexorably, the United States shifted from a smokestack to a service economy.

Technology and industrial methods of production were changing as well. Machines were developed which could take the place of human workers, accomplishing tasks more cheaply and with greater efficiency. Computers, cap-able of organizing and storing thousands of pieces of information which could then be retrieved with the push of a button or the touch of a key, became common-place.

American industry was slow to change, in retrospect, too slow. The indus-trial age was fast becoming the information age, though American captains of industry seemed to take too little notice. America, it seems, had 'taken a tempor-ary historical accident [post-war prosperity] and construed it as a permanent condition' (Halberstam, 1986).

As America was struggling to understand why it was losing industrial pre-eminence, Japan, a country humbled during World War II, was creating a modern, technologically sharp economy. By the 1970s, the United States found itself the unwitting participant in a not-always-friendly game of industrial catch-up with the Japanese. Where once 'made in Japan' was an expression of derision, increasingly it was becoming an economic threat. Moreover, in the early 1980s, the United States found itself importing from Japan more than it was exporting to its Asian ally. A trade deficit loomed ever larger. As the decade of the 1980s dawned, Japan's advancing technological and trade hegemony placed increasing pressure on the United States and the nation's sagging industrial base. Many began to assert publicly what they had feared privately. The American economy, and perhaps the American worker, had lost their way.

Japan's education system widely is touted as key to that nation's economic rise from the ashes following World War II. American newspapers and magazines are replete with detailed stories about how much time Japanese students spend in school, how hard they study, and how academically demanding their courses are. Not only, it is claimed, is Japan producing a superior 'top half', but that nation is reputed to have the best bottom quartile as well (Kirst, 1988). Education, Americans are told, has served as the engine propelling Japan's economic surge forward.

American school-reform reports of the 1980s, beginning with *A Nation at Risk*, have echoed a similar and repeated theme: The road back to economic security for the United States, the path to regaining economic competitiveness, leads from the nation's schools. *A Nation at Risk*, in its purposely inflammatory language, warned that:

Our [the United States] once unchallenged preeminence in commerce, industry, science, and technological innovation is being overtaken by competitors throughout the world. If an unfriendly foreign power had attempted to impose on America the mediocre educational performance that exists today, we might well have viewed it as an act of war. We have ... been committing an act of unthinking, unilateral disarmament. (*A Nation at Risk*, 1983)

The Committee for Economic Development sounded the same theme when it asserted:

Many of our schools stand accused of failing the nation's children and leaving the economy vulnerable to better-educated and more highly trained international competitors ... Education has a direct impact on employment, productivity, and growth and on the nation's ability to compete in the world economy. (*Investing in Our Children*, 1985)

The Carnegie Forum on Education and the Economy likewise linked resecuring the nation's economic advantage to improving the education system:

America's ability to compete in world markets is eroding. The productivity growth of our competitors outdistances our own. The capacity of our economy to provide a high standard of living for all our people is increasingly in doubt. ... Americans [are] turn[ing] to education. They rightly demand an improved supply of young people with the knowledge, the spirit, the stamina and the skills to make the nation once again fully competitive. [Education is] the foundation of economic growth, equal opportunity, and a shared national vision. (*A Nation Prepared*, 1986)

Perhaps the most succinct statement of the invisible bond between education and the economy was issued by David Kearns, chief executive officer of the Xerox Corporation. Said Kearns, 'If we do not restructure our schools, this nation will be out of business by the year 2000' (Kearns, 1987).

Pleas for American school reform continue to be mounted against a backdrop of anxiety about the nation's economy, the United States' ability to compete in the global market, and the capacity of the American workforce to adapt to the work-place challenges of the twenty-first century. Business leaders increasingly assert that the education system is functionally related to employment and that public education is failing to prepare sufficient numbers of individuals to function productively in an increasingly complex job market. Investment in human capital is touted as the way to compete economically. 'Invest in brains, not brawn' appears to have emerged as the new American credo.

The Rhythm of Reform

Education in the United States is a 'local responsibility, a state function, and a national concern' (Thomas, 1975). Through a complicated set of historical and constitutional arrangements, the provision of public education is the responsibility of each of the fifty states, though much of the actual policy-making authority resides with the governing boards of the 15,200 local school districts.

Initial responses to calls for education reform were generated by individual states. Because each state maintains substantial governmental autonomy over education matters, the kinds of schooling reforms enacted and the rates at which they have been adopted have varied greatly. Moreover, policy initiatives directed toward school reform have not been a one-time occurrence. Often one set of education-policy enactments in a state has been followed by another in what has come to be known as 'waves' of reform.

The First Wave of Reform

The three-year span from 1983 to 1986 encompasses what is commonly referred to as the 'first wave' of education reform. Marine metaphors aside, this period represents the first phase of the contemporary American education-reform movement. Coming close on the heels of the release of *A Nation at Risk*, reform policies enacted during this period contemplated an incremental approach to school change.

During the first wave of reform many states increased high-school graduation requirements, adding more academic core courses. As a consequence, high-school course enrolments shifted dramatically, with more emphasis on mathematics, science, history, and foreign language, and a de-emphasis of vocational and academically 'soft' electives (Kirst, 1988). Academic course content became more rigorous as courses began to require more critical thinking and problem-solving and less rote memorization.

A number of states tightened teacher-certification procedures, making it more difficult to become a teacher, and raised teacher salaries, making it more remunerative to choose a teaching career. Many states enacted or enhanced statewide student-assessment programs designed to measure pupils' academic progress. Some states lengthened the school day or the school year or both. A number of states enacted new homework policies. Textbooks were also a common target of first-phase school reformers. Many states, such as California, Texas, and Florida, revised their textbook-selection procedures, forcing textbook publishers to abandon the practice of 'dumbing down', or playing to the academically lowest common denominator.

Legislation emanating from this first phase of reform tended to be top-down and prescriptive. New laws flowing from capital statehouses often consisted of a series of tightly assembled but seemingly disconnected reforms packaged into a single statute. California's Senate Bill 813 is a prime example of this type of legislation. Containing more than eighty separate reforms covering issues ranging from lengthening the school day and school year to establishing the 'mentor teacher' program (an initial rung of a teachers' career ladder), Senate Bill 813 was typical of many states' attempts to establish uniform blueprints for educational change.

First-stage reform activities consisted principally of those policy alterations which might be characterized as 'safe' reforms. They represented add-ons to the existing educational structure. Initial reforms did not require anyone to do anything differently. They did not prompt a rethinking of the structure of schools, a re-examination of the traditional roles of school personnel, or a review of the conventional methods of delivering instruction.

'Intensification' best describes early state-reform activities. There was a prevailing sense that the existing system of education was basically sound, but that what was required was more: more tests, more academic rigour, more time in the classroom, more requirements for professional certification. In addition, first-stage reform policies often were employed as pumps to inject badly needed state dollars into inflation-diluted, fiscally sagging local-education systems. Money, in other words, was offered in exchange for incremental alterations to the existing educational structure.

An Emerging Shift in Reform Direction

As initial reform efforts proceeded, a growing chorus of education-reform advocates began to express concern that incremental changes were insufficient. Many of those seeking solutions to America's educational problems turned for guidance to that sector of society now squarely facing the nation's economic difficulties: the business community. Far-sighted American corporate leaders, reacting to declining productivity and increasing international competition, had triggered seismic alterations in the world of work. While schools are not profit-making institutions, and educational productivity cannot be measured as easily as counting the number of cars that roll off an assembly line, nonetheless, parallels between schools and businesses were striking. These similarities were not lost on school-reform advocates.

They found that while successful businesses were governed by a deeply ingrained corporate culture, most schools lacked this level of shared commitment. While modern corporations encouraged autonomy and entrepreneurship, most schools adhered to standardized curricula and tolerated little deviation from standard practice. Finally, while forward-looking companies had stripped bureaucracy to its bare essentials, most school districts continued to manage through layers of administration. Lessons from the corporate book became an essential part of the text of 'second-wave' education-reform reports.

Beginning in 1986, then, another series of reports calling for higher educational standards, increased course requirements, and for a panoply of reforms designed to improve the quality of instruction was issued. These reports, like their recent predecessors, sounded the theme of the need to improve schools in order to enhance economic competitiveness. Significantly, however, each of these so-called 'second-wave' reports, among them Carnegie's *A Nation Prepared: Teachers for the 21st Century*, the National Governors Association's *Time for Results*, and the Holmes Group's *Tomorrow's Teachers*, argued that serious attention must be paid to the job of teaching and the organization of schools. Without substantial changes in the teaching occupation and significant alterations in the underlying organizational structure of American public schools, declared these reports, incremental education reforms, however soothing initially, could well prove ephemeral.

These reports asserted that bureaucratic structures of conventional American schools, characterized by standardized, highly regulated environments, are ill-suited to serve as training grounds for jobs of the twenty-first century. In addition, they said, the new skills students will need to master are unlikely to be conveyed successfully by individuals who function comfortably within the confines of a hierarchical bureaucracy, in which the essential scope and sequence of their professional work life has been predetermined by others.

Thus these reports advocated a bottom-up approach to school improvement. They acknowledge that schools must alter their method of operation so that students become producers of knowledge rather than consumers of facts, able to manipulate information rather than simply to absorb it. These reports challenged school districts to re-examine with a critical eye the fundamental content of academic course offerings. They implored school districts to re-evaluate and to modify the structure of educational decision-making, and realign the balance of authority among teachers, administrators, and parents. 'Accountability' became a potent reform buzzword as states were urged to adopt both positive and negative sanctions intended to enhance the performance of schools and school districts.

Designed to alter the tone of education-reform discussions, these new reports succeeded in raising by several decibels the volume of debate. Representing a radical departure from the *status quo*, 'second-wave' reform reports argued that school as usual and teaching as usual produced business as usual, and that, they asserted, was the essence of America's economic dilemma.

In sum, this new spate of education-reform reports called for wholesale re-evaluation and reform of American schooling. Incremental changes envisioned by first-phase reform recommendations were declared insufficiently bold and altogether too timid. Tinkering at the educational policy margins would not serve as an adequate springboard to an American economic renaissance. The question was: Would American schools rise to meet the challenge?

Some Examples of Reform Efforts

What does American school reform look like? To be sure, reform has taken a variety of forms. A 1989 survey by the American Governors' Association indicated that thirty states had adopted or were implementing state-level initiatives to promote school reform (David, 1990). Additional reform efforts are being generated at the local school-district level.

While no catalogue exists which neatly indexes school-reform efforts across the nation, nonetheless some identifiable categories of reform effort are emerging. These include:

1 More intensive pre-service preparation for teachers, including the elimination of the undergraduate degree in education. This idea is being promoted most forcefully by the Holmes Group, a consortium of research universities;

2 Enhanced in-service possibilities designed to update and upgrade teachers' skills and widen their professional horizons;

3 Site-based management programs, in which essential educational decisions, including budgeting, personnel selection, and curriculum, devolve to the school site. Decisions are made jointly by teachers and site administrators;

4 'Choice', a system which enables parents to select their children's schools from among a range of educational alternatives;

5 Increased use of educational technology, including extensive classroom programs produced by organizations such as the National Geographic Society;

6 Teacher professionalization, a broad category that generally encompasses expanded professional roles for teachers, including providing opportunities for experienced practitioners to function as mentors to their novice colleagues, develop curriculum, provide staff development, participate in peer assistance and review programs, and serve as adjunct faculty in college and university education programs.

In addition, both the American Federation of Teachers and the National Education Association have established national centres on school restructuring; national organizations, such as the National Council of Teachers of Mathematics, are developing new ways to teach specific subject areas; and efforts are underway to devise improved means to measure student achievement.

What follows are some illustrative examples of current school-change efforts. Many of the most promising of these efforts combine several of the alternatives listed above.

California exemplifies state-directed efforts to restructure the school curriculum. In mathematics, the sciences, history, and English, California's education authorities recruited nationally acclaimed academic specialists and solicited their views regarding what should be taught. This effort resulted in the development of state-promulgated 'curriculum frameworks', which not only shaped what classroom instructors taught, but also influenced the content of textbooks and the nature of state-administered pupil-performance tests. The goal of California's curriculum undertaking was to render what was taught more coherent, cohesive, and intense.

New Jersey illustrates a different reform approach. Selected, urban school districts in the state repeatedly were unable to escape charges of petty corruption, nepotism, and mismanagement. Consequently, state policy makers enacted an 'educational bankruptcy' plan whereby the state, after sufficient advance notice and systematic efforts to assist local authorities, could take over a local school district, appoint new school-board members and school administrators, and begin to operate the schools in a different direction.

Minnesota pioneered yet another kind of reform: parent choice among public schools. A controversial open-enrolment plan, whereby students can attend public schools other than in their local school district and attendance area in which they reside, was proposed and enacted.

The Dade County (Florida) school system, which includes the city of Miami, has most comprehensively embraced the site-based management approach to school reform. Dade County's school-based 'Management/Shared Decision-making Program has provided more than 100 Miami-area schools with the authority to reinvent their instructional programs. Under this program, site-based teams of teachers and school administrators maintain control over budgets, staff allocations, and the organization of the school day. Dade County's shared governance approach is resulting in a variety of programs designed to meet the needs of schools' particular students. The district and the local teachers' union have agreed to waive board policies, administrative regulations, and union contract provisions which impede implementation of school-determined programs.

Rochester (New York) has pioneered an innovative career-ladder program which provides teachers with enhanced professional responsibilities in exchange for increased pay, and is designed to provide incentives for outstanding teachers to remain in the classroom. The first rung of the career ladder is the intern teacher, a novice with no teaching experience who must teach under the guidance of a mentor. The second rung of the career ladder is for resident teachers, who have successfully completed the one-year internship but are not yet permanently licensed. The third step of Rochester's career-in-teaching plan is the professional teacher, who has earned a permanent teaching certificate. The final step, the lead teacher, is a competitively selected position. Lead teachers, who must have a minimum of ten-years classroom experience and, if selected, have the opportunity to earn an annual salary of $70,000, work as mentors, select textbooks, write curricula, plan staff-development programs, and serve as adjunct professors in teacher-preparation programs. Importantly, lead teachers must agree to relinquish seniority for purposes of assignment with the result that the most experienced teachers are assigned to teach the most challenging students.

Yet another approach to school reform is the National Board for professional teaching standards. An outgrowth of the Carnegie report, the National Board is developing assessment mechanisms designed to identify outstanding teachers who effectively enhance student learning. Transcending state and local standards, the National Board will identify 'what teachers need to know and be able to do' and certify teachers who meet that standard. The expectation is that school districts will compete for board-certified teachers and these individuals may assume broader-than-traditional professional responsibilities. The National Board planned to begin certifying teachers by 1993.

The Players in the School-reform Theatre

Education reform is not the private property of a single constituency group or an individual level of government. To varying degrees, the President, Congress, states and their governors, business executives, teacher-union leaders, and individual school districts have been guiding the hand of school reform.

Education Reform, the Federal Government, and Ronald Reagan

President Ronald Reagan, who initially had disassociated himself from the National Commission on Excellence in Education and had refused the prospect of it being labelled a 'Presidential Commission', correctly sensed the depth of public concern about education once *A Nation at Risk* was released. Thus he subsequently associated his administration with the report and used public forums to prod states and local school districts to initiate and implement education-policy reforms.

But the President's attention to school reform was largely rhetorical and relatively short-lived. His political concentration on the topic of education lasted approximately a year and a half, ebbing, not coincidentally, with his re-election to a second term in November 1984. Reagan's Secretary of Education, Terrel Bell, in his book, *The Thirteenth Man*, writes most poignantly about this:

> In my mind, nothing could have assured Ronald Reagan's place in history more than his enduring commitment to the school reform movement that he supported so effectively for eighteen months, only to abandon it after the election. [But] there was simply no commitment to a federal leadership role to assist states and their local school districts in carrying out the recommendations of *A Nation at Risk*. [Yet] we would have changed the course of history in American education had the president stayed with us through the implementation phase of the school reform movement. And this would have won a place in history for Ronald Reagan as the man who renewed and reformed education at a time when the nation was, indeed, at risk because we were not adequately educating our people to live effectively and competitively in the twenty-first century. (Bell, 1988)

A review of the President's budget requests for education reveals Ronald Reagan's plans for an ever diminishing role for federal aid to education even at the height of his public enthusiasm for a revitalized school system. The executive branch's 1983 K-12 budget request of $9.95 billion, the lowest during the eight Reagan years, was nearly 33 per cent below the previous year's level of federal education spending. In 1984, the first full year following release of *A Nation at Risk*, the President asked for a substantially higher amount than he had the preceding year, but he still requested 14.5 per cent less ($13.20 billion) than the education appropriation approved by Congress the previous year (Verstegen and Clark, 1988). While the President used the bully pulpit to prompt reform, substantive school-change efforts and support would have to emanate from outside Washington, DC.

The Role of State Governors

State governors emerged among the most forceful proponents of school reform. Activist governors, such as Bill Clinton of Arkansas, put forth and achieved legislative and public approval for bold proposals for school reform. Many of these state-based education-reform efforts received play not only in the hometown papers but in dailies such as the *New York Times* and *Washington Post* as well, spreading the word and creating a reform 'ripple effect'.

The National Governors Association (NGA), an organization of which the majority of Americans was previously unaware, became a public driving force behind efforts to alter the structure of American schools. The NGA's 1986 report, *Time for Results*, became the catalyst for significant state-level education-reform policy activities. Statewide campaigns for political office, which traditionally allowed higher visibility issues to eclipse education, now began to focus on schools and education reform. One of the major issues in the Texas governor's race in 1986, for example, concerned the provisions of a controversial Texas school-reform law supported by the gubernatorial incumbent.

State-level political officials who supported school reform also found they either had to foot much of the bill for it, or use their powers of political persuasion to convince local authorities to share the financial burden of school change. Between 1980 and 1986 an additional $4.20 billion in constant dollars was made available by states and local school districts for elementary and secondary education (Jennings, 1987).[1]

The Business Community

In addition to state governors, another group of individuals who came to the surface as early champions of school reform were American business leaders. Traditionally more comfortable in corporate board rooms than in legislative chambers, business leaders took up the educational reform challenge because they could see the economic handwriting on the corporate wall. Said Charles Marshall of American Telephone and Telegraph in testimony before Congress:

> We are not interested in education simply for altruistic reasons; we need knowledgeable, well-educated, highly-skilled employees if our business is to succeed. The educational system prepares young people from whom we will enlist our future employees. If their preparation falls short, we wind up with less able employees and it is more difficult for us to reach our goals. (March, 1987)

Professional Educators

Contravening conventional wisdom which held that organized teachers were likely to resist large-scale change to existing school structures, the national teacher unions became enthusiastic proponents of school reform. The American Federation of Teachers, through its president, Albert Shanker, has been a particularly outspoken advocate of reform, and many of the most innovative reform programs are underway in school districts in which the teachers are affiliated with the AFT. A 1988 study, commissioned by the United States Department of Education and conducted by the Rand Corporation, concluded that both the AFT and the National Education Association (NEA), the nation's two major teacher organizations, have been 'committed to their role as change agents' (Jennings, L., 1988). Based on a study of 151 collectively bargained contracts and interviews with more than 600 policy makers and educators in six states, the report concluded that 'in no state were teacher organizations a major obstacle to the enactment of reform legislation'. Instead, teacher unions' 'modal response has been accommodation, even in those instances where a specific reform initiative has run counter to their organization interests or has been at odds with the professional judgment of their members'.

The Federal Response under George Bush

George Bush campaigned for the presidency of the United States saying he wanted to be the nation's 'education President'. In September 1989, the President convened the nation's governors at a summit in Charlottesville, Virginia. At this historic meeting the President told the state's political chief executive officers 'The first step in restructuring our education system is to build a broad-based consensus around a defined set of national education goals' (*Education Week*; 4 October 1989). The National Governors Association taskforce on education agreed to cooperate with the President's nominees to recommend such goals.

In the President's annual State-of-the-Union address on 31 January 1990, George Bush released his own set of goals for the nation's schools. These include:

1   Having all children ready for school by the time they enter kindergarten;
2   Increasing the national high-school graduation rate from 72 per cent to 90 per cent by the year 2000;
3   Ensuring that American students are 'number one' in science and mathematics by the year 2000.

If national standards, either those proposed by the President or those that emerge from a process of political compromise, are adopted, then states will likely be under considerable political pressure to adopt them as goals for their own schools and districts. This would be the first time in this nation's history that specific education targets would guide nationwide schooling efforts.

The President's budgetary proposals for federal aid to education were not as upbeat as his statement of national education goals. The Department of Education's request for fiscal year 1991 reflects an increase of $507 million, or 2 per cent above the preceding year. This amount was still more than 2 per cent below the congressional budget office's inflation estimates (American Education Research Association, 1990).[2]

A related federal-level effort involved the National Assessment of Educational Progress (NAEP). In 1966 Congress authorized formation of NAEP. This nationwide achievement-testing activity was funded by the federal government, but operated under contract by a bidder agency. The proviso at the time of enactment was that testing, while involving a national sample of students, should not be undertaken in a manner which would permit comparison of academic achievement among states or among school districts within states. Over time, political views regarding the wisdom of this prohibition changed and in 1988, Congress reauthorized the NAEP with a new provision permitting states voluntarily to participate in state-by-state NAEP, the results of which could be generalized to a state and thus permit the comparison of student achievement in one state with that of another.

The Status of Reform and Prospects for the Future

This chapter has explored, in necessarily abbreviated fashion, contemporary efforts to alter American schooling. The school-reform movement, which began with the release of *A Nation at Risk* in 1983, is continuing. This is not the first time the United States has undertaken school-reform efforts that are national in scope. Likely it will not be the last.

Those who pay for, work in, and employ the 'products' of American public schools rightly are beginning to ask probing question about contemporary school-reform efforts. Is reform 'working'? How is 'reform success' to be measured.[2] Is it to be in increasing scores on standardized tests, in teacher attraction and retention rates, in the ability of students to secure and hold jobs a decade from now? How long will reform efforts continue? Will there be a 'third wave' of reform?

One can look to various pieces of research and anecdotal evidence and find suggested vastly differing answers to these questions. For example, a study of reform in six states, conducted by the Center for Policy Research in Education (CPRE), concluded that incremental reforms appear to have achieved the upper hand over more difficult structural alterations. 'Reforms aimed at changing the organization of instruction or altering decision-making practices within schools [have] not generally garner[ed] much support.' (CPRE, 1989) One might conclude from this study that the impetus for structural reform is spent, if indeed it ever caught fire in the first place. Moreover, one might speculate that in the absence of significant, tangible progress, the public's enthusiasm for reform efforts would diminish as well.

Yet the public's ardour for improved schools remains steady. Significantly, the public remains favourably disposed to increasing its tax burden in support of education. A 1989 Gallup poll assessing the public's attitude toward public schools found that nearly two-thirds (62 per cent) of people would be willing to pay more taxes to increase the quality of public schools, particularly in poor states and poor communities.

School reform as an antecedent to enhanced economic competitiveness remains on the federal legislative agenda as well. A bill introduced in February 1990 by Democratic Senator Edward Kennedy of Massachussetts and Republican Senator Mark Hatfield of Oregon aimed to authorize $125 million in spending in 1991 to promote mathematics, science, and engineering education. The authors of this legislation described it as 'an essential first step in re-establishing the United States' economic pre-eminence' (Bell, T., 1990).

Finally, initial reform efforts seem to be having a salutary effect on the teaching force. A *Metropolitan Life* survey of American teachers in 1989 found that nearly half believed they now earn a decent salary (up from 37 per cent in 1984), more than half (53 per cent) felt respected by society (up from 47 per cent 1984), and more than two-thirds (67 per cent) would advise a young person to become a teacher (up from 45 per cent in 1984) (*Metropolitan Life*, 1989).

Yet, examples of reform are fragile and geographically scattered. Those who follow education reform, even intensely, can name few states and districts which have immersed themselves in school-restructuring efforts.

What, then, are the prospects for continued school-reform efforts? More importantly, what is the possibility of lasting educational improvement? Conservatism remains a powerful influence in American institutions, including schools. It may, indeed, 'be America's curse or its genius that we wish to reform as many things as possible while changing things as little as possible' (Renshaw, 1986). The folk-ways of teaching and schooling continue to exert enormous inertial force on an institution, which has the increasingly complex mission to prepare young people for a world far different from the one their forebears knew.

Some have begun to assert that it is time now to 'ratchet up' reform efforts another notch. Albert Shanker, President of the American Federation of Teachers, writing in the January 1990 issue of *Phi Delta Kappan*, called for the creation of a new incentives plan for school restructuring. Shanker asserted that school achievement must be more productively and explicitly linked to students' ability to secure employment. In addition, Shanker called for federal investment in a program that would allow all schools voluntarily to experiment with bold structural innovations and would financially reward the 10 per cent of participants which achieve the greatest educational strides.

Inner-city schools present a special situation. Urban schools particularly face increasingly tough times. As their student populations become increasingly poor, minority, and non-English-speaking, educational challenges continue to mount. The host of social services, which these children need in order to learn well, often is inaccessible or unavailable. While schools cannot be expected to provide 'all services to all children', it is probably the case that providing adequate social services to children must become coupled with education reform on the political agenda if school-change efforts are to produce the desired results.

It seems clear that, at a minimum, continued school reform will require a sustained investment of both political will and financial capital. Hopeful signs remain on the horizon. National consensus about the need for dramatic change in the education system has, if anything, intensified since 1983, although as a nation the United States has not agreed on the form structural change should take. Hurling blame for the state of the schools has been kept to a minimum. The nation seems to have recognized that 'We have met the enemy and it is us'. The breadth of players from different arenas who have sustained national attention in the schools is, indeed, impressive. The dialogue among policy makers, government administrators, teacher-union leaders, and corporate officials continues. Bold experiments are on-going.

Yet significant questions about the lasting impact and penetration of contemporary education-reform experiments remain unanswered. Assessing the effects of reform efforts, if such efforts are to be measured in long-term economic gains for the nation, must await a still-to-come glance back.

Contemporary Education Reform and High Politics

In a previous chapter in this volume we posited a theory of national education-reform politics. We asserted that the bursts of policy activity which are reflected in reform movements are occasioned by a shift in the political environment from routine, everyday politics to what may be termed 'high politics'. We established a set of testable propositions describing threshold political conditions that must be met in order for an issue to assume 'high-politics' status, make its way to the political reform agenda, and pave the way for the enactment of reforms. We conclude this chapter by revisiting those political preconditions and employing them as a template used to measure the degree to which contemporary American education-reform movement has achieved high-politics status. First, what is high politics?

Policy formation is a political process. New legislation is proposed, new laws are enacted, and new policies are implemented on a daily basis. Sometimes these new policies make news. Most often, however, the world outside the immediately involved or affected community is little aware of policy alterations.

The vast majority of government policy-making, then, occurs under routine political circumstances. Changes are incremental and do not threaten the *status quo*. The political bargaining, which is an indispensable component of public policy-making, occurs within the confines of the classic 'iron triangle' of interest-group representatives, minor government officials, and a small group of legislators who have taken a particular interest in the issue at hand. This is politics-as-usual, routine politics.

Sometimes, however, an issue explodes out of its traditional, narrow, rule-making world. A host of additional actors appears on the policy scene and the issue receives widespread public attention. The added policy players may include high-ranking government officials, legislative leaders not usually involved in the newly prominent issue, or individuals for whom politics may be foreign territory. High-politics results in 'policy-making out loud' as debates about the course of policy shifts become increasingly public and both the audience for and participants in political discussions expand. The issue which has been elevated to high-politics status captures mainstream-media attention as the nightly news and daily newspapers focus on a pivotal issue.

This 'high-politics' issue also becomes the subject of concentrated political attention, making its way into legislation, party platforms, and campaign speeches. An issue that typically might be consigned to the political backwater now becomes the topic of intense, often partisan, politics.

High-politics status is not divinely conferred upon a social-agenda issue. Certain threshold conditions must be met in order for an issue or problem to become a candidate for high-politics status. The first of these qualifications is an obvious one: The problem must enter the political realm. A concern, no matter how genuine or widespread, cannot be a topic of high politics if it is not a subject of politics at all. Thus an issue must be defined as a political problem, amenable to political solution.

School reform has been defined as a political issue. Among the most ardent advocates of education reform are the nation's governors. Other elected officials and candidates for elective office include school reform as a standard colour on their political palette. President Bush's pledge of national-education goals as a centre-piece of his State-of-the-Union message continues to focus policy makers' attention on schools. The first precondition for high-politics status, placing the issue on the political agenda, seems to have been met.

Another precondition, we asserted, is that an issue is more likely to achieve high-politics status and the attendant policy receive attention during periods of value disequilibrium. Policy preferences within the American political culture are shaped by the dynamic interplay of three values: liberty, equality, and efficiency. During any given period one value may hold greater sway over policy outcomes than another. Shifting political or economic tides will cause yet a different value to gain policy precedence. For much of the 1960s, for example, public policy preferences with regard to American education focused on the value of equality. Providing equal educational opportunity for all schoolchildren guided legislative and judicial efforts to alter schooling.

In the 1980s, mounting, national economic pressures began to manifest themselves in shifting public-policy preferences. Political discussions about contemporary education reform consistently have revolved around the national imperative to enhance education capacity as a means to increase economic productivity. In this period of uncertainty, another value, efficiency, has come to the fore.

A third crucial ingredient in this recipe for high politics and education reform is the presence of alternatives. Reform is represented by significant policy alterations. For policy direction to shift, alternative policies must be waiting in the political wings. Moreover, policy choices which will be linked to emerging reform strategies in an atmosphere of high politics must bear the possibility of success. In other words, a set of policy alternatives must exist which is already available, politically acceptable, likely affordable, and potentially implementable.

With regard to current school-change efforts, a number of alternatives, among them curriculum reform, 'choice', site-based management, the enhanced use of educational technology, revised pre-service preparation, and teacher career ladders continue to float in the education-policy wind. Whether these particular proposals, or any combination of them, ultimately will be the bricks and mortar of a reconstituted school system is not the issue here. What is key is that these ideas, as well as others, continue to circulate as viable alternatives to current education policy.

Fourthly, the charged atmosphere characteristic of high politics, which carries with it the possibility of reform, is propelled by the opening of a window of political opportunity. This open window is created by a catalytic event or galvanizing series of events. Suddenly society feels threatened, and disequilibrium replaces quiet acceptance of uncomfortable conditions or general malaise. The realization that the United States was losing its competitive edge in the world market was not an event, captured in a single time and place. Nonetheless, the increasing realization that the United States could no longer assume global economic hegemony as part of the natural order of things served as the triggering mechanism, catapulting education to the centre of the political stage.

The fifth and final condition occasioning sustained political attention to a potential reform issue is the availability of policy entrepreneurs. Entrepreneurs strike when a policy window opens and serve as brokers of change, combining a recognized problem with an available solution or set of solutions, in a favourable political environment. These entrepreneurs then remain on the policy scene as advocates, maintaining momentum, and ensuring that the issue retains 'high-politics' status. A number of individuals, not the least of whom was the President himself, serve as policy entrepreneurs for contemporary American education-reform efforts. Governors, business leaders, members of the federal executive branch, and leaders of professional education organizations continue to attempt politically to meld their vision of the problem with their proposals for solution.

We conclude, then, that education reform in the United States has, indeed, achieved high-politics status. School reform has been defined as part of the political agenda, shifting public-policy preferences are being realized as realignments of policy direction, alternative policies are available and widely discussed, a catalytic condition has focused and sustained public attention on schools and education reform, and policy entrepreneurs continue to work their side of the political street, attempting to couple recognized problems with available solutions.

Whether contemporary American school-reform efforts will bear the hoped-for fruit, whether schools can and do change dramatically, and whether even a revolution in American education will be instrumental in forging a national economic renaissance, is the subject of a different study. Suffice it here to say that altering American schooling is the subject of high politics. We continue to be confident that as long as the subject of education remains on this dynamic political course, the possibility for education reform remains alive.

Notes

1 It should be noted, however, that the vast majority of these new state and local dollars simply offset cuts in federal aid to education.
2 The Administration claims an increase of $1.20 billion, but this figure is an accounting manipulation. An $800 million increase is scheduled for existing discretionary programs, but that would be offset by a cut in mandatory and entitlement programs of $678 million. The other $407 million requested is for new initiatives (AERA, 1990).

References

AERA (1990) Info Memo, American Education Research Association, January/ February 1990.

NCEE, *A Nation at Risk* (1983) Report of the National Commission on Excellence in Education, Washington, DC.

TFTP, *A Nation Prepared; Teachers for the 21st Century* (1986) Report of the Task Force on Teaching as a Profession, May, Carnegie Forum on Education and the Economy, Washington, DC.

BELL, T. (1988) *The Thirteenth Man: Reagan Cabinet Memoir*, New York, The Free Press.

BELL, T. (1990) 'Bill Pushes Education in Math and Sciences', *San Francisco Chronicle*, 9 February.

BELL, T. (1990) ' "C" Stands for Company, Turned into Classroom', *Wall Street Journal*, 1 March.

C.E.D. (1985) *Investing in Our Children*, Washington, DC, Committee for Economic Development.

CPRE (1989) *State Education Reform in the 1980s*, New Jersey, Center for Policy Research in Education.

DAVID, L., PURKEY, S. and WHITE, P. (1990) *Restructuring in Progress: Lessons from Pioneering Districts*, part of the Results in Education Series, Washington, DC, National Governors' Association.

DAVID, L., COHEN, M., HONETSCHLAGER, D. and TRAIMAN, S. (1990) *State Actions to Restructure Schools: First Steps*, part of the Results in Education Series, Washington, DC, National Governors' Association.

ELAM, S.M. and GALUP, A.M. (1989) 'The 21st Annual Gallup Poll of the Public's Attitudes Toward the Public Schools', *Phi Delta Kappan*, 71, 1, September.

GUTHRIE, J.W. and PIERCE, L.C. (1990) *The International Economy and National Education Reform: A Comparison of Education Reforms in the United States and Great Britain*, Oxford Review of Education.

HALBERSTAM, D. (1986) *The Reckoning*, New York, William Morrow.

JENNINGS, J.F. (1987) 'The Sputnik of the Eighties', Phi Delta Kappan, 69, 2, October.

JENNINGS, L. (1988) 'The Unions Not an Obstacle to Reform', *Education Week*, 25 May.

KEARNS, D.T. (1987) 'Economic Recovery: Business Must Set the Agenda', Speech delivered at The Economic Club of Detroit, 26 October.

KIRST, M.W. (1988) 'Recent State Education Reform in the United States: Looking Backward and Forward', *Educational Administration Quarterly*, 24, 3, August.

MLIC (1989) *The American Teacher 1989*, New York, Metropolitan Life Insurance Company.

NBPTS (1988) *Toward High and Rigorous Standards for the Teaching Profession*, Report of the National Board for Professional Teaching Standards.

NGA (1986) *Time for Results: The Governors' 1991 Report on Education*, Washington, DC., National Governors Association.

RAVITCH, D., CHESTER, E. and FINN, C.E. Jr. (1987) *What Do Our 17-Year-Olds Know?*, New York, Harper and Row.

SHANKER A. (1990) 'The End of the Traditional Model of Schooling and A Proposal for Using Incentives to Restructure Our Public Schools', *Phi Delta Kappan*, 71, 5 January.

THOMAS, N.C. (1975) *Education in National Politics*, New York, David McKay Company.

THG (1986) *Tomorrow's Teachers*, Michigan, The Holmes Group.

VERSTEGEN, D.A. and CLARK, D.L. (1988) 'The Diminution in Federal Expenditures for Education During the Reagan Administration', Phi Delta Kappan, 70, 2, October.

Chapter 5

The Reconstruction of New Zealand Education: A Case of 'High-Politics' Reform?

R.J.S. Macpherson

In 1988 and 1989 there was political intervention into education on a scale never seen before in New Zealand. While the culture and traditions of educational administration had been able to withstand an earlier bipartisan challenge from parliamentarians, an electoral backlash in 1987 triggered major political intervention. In 1988, as part of the Labour government's wide-ranging social reform program, broader social values were deployed against 'provider capture' in education — where the providers of a service have captured their terms of service. The Picot taskforce recommended the radical devolution of power, resources, and responsibilities to education institutions and local communities.[1] The effects were dramatic. A large Department of Education (D.o.E.) was replaced by a new compact ministry, a national review agency was established to provided systemic accountability, and the terms of professional service, leadership, and governance in education were redefined.

This chapter is written by a New Zealander who was contracted to provide structural advice to the Picot taskforce for the six months prior to its reporting in May 1988.[2] It therefore draws on the perspectives of a participant observer, as well as from other research on the emergence of counter pressures to the radical reforms, and discusses the Guthrie and Koppich model of 'high-politics reform' in education.

In essence, Guthrie and Koppich assert that significant political reform is contingent on three preconditions — alignment, initiative and mobilization — and that 'high-politics' reform has particular features. The first precondition, alignment, requires the confluence of four politically related phenomena: the nature of a culture's deep-seated public-policy preferences, when the society involved defines education as a 'political problem', when alternative policies have been defined, and when political practices cohere with reformism. The second precondition, initiative, is the injection of uncertainty and other destabilizing influences. Guthrie and Koppich noted the recent international effects of economic and demographic dynamics. The third precondition they suggest, mobilization, is required so that champions and catalytic groups actually take advantage of enabling conditions and predisposing events. In other words, they claim that 'policy entrepreneurs' have to desire and advocate reforms, have the political skills to recognize and exploit opportunities when they occur, and have to be able to provide direction and to sustain the momentum of reform. The key indicators of reform, according to Guthrie and Koppich, are therefore dramatic alterations in *distribution* and *ideology*, especially in decision-making power, resource allocations, mandates and prohibitions, and ultimately in new values and constituencies. The first and familiar approach to testing the adequacy of this or any other theory is to establish how well it coheres with the context, phases, and consequences of recent events in context.

Background

A System of Sectored Incrementalism

New Zealand has had a national education service since 1877. It has long been differentially administered by sector. The University Grants Committee (UGC) advised the government and distributed allocated resources to seven universities which had their own Acts and governing bodies. The six teachers' colleges and twenty-two polytechnics were administered by the D.o.E.'s head and regional offices. And while they had governing councils, the degrees of discretion they had varied and were contested. Special schools were controlled and administered by the D.o.E.'s head and regional offices.

In 1988, the 349 public secondary schools had boards of governors that acted within the personnel, curriculum, and resources policies determined at 'the centre'. Some schools that traversed the primary–secondary divide had committees of management with unique but less power than boards of governors since they were also responsible to district education boards.

Similarly, the 2377 state primary schools had school committees for support purposes but were controlled and administered from three locations; by one of the ten education boards, by one of the three regional offices, as well as by the head office of the D.o.E. Pre-school kindergartens and play centres were administered by the head office of the D.o.E., with education boards providing support services. Although these multiple and confused patterns of administration were the stuff of legend, they had developed incrementally over decades and were welded into place with a centralist culture.

Major cracks became evident in the early 1980s. One appeared when the *Kohanga Reo* (Maori 'language nest') pre-schools refused from their inception to accept any linkages with the D.o.E. Claiming that the mechanisms of state in education had been oppressive and culturally counter-productive, they insisted on governing and leading their schools site by site. They were eventually funded via the department of Maori affairs.

Guthrie and Koppich's preconditions were therefore present, but it was more fundamental than a case of misaligned policy references. The coming sections will show that it was an example of a clash between the metavalues of two cultures. Metavalues are defined as assumptions so uncontested that they go without examination and unconsciously into all valuation processes (Hodgkinson, 1983, p. 5).

Political versus Administrative Cultures

In New Zealand traditional political action has been primarily regional or local in nature. It was settled from about 1100 AD by largely independent Maori *whanau* (extended families) who networked as *hapu* (tribes) and *iwi* (confederations). Policies had to be legitimated on the *marae* (the local meeting place) to be effective. The European settlers of the 1840s and 1850s also had an eye to local and provincial interests rather than to national agendas, and set up provincial assemblies with adjunct education boards to administer their local primary schools (Oliver, 1981).

These arrangements stood until after the end of the land wars. In 1877, the members of New Zealand's provincial assemblies handed over responsibility for education to the newly formed national government. The 1877 Education Act was modified in 1914, in an era of jingoistic nationalism, to centralize the inspection of schools and curriculum development.

In the following decades there was a series of reports that led to the establishment of universal secondary education, universities and the polytechnics, as well as to reforms to curriculum and pedagogy (Cumming and Cumming, 1978). These reforms, and policy-making since the 1880s, were explained and driven by four educational-policy myths that were each, in turn, subsumed: selective support; equal opportunity; equal outcomes; and most recently, equal power (Beeby, 1986, pp. 11–45; Renwick, 1986; Macpherson, 1987).

Although fundamental purposes had clearly changed significantly through the decades, and reflected the development of a complex and unique society, the structures and practices of governance and administration in education remained much as they were settled back in 1877. As each era brought new problems and new policies, the D.o.E. coped by elaborating its structure. New sections, new divisions, new levels, new practices and new philosophies were added incrementally until, by the 1970s, powers and responsibilities were widely diffused in complex patterns. The 'education system' operated as a number of conjoint and symbiotic bureaucracies: a head office, three regional offices, ten district offices, and two teachers' unions.

Conversely, over the same decades, there is strong evidence (Gold, 1985) to suggest that New Zealanders sought responsive political systems and caring social policies. They created a 'welfare state', dispensed with their 'upper house' in the 1940s, and today have a unicameral and unitary political system with three-year parliamentary terms. The linkages between cause and effect, the consequences of political intervention, and the outcomes of concentrating power in a nation of 3.50 million are relatively transparent. In general, there is an assumption of popular sovereignty, and centralism has remained in bad odour. As a professor of education history put it (Arnold, 1985), 'New Zealanders resent going to Wellington to get permission to live.'

And yet, as noted above, the national school-education system developed a countervailing administrative culture of centralism. This culture drew its strength from:

- The personalities of national figures in education;
- Controls exerted through examination, inspection, and curriculum development systems;

- An enduring public belief in the quality of primary education;
- Macro-economic forces for national problem-solving;
- The power of two symbiotic bureaucracies, the various agencies of the D.o.E. and the teachers' unions.

Client dissatisfaction grew. Participation in educational administration became a major policy issue in the late 1970s (Watson, 1977). It reached the stage where national non-educationalist opinion leaders, such as Professor Sir Frank Holmes (in Watson, 1977, pp. 79–96), were calling for an educational consumers' institute. Respected parliamentarians (e.g., Gair, 1986) recalled years later that, by the early 1980s, half their mail was about problems in education . . . despite the best efforts of teachers and administrators.

Relationships in the portfolio deteriorated sharply during the closing years of Sir Robert Muldoon's government. Minister Wellington's blunt challenges to the system simply polarized attitudes. And while the consultative style of the new Labour minister appointed in 1984, the Hon., Russell Marshall, did help abate some of the pressure and achieve some significant changes, it failed to attend to a fundamental tension, the mismatch between political and administrative metavalues in public education.

Political Intervention

Details available elsewhere (Macpherson, 1989a) show that the parliamentarians of New Zealand tried unsuccessfully to intervene in 1986. Briefly, a bipartisan Science and Education Select Committee used their new powers to the full and, after extensive public hearings, concluded that the quality of teaching in New Zealand's public schools was being undermined by three conditions:

- 'Provider capture', that is, where the providers of education had captured the terms of their service;
- Grossly elaborated structures in educational administration with muddled lines of accountability and communication;
- Obsolete administrative attitudes and practices.

Despite this bipartisan call for radical change, the 'education establishment' was seen not to respond. The Hon., David Lange's Labour government suffered electorally in 1987, and when 'problems in education' were found to have been a major determinant of voting patterns, the Prime Minister himself took the portfolio. Overnight the language of portfolio management changed from 'consultation' to emphasize 'responsiveness'. A non-educationalist, Brian Picot, was contracted to lead a review team.

Picot's taskforce to review education administration (1988, p. 9) was asked to provide:

- A review of administrative functions to maximize delegation;
- An evaluation of governance to accelerate devolution;
- A reorientation of administrative services to enhance client satisfaction;
- A reorganization of structure to achieve greater effectiveness, efficiency, and equity.

Despite claims to the contrary by the teachers' unions, the Picot exercise was not a cost-cutting exercise or an attempt to target teachers or unions in particular, despite the offence felt by many parliamentarians when the Scott report was ignored or ridiculed. The Picot process actually cost about NZ$400, 000, as did marketing and implementation, and all savings achieved through restructuring stayed in the portfolio. The increased costs discovered later, of localizing some functions for example, actually led to a series of additional budgetary allocations.

A broader view would instead see the Picot exercise as but one of seventeen taskforces set up by the Cabinet Social Equity Committee (CSEC) chaired by the deputy Prime Minister, the Hon., Geoffrey Palmer (later Prime Minister). The charters of these taskforces, and that of Sir Ivor Richardson's Royal Commission on social policy, overlapped and together straddled all social port-folio responsibilities. This approach provided gradual and contestable advice, and ensured that proposals cohered with ex-law professor G. Palmer's (1979) views on the desirability of integrating the reform of constitutional, administrat-ive, and social policies. It is further evidence supporting the point made above, that broader social metavalues clashed with traditional public-education adminis-trative policies, and that the former were imposed on the portfolio.

The Picot Report

The Need for New Metavalues

The Picot taskforce (1988, pp. 8–10) noted that the combined effects of new technology, changing and plural values, new cultural sensitivity, and the intensifying demands on education services had outstripped the administrative capacities of the system. They assumed the urgent need for greater responsive-ness in public education. Consistent with their terms of reference, they presumed that this could be achieved with appropriate incentive regimes at all levels for system and institutional managers.

It is also clear that the bipartisan parliamentary support for major structural reform and radical devolution took the thinking of the Picot taskforce well past relocating administrative functions closer to the client — the fairly common hori-zontal extension of bureaucracy euphemistically referred to as 'decentralization'. Instead, members came to believe that the devolution of decision-making power, resources and accountability was an effective means of altering the balance of power between the providers and the clients. Further, they assumed that this would lead to greater institutional, and hence system, responsiveness. The metavalue involved can be termed radical debureaucratism. There was some databased logic to this assumption.

Justification for New Metavalues

The Picot taskforce (pp. 3–37) found that despite the near-heroic efforts of teachers and administrators, the management of public education had a number of inappropriate features: over-centralized decision-making, too many decision

points, high vulnerability to pressure-group politics, excessive ministerial intervention, and a culture of centralism and dependence. The management systems
were shown to have complex and fragmented structures and processes, to rely
on arbitrary institutional roles and poor information, and to feature wasteful
duplications. Accountability systems measured fidelity to administrative regulations rather than how effectively educational aims had been achieved. Opportunity cost analyses were being neutralized by the weight of input economic
thinking. The team concluded (p. 29) that the D.o.E. 'holds together because of
the personal integrity of the management and their collective commitment to
education' rather than through any sound management structure, systems, or
practice'.

Perhaps the most telling argument of all put to the CSEC by the taskforce
was that the themes of low efficiency and undermined effectiveness were directly
related to client dissatisfaction and to the alienation of disadvantaged groups.
Whatever the evidence, and it appeared to triangulate well, this argument
rendered traditional administrative metavalues, at the very least, politically
obsolete.

Reform Strategy

Picot opted for radical devolution to reinforce the professionalism and dedi-
cation of individual teachers, parents, and community participants. He developed
the strategy by focussing on the organizational unit that sustains the relationship
between learner and teacher — the school or college. He proposed actions to
alter the balance of power between clients and providers at institutional level to
gain greater responsiveness. Key measures included reforming governance at all
levels, local empowerment, and dispersing as many functions as possible from
'the centre'.

In a White Paper, *Tomorrows' Schools* (1988), the government formally
accepted almost all of Picot's ideas, laid out an implementation process, and set
the 1st October 1989 as the change over date. Prior to the change over date, each
school community elected a board of trustees that began to negotiate a charter of
objectives in order to reflect local needs within national guidelines. The charter
had to be approved by a new ministry before it became the basis for local program budgeting and accrual accounting.

A national education-review agency was established to provide multi-skilled
evaluation teams to make transparent how well each school used its funds to
meet chartered objectives. A parent advocacy council was proposed as a check
on the tyrannical use of majority power or bureaucratic position. The ten
education boards were abolished. In their place, community-education forums
and education-service centres were planned to provide consultative and school-
support services.

Lange decided to use *ad hoc* policy taskforces rather than to establish the
recommended national education policy council. The new slim ministry took
up a policy advisory role, managed property, moved funds, and developed
personnel, administrative, governance, and curriculum guidelines as part of
the implementation strategy.

An implementation unit used a short-term video-based public-relations campaign, short-life working parties, and in-service activity to help administrators acquire financial management and program-budgeting skills. A good deal of 'paper progress' was achieved quickly with the preparation of guidelines by implementation working parties. The State Services Commission negotiated new terms of service for administrators and teachers in a somewhat uncompromising manner.

Other taskforces reported on early childhood education and higher education, and a range of reforms have impacted in these sectors as well as across all other portfolios. By late 1989 (and by now, Prime Minister) Palmer and his ministers were consolidating gains and calming all portfolios for 1990, an election year.

As a detailed analysis of the implications of the Picot report for institutional managers concluded (Macpherson, 1989b, p. 42), it had become crucial that 'researchers evaluate outcomes rigorously to ensure that policy makers move away from the processes of implementation, back to the fundamental questions of purpose and rightness'. At this point it appeared that all of Guthrie and Koppich's indicators were present, especially the radical change to the distribution and metavalues in decision-making power, resources, legitimacy, and constituencies.

On the other hand, some of the unexpected outcomes of this 'high-politics' intervention suggest different perspectives on these 'reforms'. It must be noted, nevertheless, that outcomes are emergent and interpretations of these recent events are contested. Two areas are now given close attention: the sources of counter-pressures and policy governance.

Data on these matters are limited. There are two surveys known to be in the public domain (Macpherson, 1989c). The triangulated views of eight very well-placed informants prepared to speak freely on a non-attributable basis were also used. Where views did not triangulate, they were set aside. Finally, there was the information regularly published by major interest groups and the new agencies. Nevertheless, given the methodological limitations involved, the position presented here should be regarded as provisional but indicative.

Sources of Counter-pressures

Role Loss and Self-discovery

The numbers of staff required at 'the centre' fell. The ten education boards went and other agencies were down-scaled. At the same time the ministry, the review agency, education-service centres and schools began recruiting expert personnel on contracts. In other words, displaced persons had to let a part of their professional selves die and be bereaved, as it were, before constructing a revalued self in an emergent organizational culture.

The traumatic existential reality of 'high-politics' reform for many have also been mirrored in Australian restructurings. There it has been shown (Pettit *et al.*, 1990) that people grieved the going of key metavalues, those never hitherto questioned assumptions underpinning a professional self in a relatively stable organizational culture.

In each case, in the midst of internal trauma, the person had to reconstruct the metavalues of self as they negotiated a place in a developing organization. The key point here is that the Guthrie and Koppich model does not offer a psychology of 'high-politics' intervention.

Dynamic Conservatism

The challenge to 'professional' metavalues was felt widely. Many encountered formative and comparative performance evaluation criteria and processes for the first time. Feelings of disaffection were evident for a period in a surge of collective activity. Temporary phenomena included the formation of peer support groups, some polarization of attitudes about management in education, and attempts by union organizers to convert the disaffection into fresh demands for representative power.

The loss of symbiotic structural relationships, the gradual development of middle-management leadership in institutions, the emergence of community-based resource policies, and the allocation of more limited central-bargaining rights severely undercut the potential for 'provider capture'. Residual resistance to modern managerial ethics began to wane as new expertise and confidence began to counter-balance uninformed fears, although market and corporate metaphors were persistently criticized for the exclusive service they gave to a new-right ideology. The concern here is that the Guthrie and Koppich model assumes but fails to explain the existence and functions of dynamic conservatism (Schon, in Pettit *et al.*, 1990) in a sociology of 'reform'.

Disturbed Bargaining Relationships

Another controversial area concerned appointments, promotions, and bargaining discretion — the politics of career. Boards of Trustees were made responsible for the appointment of principals on contracts, who in turn were to help recommend the appointment of their staff. Principals were empowered and held accountable for the day-to-day management of institutional life. National negotiations established the parameters of salaries and conditions.

An immediate response by the unions was to lobby for greater homogeneity rather that for greater differentiation and competition between members. Such member activity helped reaffirm power bases and helped sustain organizational integrity at a time when external sources of influence were being severed. This situation is a far cry from the days of diffuse powers among symbiotic bureaucracies. The government, via the State Services Commission and industrial legislation, imposed new conditions of service. Two avenues left for lobbying, therefore, are the wider Labour movement and at local levels.

The greater localization of politics had a number of effects. Trustees and teachers quickly identified 'anomalies', 'inconsistencies', and eventually 'injustices' and 'inequities' that were soon identified at national union level as manifestations of New-Right ideology' (Chapman 1988, p. 3). There were attempts made to move logs of claims from the parameters and details of formulae to the need for recentralized personnel practices and for more standardized conditions of service.

The foundation to these claims was the principle of equity for clients in general, and between professionals in particular, but rarely the converse. Further, the slogan of 'equity' was used to legitimize actions seeking to counter the mandated and managerial slogan of 'responsiveness'. Explaining and evaluating these and other claims to legitimacy requires philosophical machinery well outside the scope of the Guthrie and Koppich model.

The Supply of Expertise

Many primary-school principals became concerned about the availability and expertise of trustees and administrative support staff in rural communities. Many also noted that they had called in vain for leadership-development in-service education with particular features; it should have addressed felt needs, accepted and proceeded from a wide range of current mindsets, offered negotiable curricula, and established and sustained supportive professional networks during and beyond implementation.

Ironically, as these problems emerged, the affected schools, communities, teacher groups, and the teacher-training institutions began to lobby for re-regulation. Although client interests initially favoured incentive regimes that could only have taken effect in the medium and longer term, some sought a return to the centralist strategies used in the past in order to gain more immediate results. There were also actions taken by the implementation unit that contradicted the Picot management philosophy.

The point here is that while the Guthrie and Koppich model pointed to the crucial role that champions and groups have in sustaining directions, it offered no comment on their actions apart from effectiveness.

Trust in the Portfolio

It was noted above how the parliamentarians had despaired of education ever 'putting its house in order'. The process of resolving the legitimation crisis involved a cycle of death and reconstruction.

The *Tomorrow's Schools* White Paper was presented as an invitation to attend a cremation of metavalues that teachers could not refuse to attend. At the time Lange (1988) emphasized his Cabinet's determination to introduce legislation if the teachers' unions did not cooperate without disrupting the education of the students in schools. Ill-will deepened. Morale plummeted when a non-educator was appointed for eighteen months as the lead change agent. Many lamented the absence of a credible education statesperson who could give the changes an educative rather than simply a management rationale. The most intense morale problems were in the D.o.E., that is, among the very personnel expected to implement the Picot philosophy with enthusiasm.

The emotional backlash in the profession reached a peak when the effects of a highly effective print and video public-relations program began to wear off. The attitudes among primary-school principals at the time (Macpherson, 1989c) highlighted their deep need to have their service affirmed and legitimized in educational terms. Taken together, there was a loss of professional self-esteem, non-negotiable and new definitions of expertise, new limits to collective bargaining, fading trust in others, and a process of reconstructing purposes and legitimation. In other words, in addition to the political processes of realigning social reality, the cultural processes of legitimating changed practices were part of 'high-politics' reforms.

In general, then, the Guthrie and Koppich model does not appear to explain how answers are found during 'high-politics' reform to some key questions:

- What is right?
- What is significant?
- How is social reality realigned?
- How are changed practices legitimated?
- What is responsive management?
- What is responsible educative leadership?

The importance of these six questions is established by considering some of the unanticipated outcomes of changes made to policy governance at local levels.

School Governance

An Essential Service

The major policy documents specify that New Zealand institutional managers will have four major parts to their new role: facilitating governance, corporate planning, educative leadership, and management services (Macpherson, 1989b). The first and essential service expected by *Tomorrows' Schools*, the facilitation of school governance, created instructive outcomes directly related to the six questions above.

The Degradation of Policy-making

The first effect of the countervailing forces noted above was to distort the philosophical integrity of school policy-making. Boards of trustees were expected to develop a primary concern for the overall policy that their principal, as chief executive officer of the board, would implement. It was also widely assumed that each principal possessed a number of philosophical skills to help others use desirable ways and means of making right decisions. In brief, this implied being able to:

- Appreciate the relativity of the cultures of, and served by, the school, the school community, the region, and the broader society (Rizvi, 1990);
- Analyse, understand, and explain complex policy dilemmas;
- Unravel clashes of values and cultures so that trustees could make ethically sophisticated judgments (Evers, 1987);
- Use an advanced knowledge of teaching, learning, and educative administration when advocating policy;

- Use an educative approach to leadership and a sophisticated set of methods to implement policy with professional colleagues (Northfield *et al.*, 1987).

The evidence is that comparatively few had the education or expertise to satisfy such expectations. Hence, among the effects of the 'high-politics' intervention were that principals tended to suffer from self-doubt, felt vulnerable in industrial matters, lacked a sense of being right and felt alienated by instrumental expectations. Where false confidence was created through the adoption of managerial technicism, unfortunate multiplier effects were soon evident.

Whatever the validity of Picot's intentions, the general process helped create attitudinal conditions antithetical to the development of the philosophical services required by boards of trustees. This suggests that Picot's 'high-politics' intervention embodied a conceptually deficient theory of systemic change.

The Maldevelopment of Trusteeship

An early task for principals was to manage the conditions for the election of boards of trustees. The technical tasks included identifying the electorates, explaining the composition, role, support, and powers of boards, and then acting as returning officers. The appropriate political role for principals during this phase included making contact with local education statespersons such as *kaumatua* (Maori elders), disseminating information, and encouraging discussion about expertise without being compromised as the guardians of the democratic process.

Once trustees had been elected the principals were expected to help them prepare institutional charters within national guidelines and agreements for education. This meant drawing on sophisticated, philosophical, planning, and political skills since the draft charter had to define the purpose of the institution, the intended outcomes for students, and how programs would take account of students' and potential students' interests, staff strengths, as well as community resources and interests.

Unfortunately, it appears that many principals took a dominant leadership role at this point and, in their haste to produce charters, established approaches that retarded the learning of educative governance and the emergence of community leadership. There were, on the other hand, many examples of subtle process facilitation, cultural sensitivity and a low-key expertise in collaborative and strategic planning.

Assisting planning in a setting of new direct democracy in a wider context of plural interests also meant realizing the need and then arranging bilateral, horizontal, and vertical negotiations in a range of cultural modes and reconciling outcomes. Such an approach presumed that principals had few doubts about their professional competence or industrial position, that there was an organizational culture of trust and positive reinforcement, and that leadership at all levels was enabling and educative.

Again, it was a matter of idealist expectations born of imposed metavalues, the metavalues of debureaucratism that emphasized responsive and responsible management, but at cost to the questions of rightness, significance, realigning social realities, and legitimating practices.

Uneven Access to Resources

Politically astute principals moved quickly to acquire supportive resources and to interpret national guidelines. Some arranged appropriate linkages, for example, by inviting the D.o.E.'s liaison group to consult with community and staff elders to find policies for the school that resolved seemingly diverse national and local expectations. Others made the findings of applied research on staff-selection criteria and procedures (Chapman, 1985a, 1985b) available to trustees when the task faced them for the first time.

There were also examples of resources being held at 'the centre' to sustain policy leverage over management education, and reports that the prevailing climate was characterized by a low level of professional and support expertise, adversarial relationships and damaged self-esteem, distrustful monitoring and mechanistic management. A highly respected ex-director (Beeby, 1988) doubted the wisdom of locating the Ministry and review functions in separate agencies of state.

The irony appears to be that debureaucratism, the converse of bureaucratic rationality, reflects the limits of bureaucratic thought. The concern to encourage responsiveness and to localize responsibility appears to have given less priority to learning how to articulate what is best and significant in education (McKenzie, 1988), and to providing appropriate means (Stewart and Prebble, 1985; Cardno, 1988; Caldwell and Spinks, 1988) for educators to realign their assumptions about social reality and to legitimate new practices.

These findings from the New Zealand case of 'high-politics' reform are now deployed to locate the Guthrie and Koppich model in a more general and holistic model of leadership.

Limits to the Guthrie and Koppich Model

The sections above give substantial support to Guthrie and Koppich's modelling of the preconditions and indicators of 'high-politics' intervention. All of its components were represented in the radical reconstruction of the New Zealand public-school system. There, were, however, aspects of the reforms that out-stripped the parameters of the model that are now discussed.

Questionable Assumptions

The scope of the model is restricted to the realm of material things. The metaphors of death and bereavement prior to a professional rebirth, for example, can have no place in the Guthrie and Koppich model. The model fails to explain the existence of existential or shared social realities. The roles of reflection and interaction are not considered.

The model gives 'high politics' a privileged role in social affairs without justification. It is a model that de-emphasizes many other social structures to give political systems a primary role in the authoritative allocation of values to society. It also assumes that the three preconditions above are forms of input that culminate in a *gestalt* switch into 'high politics', an extra-ordinary process that provides unique outputs — new public choices, resource distribution, revised regulations, radical reforms — which in turn feed back values to society and reorder alliances.

The model also provides, especially through the workings of more standard politics, a benign view of social order and its political systems. In this latter standard mode, it is assumed that competition, bargaining, and compromise among plural interest groups explain the distribution of rewards, as well as produce checks and new balances. In both modes the model appears to adopt uncritically the presumed legitimacy of politicians' actions.

The key point here is that the dual model appears to use a natural system's approach to political analysis. Both standard and 'high politics' are conceived of as natural systems of inputs, processes, and outputs. The problem is that a natural system's ideology is located almost exclusively in realism, rather than in idealism, tends to reify social realities, and excludes the possibility of 'political realities' being conceived of and evaluated as arbitrary cultural artefacts (Greenfield, 1975; in Griffiths *et al.*, 1988). This has the effect of ingratiating influential people's actions and their impact on the patterns of others' assumptions about practices, context, and rightness (Hodgkinson, 1978; Macpherson, in Griffiths *et al.*, 1988, p. 180). Such an approach tends to set aside sociological or philosophical tools, and encourages the belief that political systems simply have a life of their own.

A Conflicted Theory of State

Another serious limit concerns the implicit theory held about the nature of policy steerage in public services. To explain, different theories of state assume that the policies of public institutions, such as schools and school systems, are steered in at least five ways (after Dunleavy and O'Leary, 1987, pp. 329–341):

- Pluralist theories locate steerage with citizens who vote, influence party politics and lobby through interest groups, and therefore explain the variations and the multiple directions in the policies of public utilities in terms of changing alliances;
- New-Right theories also locate steerage with citizens, but note that distortions in public choice-making make it difficult for institutions of state, however responsive, to avoid creating unanticipated effects;
- Elite theories assume that public services are steered by elites who manipulate the liberal democratic process of policy-making;
- Marxist instrumental theories locate steerage with a capitalist elite that tries to embed its ends into government policies in order to adjust public policy-making;
- Neo-pluralist theories assume that a dual polity operates. Public institutions offer multiple points of access for representatives, while these and other structures also give elites degrees of steerage over knowledge and process.

According to this typology of state, the Guthrie and Koppich dual model draws on pluralist assumptions to explain standard politics, and yet switches to neo-pluralist and elitist ideas to explain the dynamics of 'high politics'. Although the data of the New Zealand reforms can be described to a degree by the dual model, but only within the limits identified, the theoretical ambiguities involved have yet to be explained. Such a dual claim also begs the more abstract epistemological question: How do we judge between these competing theories of state or between particular combinations of theories?

Doubtful Epistemology

Where pluralist theories embody a natural system's ideology, others, respectively, employ economic neo-rationalism, structural Marxism, elitism and neo-pluralism. The problem they share is that they employ arbitrary foundational premises in their justificatory logic. In other words, all of these theories claim to be trustworthy in terms of different premises or foundational truth claims that, on close examination, turn out to be the preloved articles of faith of a 'discipline' or to be an expression of ideological commitment (Walker and Evers, 1982).

A non-foundational approach avoids this vicious regress by emphasizing internal and external coherence, between the theoretical, empirical and values components in beliefs or knowledge claims, as well as with the wider patterns of knowledge underpinning the most effective explanations of practical matters.

> How do we apply the coherence test? We extract common standards from the overlapping accounts of shared problems, or we adopt them from other shared areas of the theoretical frameworks of participants. By examining the actual content of touchstone, we discover what values and procedures each of the competing theories is committed to in common with the others, and ask which of the theories comes out best in view of these shared values and procedures. We test the competing theories or divergent solutions to one group of problems by reference to their common solutions to another set of problems. (Walker, 1987, p. 16)

Conclusion

Although the data available above and elsewhere do not permit definitive theorizing, there is potential in the overlap between elite theory and neo-pluralism. The Guthrie and Koppich model discussed the detailed mechanics of strategic intervention and political activity that, as shown in New Zealand, determines significance and realigns social reality.

The key problems noted above concerned theories of social reality, state, and knowledge. A non-foundational effective web of theories might therefore incorporate the views that:

1 There are conceptual, social, and material realities in human affairs (Hodgkinson, 1981) (wherein)
   • Conceptual activity is triggered by reflection on two key questions: What is right and what is significant?

- Social reality is recreated and transformed by interaction. One example is political activity that alters what is held to be the distribution and justification of powers and resources. Another is cultural activity that legitimates changes to professional practice;
- Material reality in organizations is sustained by managerial and evaluative services. Where responsive management is driven by a concern for what is achievable, responsible management would focus on effectiveness, efficiency, and fundamental purposes.

2 A dual polity of leadership in New Zealand existed that:

- Provided for standard politics with traditional representative structures, and with liberal corporatist and technocratic mechanisms of state being serviced by professional elites;
- Provided for 'high politics' (after Guthrie and Koppich) when the metavalues of mechanisms of state and 'provider capture' had to be challenged by leaders who would be educative, so that administrative metavalues could be reconciled with wider social metavalues.

To conclude, these propositions are not without support. They are epistemically and conceptually consistent with a practical, integrated, and holistic model of educative leadership developed and tested during a five-year applied-research project in Australian education systems (Duignan and Macpherson, 1987).

Notes

1 Taskforce to review education administration, *Administering for Excellence: Effective Administration in Education*, Chairman Brian Picot, 10 May 1988.
   Picot is a millionaire director and chairman of companies. He is a senior member of New Zealand's 'corporate oligarchy' (Jesson, 1987, p. 87) and the pro-chancellor of Auckland University. Other members included Dr Peter Ramsey, an associate professor of education at Waikato University, who, with others (Ramsey *et al.*, 1983) had researched successful and unsuccessful schools. Another member was Margaret Rosemergy, a senior lecturer at the Wellington College of Education who had helped of formulate Labour-party education policy. Whetumarama Wereta, a social statistician at the department of Maori affairs, joined the taskforce to emphasise a Maori perspective; she is from the Ngaiterangi-Ngatiranganui. The fifth member, Colin Wise, represented employers' interests. He is a successful businessman from Dunedin with active links with higher education. The taskforce secretariat was led by Maurice Gianotti, a senior D.o.E. official, and later chief executive of the national review agency.

2 This paper was developed from 'New Reform Directions for Educational Governance in New Zealand', a paper presented to the AERA conference, San Francisco, 27–31 March, 1989. By invitation, it was to comment on the appropriateness of the Guthrie and Koppich model and was then presented to the IIP conference, Manchester, 20–29 April, 1990.

References

ARNOLD, R. (1985) Interviewed 21 August.
BEEBY, C.E. (1986) 'Introduction', in RENWICK, W.L. (Ed.) *Moving Targets: Six Essays on Educational Policy*, Wellington, NZCER.

BEEBY, C.E. (1988) 'Review and Audit Agency', in *New Zealand Journal of Educational Administration*, 3, pp. 10–11.

CARDNO, C. (1988) 'School Development: A Proactive Response to Picot', in *New Zealand Journal of Educational Administration*, 3, pp. 57–62.

CALDWELL, B.J. and SPINKS, J. (1988) *The Self-Managing School*, London, The Falmer Press.

CHAPMAN, J.D. (1985a) *School Council Involvement in the Selection of Administrators*, Geelong, IEA.

CHAPMAN, J.D. (1985b) *The Selection of School Administrators: Procedures and Practices*, Geelong, IEA.

CHAPMAN, R. (1988) 'Presidential Address', *PPTA News*, 9, 19, p. 3.

CUMMING, I. and CUMMING, A. (1978) *History of State Education in New Zealand 1840–1975*, Melbourne, Pitman.

DUIGNAN, P.A. and MACPHERSON, R.J.S. (1987) 'The Educative Leadership Project', *Educational Management and Administration*, 15, 1, pp. 49–62.

DUNLEAVY, P. and O'LEARY, B. (1987) *Theories of the State: The Politics of Liberal Democracy*, Basingstoke, Macmillan.

EVERS, C.W. (Ed.) (1987) *Moral Theory for Educative Leadership*, Melbourne, Victorian Ministry of Education.

GAIR, THE HON., G., MP (1986) Interviewed 21 August.

GREENFIELD, T. (1975) 'Theory about Organizations: A New Perspective and its Implications for Schools', in HUGHES, M.G. (Ed.) *Administering Education*, London, Athlone Press.

GREENFIELD, T. (1988) 'The Decline and Fall of Science in Educational Administration', in GRIFFITHS, D.E., STOUT, R.T. and FORSYTH, P.B. (Eds) *Leaders for America's Schools: The Report and Papers of the National Commission on Excellence in Educational Administration*, Berkeley, McCutchan.

GOLD, H. (Ed.) (1985) *New Zealand Politics in Perspective*, Auckland, Longman Paul.

GOVERNMENT OF NEW ZEALAND (1988) White Paper, *Tomorrow's Schools: The Reform of Education Administration in New Zealand*, Wellington, Government Press.

HODGKINSON, C. (1978) *Towards a Philosophy of Administration*, London, Basil Blackwell.

HODGKINSON, C. (1981) 'A New Taxonomy of Administrative Process', in *Journal of Educational Administration*, 19, 2, pp. 141–152.

HODGKINSON, C. (1983) *The Philosophy of Leadership*, London, Basil Blackwell.

HOLMES, SIR F. (1977) 'Lay and Professional Participation in Educational Administration in New Zealand', in WATSON, J.E. (Ed.) (1977) *Policies for Participation: Trends in Educational Administration in Australia and New Zealand*, Wellington, NZEAS.

JESSON, B. (1987) *Behind the Mirror Glass; The Growth of Wealth and Power in New Zealand in the Eighties*, Auckland, Penguin.

LANGE, D. (1988) 'Statement to the NZEI Annual Meeting, 30 August', in *NatEd: New Zealand Educational Institute Newsletter*, September, Wellington, NZEI.

MACPHERSON, R.J.S. (1987) 'Equal Power in Adversity: An Educational Myth for Post-Renwick Policy-Making in New Zealand Education', Paper given at the AARE/NZARE Conference, 3–6 Dec, Christchurch.

MACPHERSON, R.J.S. (1988) 'Talking up and Justifying Organization: The Creation and Control of Knowledge About Being Organized' in GRIFFITHS, D.E., STOUT, R.T. and FORSYTH, P.B. (Eds) *Leaders for America's Schools: The Report and Papers of the National Commission on Excellence in Educational Administration*, Berkeley, Mc Cutchan.

MACPHERSON, R.J.S. (1989a) 'Why Politicians Intervened into the Administration of New Zealand Education', in *Unicorn*, 15, 1, pp. 38–43.

MACPHERON, R.J.S. (1989b) 'Radical Administrative Reforms in New Zealand Education: The Implications of the Picot Report for Institutional Managers', in *Journal of Educational Administration*, 27, 1, pp. 29–44.

MACPHERSON, R.J.S. (1989c) 'The Readiness of Primary School Principals to Lead Tomorrow's Schools', in *New Zealand Journal of Educational Administration*, 4 pp. 24–30.

MCKENZIE, D. (1988) 'Education After The Picot Report', *New Zealand Journal of Educational Administration*, 3, pp. 1–9.

NORTHFIELD, J.R., DUIGNAN, P.A. and MACPHERSON, R.J.S. (Eds) (1987) *Educative Leadership for Quality Teaching*, Sydney, NSW Department of Education.

OLIVER, W.H. (Ed.) (1981) *The Oxford History of New Zealand*, Wellington, OUP.

PALMER, G. (1979) *Unbridled Power?*, Wellington, OUP.

PETTIT, D., DUIGNAN, P.A. and MACPHERSON, R.J.S. (Eds) (1990) *Educative Leadership and Rationalisation of Educational Services*, Canberra, ACT Schools Authority.

RAMSEY, P., SNEDDON, D., GREENFELD, J. and FORD, I. (1983) 'Successful and Unsuccessful Schools: A Study in Southern Auckland,' in *Australian and New Zealand Journal of Sociology*, 19, 2, pp. 273–304.

RENWICK, W.L. (1986) *Moving Targets: Six Essays on Educational Polity*, Wellington, NZCER.

RIZVI, F. (Ed.) (1990) *Educative Leadership in a Multicultural Community*, Sydney, NSW Department of Education.

SCHON, D.A. (1990) 'Dynamic conservatism', in PETTIT *et al.* (Eds) *Educative Leadership and Rationalisation of Educational Services*, Canberra, ACT Schools Authority.

STEWART, D. and PREBBLE, T. (1985) *Making It Happen: A School Development Process*, Palmerston North, Dunmore Press.

THE PARLIAMENT OF NEW ZEALAND (1986) *The Quality of Teaching: Report of the Education and Science Select Committee* (Chairman: Noel Scott MP), Wellington, NZ Government Printer.

WALKER, J.C. (Ed.) (1987) *Educative Leadership for Curriculum Development*, Canberra, ACT Schools Authority.

WALKER, J.C. and EVERS, C.W. (1982) 'Epistemology and Justifying the Curriculum of Educational Studies', in *British Journal of Educational Studies*, 30, 2, pp. 321–29.

WATSON, J.E. (Ed.) (1977) *Policies for Participation: Trends in Educational Administration in Australia and New Zealand*, Wellington, NZEAS.

Chapter 6

A Decade of Educational Reform in Canada: Encounters with the Octopus, the Elephant, and the Five Dragons

S.B. Lawton

While economic challenges have forced educational reform and restructuring upon the school systems of many nations, these forces were of secondary importance in Canada during the 1980s. Instead, Canadian education, like Canada itself, was engaged in a reconstitution, the objective of which was no less than the preservation of the nation. Memories of the fierce recession of 1981–2, which devastated parts of Canada's resource-based economy, will fade; but the 1982 patriation of the Canadian Constitution under the leadership of Prime Minister Pierre Trudeau will not, as long as Canada continues to exist.

Before 1982, any amendment to the Canadian Constitution — the British North America Act of 1867 — required approval by the British Parliament, for it was, after all, its Act. As well, the British Privy Council was the last court of appeal, above the Supreme Court of Canada, and there was no written bill of rights. All that changed. When the Queen assented to British Parliament's *Constitution Act, 1982*, the Canadians became responsible for their own political and legal governance under the Crown. The Supreme Court of Canada was now supreme in fact, and in 1985 the *Charter of Rights and Freedoms* came into effect, providing Canadians written guarantees of their fundamental rights.

But, how did these changes affect the average Canadian? A review of a decade of reform without considering this question fails to place a human face on history. To ensure this not to be the case, it is good to recall what was written by C. Wright Mills, in his classic, *The Sociological Imagination*:

> Nowadays men often feel that their private lives are a series of traps . . .
> Underlying this sense of being trapped are seemingly impersonal changes in the very structure of continent-wide societies. . . Yet men do not usually define the troubles they endure in terms of historical change and institutional contradiction. . . No social study that does not come back to the problems of biography, of history and of their intersections within a society has completed its intellectual journey. (C. Wright Mills, 1959, pp. 1–3)

In the spirit of Mills, the purpose of this paper is to describe the major educational-policy developments in Canada and to describe, in part, the impact these are having on individuals.[1] The British Parliament originally constituted Canada, now with ten provinces and two territories, with a federal government that had a very limited role in education, namely, the protection of the provincial educational rights of religious (Catholic or Protestant) minorities (Fisher, 1989). In the 1980s, however, changes in social and economic goals and in federal–provincial relations affected these traditional arrangements. These changes are quite unlike those in other countries with which Canada shares a common heritage. Browne and Louden in Chapter 7 describe a phenomenal growth in the power of Australia's Commonwealth (federal) government as it tried to improve educational performance on a national basis. Hannaway and Crowson (1989) report a different approach but similar goals in the United States. In England and Wales the Education Reform Act of 1988, and in New Zealand the White Paper, *Tomorrow's Schools* (MacPherson, 1989), sharing the same goals, called for radical restructuring of these jurisdictions' national educational systems. Canada's national agenda, while echoing some of these concerns, has been distinctly different.

The title of this paper carries a set of meanings that demand explanation. The octopus, the elephant, and the dragon are metaphors that convey the behaviour of different nations or governments.[2] The octopus in this view is the federal government of Canada; its tentacles reach out to touch, embrace, and control. The elephant is Canada's giant neighbour, the United States, which has an awesome power and must constantly be considered. The five dragons are the booming economies of the Pacific Basin: Japan, Korea, Hong Kong, Taiwan, and Singapore. The influence of these jurisdictions, however, may not be immediately apparent at the local level. Canadians have traditionally been more oriented toward their provinces than the nation as a whole and tend to assume that external forces acting upon them are local and provincial rather than national and international. Today, that habit does not serve us well.

The trends in education policy in the 1980s on which I focus are four in number: minority language rights, minority religion rights, evaluation, and multiculturalism. Although discussed separately, they are linked in complex ways, as will be suggested later.

Minority Language Rights

Vignette 1
I am in a meeting with a group of educators to plan a workshop for the spring and ask a fellow from the Ontario Ministry of Education how things are going. He shakes his head and explains.

> I had a letter come in concerning a particular matter and dropped by the appropriate branch. The only education officer around was a new francophone official. He asked if the letter was in French. I indicated it was not. He said, 'I can't help you.'

Vignette 2
A student relates a, no doubt apocryphal, story.

Pierre Trudeau [Canada's former Prime Minister] is watching his three
boys who are learning to swim. As the life guard looks on, one boy gets
into trouble and begins to sink. When no action is taken, Trudeau dives
in to save his son's life. Afterwards, he demands of the lifeguard, 'What
are your qualifications?' The guard answers calmly, 'I'm bilingual.'

Vignette 3
Progressive Conservative MPs from the West are delighting each other with their
new joke about Quebec's language policy:

Premier Robert Bourassa dies, reaches the 'pearly gates' and seeks
admission into Heaven. After identifying himself, he is refused admission. He demands an explanation. St. Peter replies: 'Sorry, the new policy
is French on the outside, English on the inside.' (*The Globe and Mail*,
6 May 1989, p. A5)

These vignettes reveal the trapped feeling that many anglophones have
developed as a result of the implementation of the language clauses of the
Canadian Charter of Rights and Freedoms.[3] First, however, it should be emphasized that the patriation of the Canadian Constitution in 1982 and its bill
of rights in April 1985 was a major victory for all those believing in the continuation of Canada as a federal nation. The act of patriation was seen as a national
response to the Quebec referendum, which would have seen that province leave
the Canadian confederation. Nevertheless, the implementation of the charter is
creating a wake in which many individuals are getting caught.

The key clauses in the charter, as far as education is concerned, are found in
Section 23, which indicates that citizens of Canada (a) whose first language is
that of the English or French linguistic-minority population of the province
in which they reside, or (b) who have received their primary-school instruction
in Canada in English or French have the right to have their children receive
primary and secondary-school instruction in that language, wherever the
numbers warrant. The intent, in the long term, is to have schools with either
French or English as the language of instruction readily available throughout
Canada so that individuals may move within the nation without leaving behind
their linguistic community.

A few news releases from the Secretary of State of Canada, the office that
Hodgson (1988) refers to as Canada's Minister of Education, suggest the active
stance that the federal government has taken in implementing this section along
with Section 16 (official languages of Canada), which reads 'Nothing in this charter limits the authority of Parliament or a legislature to advance the equality of
status or use of English or French.'

January 5, 1989: French Language School Network Strengthened Across
Canada by Secretary of State. Ottawa, 'A growing trend towards French
language education and cultural retention across the country has been
further boosted by the federal government's efforts to strengthen
educational institutions which serve francophones', Secretary of State
Lucien Bouchard said here today. In New Brunswick, the 10-year-old
Sainte-Anne School Community Centre in Fredericton is the latest in

the series of official language success stories to receive federal funding from the Department of the Secretary of State. When the school opened in 1978, it had an enrollment of 356 francophone students; today, it has 616 pupils, an increase of 73 per cent. The federal contribution will equal 50 per cent of the total cost for the expansion ... Meanwhile, in Prince Edward Island, another agreement was signed in November 1988 ... A similar agreement was signed in October 1987, with the Province of Nova Scotia ... [and] a school-community centre will open in Newfoundland, at Grand-Terre on the Port-au-Port Peninsula, in September 1989 ... Western Canadian provinces have also recently seen a growing trend towards enriching and expanding education in the French language.

January 12, 1989: Canada and Ontario to Fund $100 Million French Language College Initiative ... The eight year cost sharing agreement includes the establishment of a French-language college of applied arts and technology in the Ottawa area by 1990, with new facilities expected to open by September 1992.[4]

January 30, 1989: Secretary of State Contributes $3.9 Million to Ontario for the Development of TV Ontario's French-Language Programming in 1988–89.

From a provincial perspective, perhaps the most dramatic response to the federal, official languages' program has been from Ontario. Even before April 1985 the province referred the issue of the governance of French-language schools to the courts. In 'Reference re Education Act of Ontario and Minority Language Education Rights' (Supreme Court of Ontario, Court of Appeal 1984), the court provided the legal basis for (1) eliminating restrictions as to the numbers of francophone students needed to justify creation of a French-language school (2) providing for the governance of French-first language schools by francophones and (3) altering the governance of Roman-Catholic separate schools in order to extend language rights to francophones.

Subsequently, the province introduced legislation forming (1) a French-language school board for the Ottawa–Carleton region on which both Catholic and public non-denominational supporters are represented (each group with its own powers), (2) a French-language school board to join the six Toronto-area public-school boards on the Metro Toronto school board, and (3) the creation of minority-language education sections as part of other school boards where groups with both language are represented (Education Act 1980, Ontario, RSO, ch., 129, S. 277). These latter bodies are referred to as French-language and English-language advisory committees; the latter apply in a few northern and eastern Ontario communities where francophones form the majority. School boards (both public and Roman-Catholic separate) with minority-language councils operate in large part with a dual structure, including distinct budgets, distinct administrators (except for the chief executive officer), and in most cases in distinct schools, although in some places school buildings are shared after architectural renovation to provide distinct areas for each language group. Legislation for the election of school boards in Ontario was changed to reflect these initiatives. Electors were enumerated in four distinct classes: public anglophone, public francophone, separate anglophobe, and separate francophone. The public electors select trustees for the non-denominational public boards; the separate electors, trustees for the Roman Catholic separate school boards. In each case, where applicable, they vote for trustees who are either anglophone or francophone (Humphreys *et al.*, 1986). And, as suggested in the opening vignettes, staffing and authority within the Ministry of Education have been affected by the changing status of the French language in Ontario.

It must be said that the change in school-board organization and elections did not transpire without difficulty. In 1988, the province conducted the enumeration for municipal elections by mail for the first time. Either because of a lack of knowledge, a lack of understanding, or poor translation, the number of francophone electors fell short of estimated numbers. In Sudbury, the Roman-Catholic separate board, which has a majority of students who are francophone, found itself with a school board composed primarily of anglophone trustees! A court challenge ensued followed by some amendments that gave, in effect, veto power to trustees of either language group to ensure that the anglophone majority could not use its majority for mischievous purpose in those few areas where the French-language section of the board did not have exclusive jurisdiction (such as control over facilities).

Paralleling the impact of minority-language rights has been the expansion in anglophone schools of French-language immersion programs. These programs, often starting from kindergarten, use French as the language of instruction for non-francophone children (Lapkin, Swain, and Argue, 1983). The intent is to develop children who are bilingual in both of Canada's official languages. The programs are in large part subsidized by the federal government, although the funds are routed through provincial governments and ministries of education on their way to school boards (Hodgson, 1988). Promoted by the Canadian parents for French association, a group subsidized by the federal government, French immersion has been particularly popular in middle and upper middle-class neighbourhoods. In some cases 50 per cent of the children in the neighbourhood have selected a regional French-immersion program over the neighbourhood school.

In no other aspect of education, it seems, do the tentacles of the federal government reach deeper and further than in the area of language. Their grasp is with a purpose: to hold the country together.

Minority Religion Rights

Vignette 4
A staff officer of a trustee association telling how Bill Davis, then Premier of Ontario, is said to have told the cabinet of his decision to fund Catholic high schools.

> 'I've decided to make Ontario officially bilingual.' As the faces paled, he announced, 'Just kidding. We're only going to fund Catholic high schools.' Sighs of relief.

Vignette 6
A student explains why he's coming into a Ph.D., program.

> In Quebec City, there are maybe three Protestants left within the original borders of the Protestant school board. If the Quebec government moves to align boards on the basis of language rather than religion — and only the original borders of the board receive constitutional protection — there won't be any job left for me.

Vignette 5
A student explains why he's not coming in full-time for an MA program.

> I've been offered the headship of the technical department in a Catholic high school. With full funding, there are career opportunities I can't pass up.

Apocryphal or not, the first story illustrates well the sensitivity of language and religion, their relative priority, and their interconnection in the Canadian context. In Ontario, it is unlikely that French-language education could have been expanded to reflect charter commitments without also extending the publicly funded Roman-Catholic separate school system from an elementary-only system to a complete elementary and secondary system (Lawton, 1986, 1989). Certainly, when the challenge to the legislation extending the Catholic system was heard by the Supreme Court of Canada, the court found that Ontario Catholics had a right to a complete elementary and secondary educational system (Reference re Bill 30, 1987).

The original Canadian constitution gave the federal government one role in education: the protection of the rights of Catholics or Protestants who were in a minority. This role had lain dormant since 1941 when the last of the major cases, the Ford Motor Company case, challenged the practice of allocating to public-school boards all property assessment not assigned by its owner to a public or separate school board (Sissons, 1959). That case, like many key cases before it, had been decided by the Privy Council in the United Kingdom, which was the court of last appeal until the patriation of the constitution in 1982. In the Ford Motor case all courts in Canada made decisions favouring Catholic school boards; the Privy Council reversed the decision. Now, the Supreme Court of Canada is the court of last appeal.

The influence of the Supreme Court of Canada has been enhanced both by its new status as the court of last appeal and its responsibility for interpreting the new Charter of Rights and Freedoms. In the first instance, its decision upholding the extension of the Catholic system in Ontario paralleled decisions that upheld the rights of Protestant-separate school boards in Quebec against attempts to realign school boards along language lines (see, for example, Attorney General of Quebec vs. Greater Hull School Board, *et al.*, 1984). Any future attempt to realign Quebec school boards will also, no doubt, be adjudicated by the Supreme Court of Canada. While the Charter of Rights and Freedoms offers protection for speakers of the minority language (English in Quebec), the ability of the province to pass exemptions from the charter means that most anglophones would rather trust the more secure protection of their religious system (most anglophones are Protestant) than to risk the less secure protection of the charter. The 1989 action of the Quebec government in setting aside the Supreme Court's first decision on minority-language rights did nothing to change this situation.[5]

Roman Catholics in Manitoba have considered making a judicial attempt to regain public support for a separate school system by challenging a political compromise that was reached in 1986 to settle the Manitoba schools question, an issue that nearly split confederation (Tenszen, 1986). Even without a court case, the issue has already had impact: 'for 1986 the province ... raised its grants to private schools [including private Catholic schools] to $792 from $662 per pupil in 1985, an increase of about 20 per cent, far in excess of the percentage increase in provincial grants to public board (Lawton, 1987, p. 54).'

The courts have also been actively involved in supporting the right of denominational schools, including those separate school boards that operate with government funding and under government regulations, to enforce religion-based conditions of employment. In a series of cases testing the Charter of Rights and Freedoms the courts affirmed the right of denominational school boards to dismiss individuals for denominational cause (Lawton and Wignall, 1989; MacKay, 1984). In Newfoundland, which operates four publicly supported denominational systems, a Roman-Catholic school board was challenged for dismissing a teacher who, although hired while a Roman Catholic, had become a member of, and married within, the Salvation Army Church. Such discrimination, the teacher claimed, ran counter to the charter's clauses affirming equal treatment and non-discrimination. In its decision upholding the school board, the court noted that Section 29 of the charter reaffirmed denominational rights in education; denominational school boards had always had the right to discriminate on the basis of religion and could continue to do so (Walsh and Newfoundland Teachers' Association v.s. Newfoundland (Treasury Board) and Federation of School Boards of Newfoundland, 1988).

While the courts have been very supportive of minority religious rights, especially as far as Roman-Catholic minorities are concerned, they have been far less supportive of public-school religious instruction for members of the religious majority in provinces where Protestants have been the traditional majority.

Evaluation

Vignette 7
A private-sector vice-president's indictment of the Canadian educational system at a conference for educators concerned with the transition from school to work.

> In a recent study Canadian science and math achievement scores were at the bottom, along with those of the Americans. The Koreans were at the top. We have the worst high-school drop-out rate among industrialized countries ... One of the best things we could do to improve Ontario education is clear out the Ministry of Education and start fresh.

Vignette 8
'B.C. Students excel in international survey.' Title of a *Toronto Globe and Mail* article reporting on the same study (MacKenzie, 1989).

Vignette 9
Highlight in an article about the same report by Associated Press writer Jill
Lawrence.

> 40 percent of the Korean students understand measurement and
> geometry concepts and can solve more complex problems, such as
> figuring out the radius of a circle. That compares with less than 10
> percent in the United States and French-speaking Ontario.

A World of Differences (Educational Testing Service, 1989), the publication
referred to in these vignettes, might have an appropriate title to describe the
varying portrayals of its contents. The study in question is part of a series of
international comparative studies of educational achievement, in which one or
more Canadian provinces have been involved. The willingness of a number of
provinces to admit to the world how good or how bad their educational systems
are is striking. How and why did this openness come to be? A few of the factors
influencing their decisions are suggested here, but the complete story is yet to be
told.

There is no doubt that the prolonged economic problems of central Canada
brought on, in large part, by the energy crisis of the 1970s followed by the great
recession of 1981–2 that savaged, as well, the energy-based economies of the
western provinces forced Canada to attend to fundamentals. Among these was
the quality of its educational system, or more accurately, of its provincial
educational systems. The key document of this introspection is the *Report of
the Royal Commission on the Economic Union and Development Prospects
for Canada* (The McDonald Commission). Appointed by order in Council in
November 1982 by the Liberal government of Pierre Trudeau, it reported in
August 1985 to the progressive Conservative government of Brian Mulroney.
Among its salient recommendations was that a free-trade agreement be negotiated with the United States.[6]

Only three pages of the McDonald Commission's three-volume report of
nearly 2000 pages are devoted to elementary and secondary education. After
making a brief argument in support of a national interest in the field and of
increasing concern over the issues of quality and standards, the commissioners
stated:

> We do not believe that the federal government should become more
> deeply involved in primary and secondary education, but we are con-
> vinced, in view of general public concern about educational standards
> and quality, that there is a need for a national body to develop
> achievement-testing procedures and to monitor standards of achieve-
> ment across Canada.

> The national body we recommend for Canada should consist of some
> members who have direct experience in education and some who have
> had no direct connection with the sector. It must represent both
> Canada's charter-language groups .... Although it could be formed
> under the aegis of the Council of Ministers of Education, its credibility
> might be enhanced if it were not directly financed by government. (1985,
> 2, pp. 739–40)

Support for this type of policy initiative came from The Fraser Institute, a neo-conservative 'think tank' located in Vancouver, British Columbia, which conducted an investigation into the economics of the service sector in Canada, and which was funded by the federal department of regional industrial expansion. The institute's education report in the series is *Education in Canada*, written by economist Stephen T. Easton. In his contribution (which incidentally was printed in Singapore), Easton states:

> One potential role for the federal government in the educational process is as a disinterested monitor of what is taking place nationally. In particular, the federal government could provide a framework by which individual provinces could assess their performance in education ... The federal government could provide a Continuing Survey of Educational Performance ... Such a survey could develop data on a longitudinal basis to capture not only the performance of individuals in school but the achievements after elementary and secondary education. A survey that was national in scope would help to provide benchmarks for policies by drawing on a sample that is broader than any particular provincial environment. (Easton, S.T., 1988, p. 108)

For all intents and purposes, the McDonald commission's assessment was also seconded by Ontario's Premier's Council (the official quoted in Vignette 7 was a member) which released its report *Competing in the New Global Economy* in 1988. The report's preface notes that the Council was established in the 22 April 1986 speech from the Throne with a mandate to 'steer Ontario into the forefront of economic leadership and technological innovation'. A multipartite advisory body chaired by Premier David Peterson, the Council is composed of a number of cabinet ministers and leaders of business, labour, and academic communities. All of the representatives of the academic communities, with the exception of the Minister of Education (a politician), were representing universities, yet most of the pronouncements concerning education that were contained in 'Investing in People', Chapter 10 of the report, referred to elementary and secondary education.

The Council was particularly distressed by results of the Second International Mathematics Study (SIMS). This authoritative comparison of secondary-school student achievement in some twenty countries placed Canadian and American students well below their international competitors in applied mathematical skill levels. Ontario students' consistent average performance on SIMS was in stark contrast to the consistently superior performance of students from Hong Kong and Japan. Ontario's students did outperform students from the US and British Columbia, among other locations, but such success offered little comfort when all jurisdictions in North America trailed so far behind their leading competitors in Asia and Europe (p. 219). Ultimately, the Council (pp. 224–5) called for:

1 Provincial standards maintained by regular province-wide testing;
2 Initiation and participation in national and international performance comparisons of its students and school systems;

3 Public accountability strengthened through reports to parents of the performance of individual schools and the province in comparative testing;

4 A thorough review of the overhead cost structure of the educational system with a view to reallocating resources from administration to teacher improvement.

The Council's views paralleled those of two studies by Radwanski (1986; 1987) commissioned by the Premier's office to guide the development of the province's service sector and to reform education in order to reduce the numbers of high-school drop-outs.

Had *A World of Differences* been available to the Council or Radwanski, it is doubtful their opinions would have changed much. According to MacKenzie (1989), this five-nation comparison designed by the Educational Testing Service, a US firm best known for its college board of entrance examinations, indicated that, in mathematics, South Korean children were clearly superior, while French-language students in Quebec were next. They were followed by those in British Columbia, English-language Quebeckers, English New Brunswickers, English Ontarians, students in Spain, Britain, Ireland, French Ontarians and, finally, US students. The science findings were similar, although BC students were tied with the South Koreans at the top of the list. Students in Britain came next, then anglo-Quebeckers, English Ontarians, French Quebeckers, New Burnswick anglophones, students in Spain, the United States, Ireland and, in a virtual tie for last, students in French schools in Ontario and New Brunswick. (The French-language schools of Ontario do not refer to immersion school for English-speaking students).

Aside from the content of the findings, there are characteristics of this international study that reveal Canada's peculiar approach to the national evaluation of its educational system. First, unlike the other nations, Canada as a nation did not participate. Instead, four individual provinces, albeit four that enrol about 80 per cent of all Canadian students, participated in a voluntary, cooperative arrangement. Second, in the three provinces with significant numbers of francophones (New Brunswick, Quebec, and Ontario), evaluation was done on the basis of language group. Third, although the data were processed at Université Larval in Quebec City, the project management and publisher was an American company. We may yet see a national body set up to conduct educational evaluation in Canada. Fisher (1989, p. 11) hints of this possibility when he speaks of 'the federal government's firm commitment to the creation and administration of a national test of scientific awareness and competence as an eligibility indicator for those students being considered for [federal science] scholarships'. Ironically, it might be easier to commission a foreign company to do the job privately than to secure unanimous agreement among the provinces.

Actions have been taken to improve the effectiveness of educational systems at the provincial levels, although the actions have often been far removed from the free-market solutions inevitably advocated by economists and adopted in jurisdictions such as Britain and New Zealand. Economists seem convinced that if a bit of market discipline is introduced into the educational enterprise, higher quality (and efficiency) will result. Instead, Ontario and British Columbia at least have chosen to alter the process technology of education. That is, the provincial governments have decided to tell school boards and principals how to run their schools. (The proverbial faith of Canadians in government bureaus is alive and well!) British Columbia has mandated non-graded primary schools with dual (twice per year) entry for kindergarten students, recommendations made by its Royal Commission (1988). Ontario has mandated the de-streaming of Grade 9, the reduction of class sizes in the Grades 1 and 2, and the provision of junior and full-day kindergartens. The latter steps were based on a series of reviews, research projects, and reports (Radwanski, 1986; 1987; Lawton *et al.*, 1988). The intent of the changes was to reduce the difficulty that children, especially those from less favoured backgrounds, have in school and, in the long term after the year 2000, to provide Ontario with a better educated labour force.

> Although Canada spends a relatively high proportion of its gross national product on education — 7.7 per cent vs. 6.9 per cent in the United States and 5.9 per cent in Japan (Premier's Council, 1988, p. 224) — the major thrust of educational critics, who come primarily from the private sector and rely upon the analyses of economists, is the effectiveness of the educational system — the quality of its products — rather than its cost. The title of the Premier's Council says it all: competing in the new global economy. Canada, as a nation, has always relied in large part upon its natural resources (and offshore capital) for its prosperity, which still ranks second only to the United States among major industrialized nations in terms of its standard of living. (Lawton, 1988)

> The nation's primary concern is that, with changes in the world economy and the role and availability of natural resources, Canada will have to live by its wits. Its competitors and collaborators in this future will be not its traditional partners, England and Europe, but the United States (the elephant) and the industrialized nations of the Pacific Basin (the five dragons). (Hervouet, 1988)

Multiculturalism

Vignette 10
A parent explaining to a new neighbour why his children are attending the French-immersion school two miles away rather than the neighbourhood school around the corner:

> I figured if my kids were going to learn a foreign language, they might as well learn French [rather than Chinese].

Vignette 11
A Cantonese language teacher explaining an appeal for donations to a parent:

> The school board in this community doesn't fund the Chinese heritage language program the way other Metro Toronto school boards do. Our fees and the federal grant we receive are too low to pay the teachers a decent wage.

Vignette 12
The debate in one traditional community over the Ministry of Education's new policy that the exclusive use of the Lord's Prayer during opening exercises does not reflect Ontario's multiculturalism:

> Politicians are so caught up in multiculturalism that they don't see the rest — global Canada, its history and what we based our whole country on. Secular humanism relegates Judaeo-Christian religions to equality with all the others ... Intolerance looms on the horizon with the rise to primacy of secular humanism and its coercive demand that all ... conform to its ideas. (Perkins, 1989)

The gathering force of multiculturalism in Canada is often traced to the reaction, especially in western Canada, to the federal government's Royal Commission on bilingualism and biculturalism (Royal Commission, 1967). In several western provinces, those of Ukrainian and German descent outnumbered by far those of French descent; the attempts these other groups were making to maintain their languages and cultures seemed neglected by the Commission's focus on the two founding peoples, the French and the English. The response from the federal government was to enunciate a multiculturalism policy, create a multiculturalism directorate within the office of the Secretary of State, and to fund research and programs concerned with languages and cultures of origin (Cummins, 1983; Hodgson, 1988).

In the 1980s, the most important codification of multiculturalism occurred in the Charter of Rights and Freedoms, Section 27, which states, 'This charter shall be interpreted in manner consistent with the preservation and enhancement of the multicultural heritage of Canadians'. Complementing this section are clauses guaranteeing equal protection and benefit before and under the law (Section 15 (1)) and assurance that affirmative action programs are permissible (Section 15 (2)) to ameliorate conditions of groups disadvantaged due to race, national or ethnic origin, colour, religion, sex, age or mental or physical disability.

One of the first tests of the impact these rights would have occurred with the Supreme Court of Canada's decision concerning the extension of the Roman-Catholic separate school system in Ontario. Some commentators believed that the Sections 15 and 27 of the charter would mean that Ontario would be forced by the court to fund schools operated by various ethnic and religious groups. The court quashed this hope by approving the laws that Ontario had passed holding that provincial plenary powers over education guaranteed since confederation allowed them full scope to do what they pleased, so long as the Catholic minorities' rights and benefits were not lessened (Lawton, 1989).[7]

Although other ethnocultural groups have yet to benefit directly from the charter's provision of benefits, a legal attack on the role of religion in non-denominational public schools has succeeded, at least in Ontario, in reducing the predominantly Christian ethos of public schools. Until a recent, provincial court decision barring practice, the Lord's Prayer was used as a routine part of opening exercises in many elementary and secondary schools. In its place, the Ontario Ministry of Education indicated that a minute of silence or a selection of appropriate readings be used; if the latter was preferred, no one religion or philosophy was to receive special emphasis.

In some communities and with some individuals, the demotion of the Christian religion was not warmly received. Vignette 12 reflects the view that the majority — in this case Protestant Christian — were being discriminated against because of the few. Given that the Roman-Catholic separate system was set up so that Catholics could escape the religious instruction of the Protestant majority that was purveyed in nineteenth century Ontario, it seemed particularly unjust to the Protestants that the Catholics were not told, in effect, to keep their religion out of the Protestant schools. As the comments made about secular humanism suggest, however, the battle over the Lord's Prayer is as much civil strife among the descendants of the nineteenth century Protestants as it is a reaction to new immigrants.

But new immigrants — New Canadians — are an important part of the equation. Before 1967, the year of Canada's centennial and of the report on bilingualism and biculturalism, most Canadian immigration was from Europe and immigrants were white and Christian. Now most immigration is from every place except Europe — the Caribbean, South America, Asia, and Africa — from which immigrants are not white and many are not Christian. The impact of this immigration, now estimated at about 150,000 per year, is concentrated in a few geographical areas; it is particularly evident in major cities like Vancouver, Montreal, and Toronto. Culturally these cities are rapidly being transformed into societies that have little in common with rural and small-town Canada. As Perkins (1989) comments, the new rules emphasize 'the perception that laws — the approval of Sunday shopping, the ban on wolf bounties —are made for people in Toronto.'

Immigration is not about to end, although many Canadians wish it would. A 1987 report prepared for the federal government, which controls immigration, indicated:

> Canada must accept more immigrants or risk having its door battered down by desperate people fleeing Third World poverty ... If immigration policy should remain restrictive and selective, Canada would have to increase the resources and military personnel used to patrol the seas, air corridors and the Canada-US border ... Public opinion polls indicate most Canadians want immigration levels to remain where they are, or lower. A 1987 Gallup poll suggested only 13 per cent favor an increase ... Meanwhile, the birth rate for Canadian women of child bearing age has dropped to 1.67 from a high of 3.84 in 1961. There is no indication the fertility rate is on the way up. (Canadian Press, 1989)

Canada, of course, is not alone in facing a multicultural future (OECD, 1987).

Conclusion

Vignette 13
Author's bio: male; age, 47; Anglo-Saxon Scotch-Irish descent; unilingual English; 75 per cent secular humanist and 25 per cent Protestant; married. Wife: age, not given; Chinese descent; Cantonese and English; religion, not given. Two

children. Son: age, six; Cantonese and English; said the Lord's Prayer in public school until February 1989. Daughter: age, two; Cantonese and four words of English — mine, come, no and ice. Family residence: Agincourt ([racist] slang Asiancourt), northeast Metro Toronto, Ontario.

What you see depends on where you sit. What one experiences depends on who one is. To be sure, it is possible to portray the expansion of French in Canada as a marvelous accomplishment in the task of nation-building; the extension of Ontario's Roman-Catholic separate school system as the rectification of an ancient wrong; the development of a national, educational assessment system as a necessary measure to assure Canada's place in the sun; and the implementation of multiculturalism as the transcendence of narrow ethnocentrism. Such a portrayal must ring false, however, as it suggests that in the process of making these changes everyone wins and no one loses. That is not the case. Perhaps there is a social utility function that could demonstrate in quantitative terms that Canada is winning a net gain by the changes outlined in the paper, changes actively promoted, funded, and policed by the general and provincial governments. I have not seen it, however.

What I have seen is a range of impact, sometimes negative and sometimes positive. Given my descent, language, religion, and profession, I have probably had more contact with losers than winners. This comes through in the vignettes provided. Given my province of residence and working experience, my perspective is one from central Canada, especially Ontario. This, too, is evident in the vignettes. I have seen gains in the one area that is a lived reality for me, multiculturalism. Our new school trustee is of Chinese descent and, in November 1989, our school system began providing Cantonese and other heritage language classes free of charge, but only because the province adopted legislation mandating that such classes be offered. The reluctance with which the school system introduced these programs is evident in their scheduling: all classes are offered either Saturday morning or from 6.00–7.30 p.m. in the evening. Principals, I was told, do not want them to interfere with their regular program, including the extra-curricular program offered from 3.30–5.00 p.m. Parents were not asked at what time they would like to have the courses offered.

Had this paper been written by a francophone from Quebec, an anglophone Catholic from Ontario, or a Sikh from Vancouver, a different paper and different perspective would have been portrayed. That is as it should be. At the same time, there is no doubt that the four trends I have described — minority language rights, minority religion rights, evaluation, and multiculturalism — are dominant trends in Canada and that the federal government has played a significant role in each of them. And where political action on the part of government stops, the influence of the courts, and especially the Supreme Court of Canada, begins. Its impact on the definition of Canada and Canadian schools is only beginning. One important theme has been omitted, however: the education of native peoples. This topic is complex in its own right and is part of a process of developing a place for these people in Canada's Constitution, a process that is as yet unfinished.

Contrasting Canada with nations that share much of Canada's political, cultural, social, and religious characteristics — Australia, the United States, the United Kingdom, and New Zealand — suggests a number of parallels and differences. Canada's struggle with bilingualism is unique among them, devoted as it is to the preservation and enhancement of two national linguistic communities (but hopefully not an eternity of two solitudes). The only close parallel has been the national struggle in the United States to end racial segregation, a struggle that has seen the rearrangement of school-district lines, political action at all levels, and the strong arm of the US Supreme Court. Ironically, the US has put these powers of state to the removal of differences between two groups in order to achieve equality, while Canada has used the powers of state to segregate and preserve differences while ensuring equal provision of services and opportunity to the two groups. However, at no time during the civil-rights struggle in the United States could it be said that the very existence of the nation was in question. In the future, with Hispanic immigration, the US may find itself a bilingual nation, *de facto* if not *de jure*. Its English-first movement often points to Canada and Quebec as the example **not** to follow.

The extension in parts of Canada of public funding to the schools of a religious minority, in this case Roman Catholics, does have its parallels in Australia, where the government is heavily subsidizing the private Catholic school system, New Zealand with its Integration Act, and the United Kingdom with its grant-aided schools in England and Wales. Although Australia's method of direct, federal grants to religious schools is foreign to Canada, federal equalization payments to low-wealth provinces may accomplish the same end. In the United States, Roman Catholics have long sought public support for their schools. As in Canada, outside of Quebec, and in Australia, Catholics in the United States are the largest religious minority; but of the five nations considered, only in the US has Protestantism managed to contain the flow of funds to Catholic schools.

In all five countries, the abandonment of religion by public school has met with a significant response from evangelical Christian groups that have withdrawn from the public system and formed their own private schools. In some Canadian provinces (Alberta, British Columbia, Saskatchewan, Manitoba, and Quebec) their schools have qualified for funds provided to all private schools. Canada's national government has done nothing to ensure this privilege is extended elsewhere, as governments in Australia and Britain have done.

The questions of educational quality, high-school drop out rates, and economic success have become highly visible issues in all five nations. Canadian schools are more democratic and less elitist than those in many Commonwealth countries: approximately 70 per cent of its youth complete high school, a completion rate comparable to the United States and far above that of the United Kingdom and Australia in the 1980s. Several Canadian provinces, especially British Columbia and Ontario, have been among the leaders in subjecting themselves to this type of international scrutiny. However, the Canadian government has used its offices more to influence the debate than to initiate action. Its efforts, reflecting restrictions on its powers, are far less than those in the US, Australia, or New Zealand. All four nations look toward their Asian competitors across the Pacific Basin to assess whether they are keeping up educationally and economically; they wonder if joining them is not easier than beating them.

Multiculturalism is in fact joining nations together. The impact of immigration from Hong Kong alone is having a significant impact on a number of Canadian cities; the situation is no doubt similar in American and Australian cities, although Canada's policy of offering citizenship for cash (that is, admitting individuals who have sufficient assets to create jobs in Canada) makes Canada particularly attractive. In any case, Canada and Australia support heritage language classes and the US federal government has supported sometimes controversial programs in bilingual education. Commonwealth links with the Caribbean have made it a natural source of immigration to Canada; only now is Canada beginning to receive an influx of immigrants from South America who have made their way across or over the United States. The settlement of individuals from these areas presents more difficult issues educationally since, unlike most school-aged immigrants from Asia, they arrive without a strong tradition of educational accomplishment.

What lessons can we draw from these similarities and differences? Several conclusions are suggested under three themes: education and the constitution of nations; education and the economy; and the structure of educational systems.

Education and the constitution. Education is an important part of the process of inducting children into society. Education in Canada, and especially Ontario, went through major reforms in the 1980s because Canada was trying to reconstitute itself in order to ensure its continued existence, an outcome which is by no means assured. The debate over a proposed constitutional amendment that would recognize Quebec as a distinct society suggests this constitutional crisis will continue into the next decade. It is because education is so fundamental that constitutional issues are involved; it is the rare nation that has not lodged its solutions concerning the structure of its educational system in its constitution (Lawton, 1985). It is little wonder, then, that education in Canada has been, in Guthrie and Koppich's terminology, a question of high politics for the entire decade of the 1980s.

Education and the economy. Economic pressures of the 1980s, most of which can be traced to the severe recession of 1981–2 and the globalization of the economy, have raised the links between education and the economy to a visible position on the political agenda. The call, in simple terms, is for more effective educational systems: the human capital imperative identified by Guthrie and Koppich. To achieve this end, many nations have adopted reforms based on the assumption that the operation of a free market in education will prove more successful and more efficient than a state bureaucracy. In Canada, to date, reforms of this nature have be muted or limited to individual school districts;[8] instead the primary concern has been on social reform, especially as it concerns the education of francophones, and on the evaluation of student learning. Provincial bureaucracies have been the agents of change rather than for change. Questions of efficiency did not seem to be particularly important.

This situation may be changing, however. The federal budget deficit was the order of $30 billion per year for most of the decade, a deficit triple that of the United States on a per-capita basis. Overall, thirty cents of every tax dollar now go for interest payments. As a result, the federal government reduced transfer payments to the provinces and proposed a national sales tax, a goods and services tax (GST), dubbed the 'gouging and screwing tax' by an irreverent member of parliament, of 9 per cent for implementation in 1991. As the full impact of these cutbacks and tax increases are felt, one can expect the call for efficiency in government services to increase.

School system structures. Where reform has meant a radical change in the allocation of power in education, a radical change in the system of financing education may follow. The case of the United Kingdom with its emphasis on financial delegation and the local management of schools is a good example (Thomas, Kirkpatrick and Nicholson, 1989). In Canadian provinces where alternative strategies for investing in education have been developed (e.g., Ontario and British Columbia) the provincial governments have used targeted funds and regulatory control to achieve their objectives. Although the two strategies appear to be in direct opposition to one another, one calling for decentralization and the other for centralization, both approaches may reflect the same impetus: a distrust by the central government of the intermediate (school-district) level and a fear that funds will be squandered on a pampered bureaucracy.

Administrative practices in Canada, it seems, are out of step with those in nations sharing a similar heritage. There seems to be a continued reliance on central authority at a time when other jurisdictions are adopting a radically different strategy. In defense of a strong central presence in Canadian education, one can point to the results of international comparisons. Canadian provinces have done relatively well, judged against their peers, in international comparisons of student achievement. As the saying goes, 'If it ain't broke, why fix it?'

Central regulation can result in both fiscal and political inefficiencies, however. By way of example, Ontario's mandating of class sizes of twenty in grades 1 and 2 removed the power from schools and school districts to assign teachers in the most cost-effective manner. In one school system, this provincial mandate disrupted a successful program of allowing schools to allocate personnel resources in a flexible manner. For over a decade schools had been able to trade off staff positions for teachers, principals, vice-principals, secretaries, and clerical aid according to a 'unit of strength' formula. Ontario schools and their communities are now no longer able to tune a school's staff to the local situation, local values, and local needs. Even the use of school-district authority often has had the same effects. School boards are often local oligarchies that rule as a one-party system, lacking even the loyal opposition present in provincial and national parliaments (Humphreys *et al.*, 1986).

In short, there is in Canada a high reliance on more senior levels of government to make decisions about education at a time when economic pressures are growing. As well the institutional structures built up over the years are large, distant, and often unresponsive to local preferences. However, if its constitutional crisis can be resolved, Canada may find itself following the global trend of restructuring education: of moving decisions down to the school-community level as funding declines and the inability of school systems to satisfy competing demands increases. Schools would then be forced to turn to their immediate communities for the resources, political and economic, that are necessary for their operation, while the provinces and, in all probability, the federal government concern themselves with the assessment of student achievement on a core of subjects seen as crucial to national prosperity.

Notes

1 This chapter is a revised version of a paper presented at the annual conference of the American Educational Research Association, San Francisco, CA, 27–31 March 1989. Another version was also presented at Oxford International Round-table on Education Policy, St. Peter's College, University of Oxford, 13–19 August 1989.

2 The animal metaphors are drawn from various sources. The octopus is from Frank Norris's book of the same name. The elephant comes from Pierre Trudeau's often quoted concern about Canada's position: 'Living next to you', he reminded a US audience, 'is in some ways like sleeping with an elephant. No matter how friendly and even-tempered the beast, one is affected by every twitch and grunt.' (*MacLean's*, 1989). The dragons are from Roy A. Mathew's book (1983), *Canada and the Little Dragons: An Analysis of Hong Kong, Taiwan and South Korea and the Challenge Opportunity They Present for Canadian Interests in the 1980s*, Montreal, Institute for Research on Public Policy.

3 I was witness to the scenes described in the first two vignettes, although the comments are paraphrased from memory rather than direct quotations.

4 Canada's capital, Ottawa, is a city in the province of Ontario; there is no separate federal territory although federal offices spread across the Ottawa River into Hull, Quebec.

5 Whether anglophones in Quebec, a province that has French as its official language, feel the protection offered by the federal government is open to debate. Recently, the Supreme Court of Canada found that a Quebec law, forbidding the use of English (or any other language except French) in store signs, to be a violation of the charter. The Quebec government utilized Section 33 of the charter (the so-called notwithstanding clause) to exempt the sign legislation from the charter for a period of five years. For Quebec, the social issue of concern is maintenance of a French community within its own borders. With a birth rate well below replacement levels it must depend on immigrants for new recruits; yet historically most immigrants have gravitated toward the anglophone community. Hence its desire to minimize the visibility of English and other languages. It is this situation that is the butt of the joke in the third vignette.

Another divisive issue in late 1989 was the so-called Meech Lake accord, a constitutional amendment to recognize Quebec's distinct status within the confederation. Seven of the ten provinces approved; the three remaining provinces rejected the notion that one province should have special status. The accord, which meant to gain Quebec's approval of the 1982 patriation of the Constitution (which it alone opposed), had to be approved by all ten provinces by June 1990 to become a part of the Constitution.

6 The free-trade recommendation was first rejected and then accepted by the progressive Conservatives, and accepted, and then fundamentally rejected by the Liberals. In fall 1988, the latter party, under the leadership of John Turner, fought a bitter election campaign committed to the tearing up of the tentative free-trade agreement that the Tories had negotiated with the US. With the Tory victory, the key recommendation of the Liberal-appointed MacDonald Commission was assured implementation.

7 It is worth noting that the workload of making fundamental interpretations of the new charter has already caused three judges on the Supreme Court of Canada to retire, their health broken.

8 The public-school system in Edmonton, Alberta, is noted for its plan to decentralize authority and budget to the school level. Researchers and administrators from Australia, the United States, the United Kingdom, and parts of Canada have visited the system to study its plan.

References

ATTORNEY GENERAL OF QUEBEC VS GREATER HULL SCHOOL BOARD *et al.* (1984) 2 R.C.S., 575.

BROWNE, R.K. and LOUDEN, L.W. (1989) 'Developments in Education Policy in the Eighties: An Australian Perspective', Paper presented at the Annual Conference of the American Educational Research Association, San Francisco, CA, 27–31 March.

CALDWELL, G. and WADDELL, E. (1982) *The English of Quebec from Majority to Minority Status*, Quebec City, Institut Québécois de Recherche sur la Culture.

CANADIAN PRESS (1989) 'Canada Urged to Accept More Immigrants', *The [Toronto] Globe and Mail*, 6 March.

CUMMINS, J. (1983) *Heritage Language Education: Issues and Directions*, Ottawa, Multiculturalism Canada, Minister of Supplies and Services.

EASTON, S.T. (1988) *Education in Canada: An Analysis of Elementary, Secondary and Vocational Schooling*, Vancouver, The Fraser Institute.

EDUCATIONAL TESTING SERVICE (1989) *A World of Differences*, Princeton, NJ, ETS.

FISHER, H.K. (1989) 'Developments in Educational Policy in the Eighties: Trends in Three Federal Systems — Australia, Canada, and the USA. The Canadian Experience', Paper presented at the Annual Conference of the American Educational Research Association, San Francisco, CA, 27–31, March.

GLOBE AND MAIL (1989) 'National Scene', *The [Toronto] Globe and Mail*, 6 May.

HANNAWAY, J. and CROWSON, R. (1989) *The Politics of Reforming School Administration*, New York, The Falmer Press.

HODGSON, E.D. (1988) *Federal Involvement in Public Education*, Toronto, Canadian Education Association, pp. 63–70.

HERVOUET, G. (1988) *About Canada: Canada and the Pacific Basin*, Ottawa, Canadian Studies Directorate, Minister of Supply and Services.

HUMPHREYS, E.H., LAWTON, S.B., TOWNSEND, R.G., GRABB, V.E. and WATSON, D.M. (1986) *Alternative Approaches to Determining Distribution of School Board Trustee Representation*, 1, 2, 3, Toronto, Ontario Ministry of Education.

LAPKIN, S., SWAIN, M. and ARGUE, V. (1983) *French Immersion: The Trial Balloon that Flew*, Toronto, OISE Press.

LAWRENCE, J. (undated, 1989) *Math, Science Scores of US Teens Fall Short*, The Associate Press.

LAWTON, S.B. (1985) 'A survey of the governance of Roman Catholic and denominational education in Canada, the United Kingdom, Ireland, Australia, and New Zealand', Unpublished manuscript.

LAWTON, S.B. (1986) 'A Case Study of Choice in education: Separate schools in Ontario', *Journal of Education Finance*, 12, 1, pp. 36–48.

LAWTON, S.B. (1987) 'Teachers' Salaries: An International Perspective', in KERN, A. and MONK, D.H. (Eds) *Attracting and Compensating America's Teachers*, Eighth annual yearbook of the American Education Finance Association, Cambridge, MA, Ballinger Publishing Company.

LAWTON, S.B. (1989) 'Public, Private and Separate Schools in Ontario: Developing a New Social Contract for Education?', in BOYD, W.L. and CIBULKA, J.G. (Eds) *Private Schools and Public Policy: International Perspectives*, Buffalo, NY, SUNY Press.

LAWTON, S.B., LEITHWOOD, K.A., BATCHER, E., DONALDSON, E.L. and STEWART, R. (1988) *Student Retention and Transition in Ontario High Schools: Policies, Practices, and Prospects*, Toronto, Ontario Ministry of Education.

LAWTON, S.B. and WIGNALL, R. (1989) *Scrimping or squandering? Financing Canadian schools*, Toronto, OISE Press.

LAWTON, S.B. and WIGNALL, R. (1989) 'Denominational Cause and Employment in Religious Schools', Paper presented at the Annual Conference of the American Educational Research Association, San Francisco, CA, 27–31 March.

MACKAY, A.W. (1984) *Educational Law in Canada*, Toronto, Edmond-Montgomery-Publications Ltd.

MACKENZIE, C. (1989) 'Students Excel in International Survey', *The [Toronto] Globe and Mail*, 1 February.

MACPHERSON, R.J.S. (1989) 'Reform of New Zealand and New South Wales Education Systems,' Paper presented at the School of Education, University of Michigan, Ann Arbor, April.

MACLEAN'S (1989) *Portrait of two nation, Special report*, 3 July, pp. 23–84.

MILLS, C.W. (1959) *The Sociological Imagination*, London, Oxford University Press.

ORGANIZATION FOR ECONOMIC COOPERATION AND DEVELOPMENT (OECD) (1987) *Multicultural Education*, Paris, Centre for Educational Research and Innovation, OECD.

PAQUETTE, J. (1989) 'The quality conundrum: Assessing what we cannot agree on', in LAWTON, S.B. and WIGNALL, R. (Eds) *Scrimping or squandering?: Financing Canadian schools*, Toronto, Oise Press.

PERKINS, M. (1989) 'Principal's Demotion Keeps School Prayer Dispute Simmering', *The [Toronto] Globe and Mail*, 6 March.

PREMIER'S COUNCIL (ONTARIO) (1988) *Competing in the New Global Economy*, Report of the Premier's Council, 1, Toronto, Queen's Printer for Ontario.

RADWANSKI, G. (1986) *Ontario Study of the Service Sector*, Toronto, Ontario Ministry of Treasury and Economics.

RADWANSKI, G. (1987) *Ontario Study of the Relevance of Education, and the Issue of Dropouts*, Ontario, Ministry of Education.

RENSHAW, G. (1986) *Adjustment and Economic Performance in Industrialized Countries*, Geneva, International Labour.

ROYAL COMMISSION ON BILINGUALISM AND BICULTURALISM (1967) *Report of the Royal Commission on Bilingualism and Biculturalism*, Ottawa, The Queen's Printer.

ROYAL COMMISSION ON THE ECONOMIC UNION AND DEVELOPMENT PROSPECTS FOR CANADA (1985) *Report of Royal Commission on the Economic Union and Development Prospects for Canada*, 1, 2, 3, Ottawa, Minister of Supplies and Services.

ROYAL COMMISSION ON EDUCATION (British Columbia) (1988) *A Legacy for Learners: The Report of the Royal Commission on Education*, Victoria, BC, Queen's Printer for British Columbia.

SISSONS, C.B. (1959) *Church and State in Canadian Education*, Toronto, The Ryerson Press.

SUPREME COURT OF ONTARIO (1984) *Reference re Education Act Ontario and Minority Language Education Rights, 47 O.R., 2, 1*.

SUPREME COURT OF ONTARIO (1987) Reference re Bill 30, an Act to amend the Education Act, 1 S.C.R., 1148.

THOMAS, H., KIRKPATRICK, G. and NICHOLSON, E. (1989) *Financial delegation and the local management of schools: Preparing for practice*, London, Cassell Educational Ltd.

TENSZEN, M. (1986) 'Manitoba's RC Trustees Plan Appeal to Ottawa', *The [Toronto] Globe and Mail*, 10 January.

WALSH AND NEWFOUNDLAND TEACHERS' ASSOCIATION VS NEWFOUNDLAND (TREASURY BOARD AND FEDERATION OF SCHOOL BOARDS OF NEWFOUNDLAND (1988), 71 Nfld. and P.E.I.R., 21.

Chapter 7

Developments in Education Policy in Australia: A Perspective on the 1980s

L. Warren Louden and R.K. Browne

The importance of a 'good education' is one of the most widely held beliefs in Australian society. As a result, in every state election, political parties make much of their education policies. To a very significant extent, however, Australian schooling has been influenced more in the past fifteen years by federal government policies than by the states. What makes this interesting is that the federal government has no constitutional power over education and provides directly less than 10 per cent of the funding of government schools.

Constitutional Responsibility for Education

Prior to 1901 Australia consisted of six self-governing states. It is important to note that all of the states had been colonies of the United Kingdom and thus shared a common cultural background. In each of the states a system of free and compulsory education for at least all pupils of primary-school age had been set up although these were of fairly recent origin. If, at the time of federation, a decision to make education a responsibility of the federal government had been taken, it would have been a relatively simple matter to reconcile the minor differences which existed at that time. This did not occur and as a result six different systems became entrenched. Despite the independent approaches there was a good deal of similarity. In general, one of two models had been followed. New South Wales, Victoria, and Tasmania opted for six years of primary education followed by up to six years of secondary education. The other states followed a model based on seven years of primary followed by up to five years of secondary education. The age at which children began schooling also varied.

Despite these differences their common background ensured that there was a good deal of curriculum commonality among states although there were differences in emphasis and approaches. Even though there is an Australian Education Council (of which all ministers are members) and frequent meetings of senior staff, until recently there has been little cooperative interaction and control of education has been a jealously guarded state's right.

The Australian Constitution

On 1 January 1901 the states federated to form the Commonwealth of Australia. Like the United States, Australia has a written Constitution. The basis of the Australian Constitution was that, for the most part, every power of the state was to continue unless it was exclusively vested in the Parliament of the Commonwealth or withdrawn from the Parliament of the state (Section 107). To amend the Constitution the proposed changes must first be passed by both houses of the federal Parliament. If this condition is satisfied the proposed amendment must then be submitted as a referendum, at which a majority of the electors in a majority of the states, must favour the change if the amendment is to be accepted (Section 128). Since 1901 only eight proposals have been passed and the substance of the Constitution remains much as it was in 1901.

The powers which were exclusively vested in the Commonwealth in 1901 were relatively limited. They are detailed in Section 51 of the Constitution. In summary, these powers (1) set up a common market between Australian states with free trade and a common, external customs tariff (2) gave the Commonwealth control over Australia's relations with other nations e.g., defence, immigration, and external affairs (3) gave the Commonwealth the power to levy taxation and 'borrow on the public credit' of the Commonwealth. While the Constitution does not give the Commonwealth any powers in respect of education, Section 51 23A which was inserted in 1946 allows the Commonwealth to provide a range of 'benefits to students'.

A unique feature of federal-state relations in Australia arises from the federal government's position in regard to taxation. Under Section 51 (ii) of the Constitution the Commonwealth has the power to levy taxation 'but so as not to discriminate between states or parts of states'. States also have the constitutional power to levy taxes including direct income tax. During World War II, however, a system of federal government-levied, uniform, pay-as-you-earn taxation was voluntarily agreed by the states. This practice has continued so that all direct income tax is now paid to the Commonwealth. States then receive 'grants' as appropriations from the Commonwealth Treasury. In addition, the Commonwealth Grants Commission (established under Section 96 of the Constitution which gives the federal Parliament power to grant financial assistance as it sees fit) recommends additional funding to states which have circumstances which make the provision of government services more costly in some states than others. As a result, there is a levelling effect between states which allows all governments to provide comparable levels of public services. The decisions concerning the distribution of these funds between different activities is a matter for decision by state governments. The result is to bring about considerable similarity between the per-capita spending of states on the services they provide. In most Australian states education accounts for about one quarter of the state-government's expenditure.

The Development of Federal Involvement in Education Prior to 1980

Although there is no specific provision for federal-government involvement in education such involvement has existed for many years. As long ago as 1951–2 the Commonwealth began to assist with the recurrent expenditure of universities, up to this time entirely a state responsibility. Further direct involvement followed in 1958 when the Commonwealth assumed some responsibility for capital expenditure in universities. In 1965 a further significant change took place, when funding was made available for capital works in technical colleges on an equal-share basis with states.

The first schools established in Australia were non-government, and these have persisted to the present day. They may be divided into schools which charge substantial fees and parish schools conducted by Catholic school authorities, which charge low fees made possible by the availability of members of religious teaching orders.

Following World War II pressure began to build on Catholic school as population growth from natural increase and migration greatly increased the numbers of students seeking places. At first this increase was accommodated by increasing the size of classes. In Western Australia, for example, in Catholic primary schools pupil–teacher ratios rose from 25.1 in 1940 to 38.1 in 1960. Continuing demand and a reduction in recruitment into the vocations, however, posed massive financial problems and consequent agitation for government aid to non-government schools.

Government aid for non-government schools had been part of the platform of the Australian Labor Party. In 1955 there was a major split in the Labor Party largely on religious grounds, and as a result, in 1957, this plank of the platform was removed. Both federal and state Labor governments were bound by this ruling. The Labor Party decision, together with increased demand for education in Catholic schools, led the issue of government assistance for non-government schools to become an important political one. It was not surprising, therefore, that the Liberal-Country Party government late in 1963 promised, if returned in the impending election, to take steps to improve facilities in both government and non-government schools. The government was duly returned.

The first step in federal support for both government and non-government schools was the provision of funds to construct high-quality science laboratories in secondary schools. The justification was the government's belief that it was essential to improve science facilities if Australia was to train scientists and technologists. Initially, funds were distributed to government and non-government schools according to enrolments. However, by 1967 the amount of money made available to non-government schools had doubled. The justification was that there were 'particular needs' in the non-government sector. This was the first time that a 'needs' basis was applied by the federal authority to the provision of funding for education. The effect of this change in policy was that by 1971 (i.e., after the scheme had been in operation for seven years) the non-government sector which enrolled less than 25 per cent of secondary-school students had received some 37 per cent of Commonwealth funding.

As the science laboratory program was moving towards completion, the Commonwealth announced its intention of providing funds to raise the standard of secondary-school libraries in government and non-government schools. The purpose of this program was clearly described as to develop 'a modern school library as a centre of learning in which a wide range of resource materials . . . is available' (Commonwealth Department of Education Annual Report 1967–8, p. 28). This statement indicated a changed direction by the Commonwealth. Up to this time, apart from specification of the standard of buildings to be constructed, no directions to schools or education authorities had been issued. The decision to build libraries indicated a preference for discovery learning as a methodology and a multi-media approach as being necessary, not a widely accepted philosophy at that time. The Commonwealth secondary-school library program was important also because members of the committee visited non-government schools and made reports on the adequacy or otherwise of the buildings and learning resources available in these schools. As a result of these visits a picture of Australia's secondary schools began to be visible to federal-government authorities.

Per-capita Grants to Non-government Schools

Perhaps the most important decision on education made by the Liberal-Country Party government in the 1960s was to provide per-capita grants to non-government schools to assist with recurrent expenditure. Prior to this, grants had been associated with the funding of capital works, not with the recurrent costs associated with providing schooling. The initial per-capita grants were modest, $35 per annum for primary pupils and $50 per annum for secondary in 1969 students. These grants were not made to government schools.

Since the Constitution did not allow the Commonwealth to make direct grants to non-government schools, the grants were made to the state authorities on condition that they would be passed on to the individual non-government schools. For their part, the states were to require the school authorities to enter into an agreement with the state that they would use the money for the purpose for which it was approved. States were willing to accept these conditions since it reduced the demands upon them by non-government schools seeking assistance.

The State-aid Controversy

The provision of state aid for non-government schools was bitterly opposed by government school-teachers' unions and parent groups. They claimed that the government's responsibility was towards government schools. They insisted that no state aid should be made available until conditions were improved in government schools. They also argued that such aid was unconstitutional. Up to 1967 this group had the support of the opposition Labor Party. However, since there was a significant political disadvantage involved in opposing state aid for non-government schools, the Labor Party's platform was changed and state aid for non-government schools became the policy of all major political parties.

A constitutional challenge was later mounted through the courts by a group known as DOGS (Defence of Government Schools). The grounds were that such aid was not consistent with the Constitution Section 96 'the Parliament may grant financial assistance to the states on such terms and conditions as the Parliament thinks fit' and section 116 'the Commonwealth shall not make any law for establishing any religion or for imposing any religious observance'. The High Court by a majority of six to one dismissed the suit of the plaintiffs and, with its

constitutional validity established and acceptance of state aid as a plank of platform of all major political parties, state aid had clearly come to stay in Australian
education.

Federal Government Influence on Education in the 1970s

While the federal government was now involved in all aspects education, its
influence in government schools had been limited to the provision of science
laboratories in the period 1964–1971 and of school libraries from 1968. The late
1960s and early 1970s was a period of growth in the size of the school population
in Australia. Between 1966 and 1971 there was an increase of over 8 per cent in
the number of children in the age range over which schooling was compulsory.
This led to problems in both the government and non-government sector for
capital funds to provide new places.

Approaches by both state and non-government schools for capital aid for
both primary and secondary schools led to the decision by the federal government in 1972 to provide such aid. The allocation to the sectors reflected the
respective enrolments in each. At the same time, the per-capita aid to non-
government schools which had been introduced by the Commonwealth in 1969
was increased to 20 per cent of the cost of educating a child in a government
school. The Commonwealth also indicated to states that they would be expected
to match this amount.

The outcome of these evolutionary changes was that during the period
1951–72, during which period a Conservative government had been in power,
the Commonwealth, which had no constitutional responsibility for education,
had advanced to the situation where in 1971–2 it was providing $161 million
for universities and university-student assistance; $65 million for colleges of
advanced education and technical education; and $50 million for primary and
secondary schools, of which $32 million went to the non-government schools.
While during its term of office the government had greatly increased its influence
on education, this was almost entirely confined to financial involvement. It appeared not to wish to affect what was happening in schools nor is there evidence
that it saw education as being a central plank of government policy. Because of
this hands-off policy the constitutional responsibilities of state governments were
not threatened and the Commonwealth's involvement was welcomed.

Revolutionary Change: The Schools Commission

In December 1972 the Liberal-Country Party government, which had held office
since 1949, was defeated by the Labor Party led by E.G. (Gough) Whitlam. It
was to be expected that there would be major changes upon its assumption of
office. The Labor Party in Australia is traditionally the party of the working
class. Its view has always been that education is an important means of reducing
inequities due to socio-economic factors. Thus equal opportunity of education
for all has been a key plank of the Labor platform. It was to be expected that
education would assume a high profile once the party achieved government. This
importance was reflected in the selection, as Minister for Education, of Kim

Beazley, one of the longest serving members of Parliament. He had been elected to federal Parliament in 1945 and was highly regarded as an intellectual who had the respect of all parties.

One of the first actions of the new government was to announce the formation of an Australian Schools Commission. An interim committee under the chairmanship of a distinguished academic, Professor Peter Karmel, was appointed to 'examine the position of government and non-government primary and secondary schools throughout Australia and to make recommendations on the immediate financial needs of those schools, the priorities within those needs and the measures appropriate to assist in meeting them' (Australian Schools Commission, 1973, p. 3 *et seq*.). However, there were several further important terms of reference which broke new ground. The first required the committee to establish 'acceptable standards for those schools, government and non-government alike, which fall short of those standards'. Instead of federal assistance for education being granted to states to supplement their funding, the Commonwealth now wished to set standards towards which they would work.

A second term of reference required the interim committee to take account of 'the particular needs of schools for the handicapped ... and of isolated children'. It was clear that the government wished to target those whose needs were greatest i.e., those who suffered the greatest educational disadvantage. The committee must also take into account 'the diversity of curricula to meet differing aptitudes and interests of the students'. In posing this term of reference it was clear that, for the first time, a federal government was to be interested in what happened in schools as well as with their funding. Finally, the additional funding made available by the Commonwealth with effect from 1 January 1974 was not in substitution for funds provided by state governments or private-school auuthorities. These authorities would be required to maintain their efforts.

The Karmel Report

The committee worked quickly and its report *Schools in Australia* was available in May 1973. Since its publication, it has been referred to as the Karmel Report. The report was based on six main values. The first was acceptance of devolution of authority. Most Australian state systems at that time were highly centralized, but the committee favoured 'less rather than more centralized control over the operation of schools' (ASC, 1973, p. 10). This view required that the Schools Commission, when it began operation, should not follow a policy of central control but should establish guidelines to give schools freedom. The second value was equality. The view was taken that all children, irrespective of their parents' income or of their own ability, should have the opportunity to receive an appropriate education of quality. The third value, diversity, included both different teaching methods and diversity in the nature of relationships between teachers and pupils. The fourth value was acceptance of the dual system of government and non-government schools, still an issue of conflict in the Australian community. The fifth value was the acceptance of community involvement in schooling. The interim committee believed meaningful involvement of the community to be essential if education was to receive parental acceptance and support. Finally, the committee affirmed the special role of schools in assisting young people towards 'the acquisition of skills and knowledge, initiation into the cultural heritage, the valuing of rationality and the broadening of opportunities to respond to and participate in artistic endeavours'. Despite this affirmation of the traditional role of schools (ASC, 1973, p. 14) it accepted that schools now had an expanded social role over that which had existed previously.

The Karmel committee highlighted a number of deficiencies in Australian education, including an overall lack of resources with great inequities between schools, many inadequately trained teachers, a relatively narrow curriculum with little provision for individual differences and an 'authoritarian and hierarchical atmosphere' (ASC, 1973, p. 139) which inhibited human relationships. Despite these inadequacies the committee recognized the need to operate through the various educational authorities. It proposed that funds should be made available in the form of block grants, which schools and school systems would be free to spend in accordance with their own preferences. It was further proposed that, to begin rectifying the inequities which existed, schools and systems should receive differential grants but that all schools should achieve minimum acceptable standards by the end of the decade.

The committee recommended seven main programs covering general recurrent resources, general buildings, primary and secondary libraries, disadvantaged schools, teacher development, and innovation. These programs in total were calculated to cost $467 million in 1974 and 1975, of which almost 90 per cent was to go to government schools. This was in addition to the existing $195 million, most of which went to non-government schools. Overall, about 28 per cent of funds were to go to non-government schools. The interim committee also recommended that the Schools Commission consist of several full-time commissioners and six par-time commissioners drawn from the widest possible cross-section of the educational community.

Throughout the 1970s the Schools Commission occupied a highly influential role in Australian education. Despite a change of government in 1975 the value of the Commission was such that it continued to operate. By the end of the decade the resource targets set in 1973 had been surpassed in government schools and Australian schools were greatly changed from what they had been only seven years previously.

The Curriculum Development Centre

In addition to the Schools Commission, the federal government also set up the Curriculum Development Centre, a move consistent with the clear intention of the new minister that the Commonwealth would not only be a funding agency but would also be concerned with what happened in classrooms. The centre had quite broad functions but essentially its purpose was to produce school curricula and associated educational materials which, because of their quality, would be widely acceptable in Australian schools and whose widespread use would bring about both improved teaching/learning and a more common curriculum throughout Australia.

Some work had already been done along these lines through the Australian Council for Educational Research which had managed the Australian Science

Education Project (ASEP). This project, which was a cooperative between states and the Commonwealth, preceded the election of the Labor government by some three years:

> ASEP demonstrated that a significant number of teachers and administrators saw Australian science teaching lagging behind most developed countries and were prepared to do something about it. It showed that curriculum developers and educationists had a voice in what happened in schools and that co-operation across State borders was not impossible. (Moran, 1980, p. 54)

This realization was reflected in a decision taken in 1974 to institute a second major project, the social education-materials project, which was assumed by the Curriculum Development Centre when it began operation. These initiatives were later repeated in the areas of Asian studies and English teaching at the lower secondary level.

Trends in Education Policy in the 1980s

While the conduct of schools is a state responsibility, attention is here devoted to the role of the federal government during the 1980s and its inter-relationship with state systems.

The defeat of the federal Labor government in 1975, after less than three years in office, diminished the reformist zeal of the federal government towards education in schools. The Schools Commission remained in existence and continued to provide advice to the government on priorities for educational funding. One important issue raised by it was the difficulty of moving towards long-term goals through annual budgets and it suggested that funding should be on the basis of a 'rolling-triennium'. In accepting the advice the Commonwealth indicated its intention to increase funding in real terms by 2 per cent per annum and to concentrate this funding in the low-fee-paying non-government schools whose position, in comparison with both government schools and high-fee non-government schools, had declined despite the Schools Commission's assistance. The special purpose programs aimed at increasing equity were continued.

By 1980 there were grave doubts about Australia's economic position. Rapid inflation, a decline in the price for mineral exports and decline in the competitiveness of Australian manufactured goods led to a severe financial crisis. As a result the government sought to effect economies. It decided not to continue the promised 2 per cent increase in recurrent expenditures for government schools but to peg these at the 1979 level. Additionally, as a one-year economy measure, the allocation for capital works was reduced by $44 million (32 per cent).

To effect economies in the non-government sector proved a more difficult problem for the government. In its report the Commission noted:

> In the non-government schools (both Catholic and other) increased recurrent resources have been financed from government subsidies with declining, or at best static, private inputs and services.... More than

three-quarters of the cash income of Catholic schools now come from government subsidies. (ASC, 1979, p. 3)

Given the reliance of the low-fee schools on government aid, it was clear that if any economies were to be made they would need to be made in the least dependent schools. In non-government schools subsidies were paid according to a system of categories, a six-level structure in which the wealthiest schools were classified as level I while those least well-resourced were level 6. In 1979, for example, the per-capita grant to level-1 schools was 16 per cent of the cost of educating a child in a government school, while in level-6 schools it was more than double this amount. In an effort to contain expenditure the federal government made no increases in the funding levels for any but the level-6 schools and, as it had done in government schools, reduced capital funding in the case of non-government schools by 19 per cent.

Some Commonwealth programs required the cooperation of government and non-government schools. In financial terms the largest of these was provided for the 'services and development' program, essentially for the professional development of teachers. At a time when, because of changes which were occurring, professional development was vitally important, funding for this program was cut by 26 per cent. Since state governments too were suffering the same financial difficulties as the Commonwealth, these reductions could not be offset through state funding and, in fact, the Commonwealth's lead was followed by some state treasuries.

The School-to-work Transition Program

Faced with rising youth unemployment, the federal government in 1980 introduced the above program to increase the opportunities for under-eighteen-year-olds in education, training, and employment. The program sought to increase retention in secondary schools and to develop either saleable skills or a capacity to benefit from further training. Because the program spanned technical education (TAFE) and schools, it was administered not through the Schools Commission but by the Commonwealth Department of Education.

In the initial year there was strong objection to the program by state authorities and schools, based on three grounds. The first arose in respect of the Commonwealth's demand that over the five years of the program the states should progressively assume financial responsibility for the initiatives involved. Secondly, schools resented the implication that it was because of their failings that high levels of unemployment existed and it was only by changes in the schools that this situation could be overcome. The third objection was that if the Commonwealth's program was successful, state governments would incur increased capital and recurrent funding responsibilities in pursuit of a Commonwealth-inspired objective. After close collaboration between the states to present a united front, the Commonwealth made a five-year funding commitment, which included the payment of transition allowances to youths returning to work experience and training.

This program was highly significant in a number of ways. It was the first time that secondary education had been viewed as a direct tool in the fight for economic progress. Secondly, the program provided for secondary and technical colleges to work together. Such a relationship had not existed in the past. The third point of significance was that since the bulk of the unemployed were students who had not done well in the traditional school, schools were faced with the problem of providing relevant courses for a hitherto largely neglected group. The experimentation to solve this problem was to have a profound effect on secondary-school practice generally since changes made to capture the interest of reluctant students, to satisfy their demands for obvious and immediate relevance, and the need to involve the community outside the school to do this have subsequently been reflected in the programs of more able students.

This program, when initiated in 1980, was given a life of five years, the first time a program had been guaranteed for such a substantial time. The school aspects were supported by a variety of other schemes conducted on the job, in TAFE colleges or in agencies conducted by community groups. Given such a combination of contributing agencies it was inevitable that there should be some confusion and overlap and even by March 1981 the Schools Commission noted that an assessment of the existing pattern of youth training and support schemes should be undertaken.

As well as breaking new ground in educational terms, the transition program broke new ground administratively. State committees, which included representatives of schools, TAFE, Departments of Employment, teachers' union, employers, and community, were set up. These committees had the responsibility for recommending projects for funding, some submitted by community agencies, some by government departments, and many by individual schools. Because these schools had access to funding they were able to undertake innovative schemes with the students for whom the courses were designed.

The transition program, which was born in disputation between federal and state authorities, was to have a significant long-term effect on the provision of secondary education in Australia and on the nature of the secondary-school population.

For those unfamiliar with Australian education the foregoing would suggest that, while states have constitutional responsibility for education, most policy changes over the last fifteen or twenty years can be attributed to federal initiatives. There would be a good deal of substance in such a perception. As a '10 per cent shareholder' the federal government had a far greater influence on state-education systems than its contribution would suggest. This is so because Commonwealth money can be directed to particular innovative purposes whereas state funds are used to pay for the basic educational fabric: teachers' salaries, transport of children, and the provision of educational services such as curriculum development and research. Despite the Commonwealth's disproportionate influence, state governments do influence educational policy-making. In recent years these influences have exhibited sufficient commonality for the resultant changes to be described as national directions rather than state-specific changes. It may seem strange in a country as large as Australia, with such differences in population distribution, with the availability of natural resources and the resultant occupational differences, that there should voluntarily be great similarities between the courses of action followed by different governments. This, however, was true of newly elected Labor governments in South Australia, Victoria and Western Australia in 1983–4 and more recently of a non-Labor government in Queensland.

L. Warren Louden and R.K. Browne

Changes in Organizational Structure

Among the changes taking place over much of Australia was organizational restructure. In all of these states wide-ranging changes in the organization of government departments have taken place. The motivation for these changes has been in resource pressures in which there are ever-increasing demands on static or declining government budgets. The necessity to improve the efficiency of the public sector has led to major reorganization and to a demand for 'better managers'. The nature of the changes in all states has been similar. Among the most important are reduced central bureaucracies, devolution of authority to the school level, increased public involvement in school-level policy formulation, and greater accountability at both school and system level. In these changes it is of interest to note that the recommendations of the interim committee of the Schools Commission, which had met ten years earlier, concerning devolution and community involvement were given expression.

Support for Non-government Schools

The question of government aid for non-government schools was a contentious one but by the end of the 1960s it was an accepted plank of platform of the major political parties at the federal level. In the states too, the political advantage of providing aid to non-government schools was recognized and they all began to provide grants to non-government schools, now a firmly established feature of Australian education. All states pay a per-capita grant expressed as a percentage of the cost of educating a child in a government school. All accept that the costs of providing education for pre-school, primary, and secondary students are different and pay different amounts to the different levels. In some states all schools at each level receive the same amount for each student. In others, a 'needs' basis is observed with per-capita differences between schools of up to 25 per cent. In addition to per-capita grants, state governments provide a variety of other forms of help. This includes such things as school stocks, interest subsidies on capital works, low-interest loans, transport of children, access to curriculum materials, advisory services, and so on.

The decision of the Commonwealth and some state governments to fund non-government schools on a needs' basis has had a significant effect on the development of non-government education in Australia. Prior to 1973 there were two quite distinct types of non-government schools: independent schools, which were responsible for raising all of their own funds, and parish schools staffed largely by members of religious orders. The independent schools, almost all of which were single-sex residential colleges, were seen as being largely the preserve of the well-to-do. The parish schools generally charged low fees and, while they were subsidized by the church, had low resource levels. The decision to fund on a needs' basis meant that low-fee schools would receive substantial assistance from the two levels of government for both recurrent and capital expenditure. Under existing conditions low-fee schools can receive up to 75 per cent of the cost of educating a child in a government school and substantial assistance with the cost of erecting buildings and servicing the cost of loans. As a result of this change, religions other than Catholic have taken advantage of setting up low-fee schools which, in effect, has opened up the option of attendance at a non-government school to most of the community.

In addition to schools which form part of systems associated with major religious groups, the way has also been opened for groups to establish schools based on different philosophies, and Steiner, Montessori and 'alternative' schools have flourished. In addition small groups of parents have established 'Christian' schools based mostly on the use of individualized materials emanating largely from the United States. These schools, once registered, become eligible for government assistance as long as their premises are acceptable, they employ trained teachers, and they provide programs which include specified subject areas.

Enrolment in the non-government sector increased from 21.4 per cent of the total enrolment of students in pre-primary, primary, and secondary schools in Australia in 1973 to 27 per cent in 1988.

Links with Business

Another initiative has been the building of closer links between schools and the business community. These links include not only the involvement of business in providing work-experience placements, visits to businesses, and the provision of guest speakers but also involvement in syllabus construction, the development of materials, sponsorship of schools in simulated business games, and even 'adoption' of a school by large businesses. The effects have been beneficial. Schools for their part have become acquainted with the expectations of business while the commercial sector has had the opportunity both to influence the content and quality of what is taught in schools and to gain some appreciation of the constraints under which schools operate.

Performance Measurement

All states gave attention to performance measurement at one or more levels. Performance indicators based upon corporate plans are subject both to the scrutiny of the auditor-general and of Parliament. A second area of performance measurement in most states relates to the evaluation of teacher performance, particularly in terms of selecting for promotion those who are most capable. Promotion by merit has strong philosophical support in all areas of the Australian schooling community but the application of the policy has proved difficult.

Student Certification

A further policy area for which states have total responsibility is student certification. As in the area of organizational review, most Australian states addressed this problem, but unlike organizational review there has been little unanimity in the responses. The reasons for concern are common. Throughout the decade retention rates increased rapidly. To cater for these students, whose academic abilities are more varied than ever before, schools must provide a wider range of relevant courses, many of which have elements which do not lend themselves to external examinations of the pen-and-paper type.

At the same time as schools were providing a wider range of courses for a more academically diverse group of students there was extreme pressure on tertiary institutions. These institutions wish to select the most academically able of those students who have applied for admission. To optimize the selection process institutions providing higher education have a strong preference for selection based on performance in a narrow range of subjects of comparable difficulty examined in the most objective way possible. The setting of a common examination done under as nearly identical conditions as possible is seen as meeting this latter condition. There are clearly contradictions between the wishes of schools to cater for the needs, abilities and interests of their students providing a variety of courses and testing the outcomes in what they perceive to be an appropriate manner and the need to place students from a large number of schools spread over a large geographical area in an equitably derived rank order.

While different states developed different systems to accommodate these conflicting needs, all now involve at least an element of a school-determined mark or grade to supplement the external written examinations. Beyond that similarity there is wide divergence involving the range of subjects, the number of subjects to count for tertiary entry, the period over which courses are studied and examined, the methods by which comparability (both between subjects and schools) are achieved, and the basis on which tertiary institutions make their selection decisions.

A Change of Government

In 1983 the coalition Liberal-Country Party government was defeated at the polls by a Labor government. This government was faced with severe economic problems, the solution of which was to be the main priority for action. In the Australian federal government's budget process allocations are normally made for a financial year which extends from July to June. State budgets follow the same pattern. From the time of the setting up of the Schools Commission, however, school funding had covered the January–December period which coincides with the Australian school year. Thus, though the federal government was elected in May 1983 its first educational budget was not implemented until the beginning of 1984.

Almost immediately upon taking up office, the Minister for Education, Senator Susan Ryan, requested the Schools Commission to define new targets since the Karmel targets had been achieved by most government schools and many of the elite fee-paying schools. As a result of the Commission's work a publication *Funding Policies for Australian Schools* (Commonwealth Schools Commission, 1984) was produced. This document, after consideration of the resources necessary to provide schooling of high quality, costed these resources and set this cost as the 'community standard'. It was realized that different circumstances in schools would require a different mix of resources but this flexibility could be achieved within the financial provision of the community standard. Improvements towards these standards were in large measure accepted by the federal government as the basis for future funding policies.

The education budget for 1984 was brought down within a few months of Labor assuming office. The directions of funding were of great interest to the educational community in view of the importance which the Labor party had, in its earlier term of office, attached to education. Given the economic situation it seemed likely that there would not be large increases in allocations and this proved to be the case. There were, however, three significant differences even though the sums involved were relatively small.

The first of these was the announcement of a new program to be entitled 'participation and equity'. The program was to subsume the previously existing school-to-work transition program, but it was much more ambitious in its intentions than simply to increase retention and to assist the assimilation of young people into the economy. The program, described by the minister as the centre-piece of the government's youth policy, stated, 'The program will make funds available to the States and non-government schools to stimulate broadly-based changes in secondary education' (Commonwealth Schools Commission, 1983, p. 1).

It must be reiterated that the federal government has no constitutional responsibility for education, yet its increasing involvement over a period of years through contributing in quite a small way to government schools had culminated in a program which bluntly stated that its objectives were to increase retention, change the organization of secondary schools, reform and diversify the curriculum, review credentialling and assessment, change and develop teacher attitudes, and improve the relationship between schools and their communities. All of these objectives were to be achieved by the injection of about $45 million annually into an annual schools education budget of some $7 billion. In addition to these quite specific classroom-related objectives, the program also sought to foster 'equal educational outcomes'. For many years educational rhetoric had revolved around providing equal educational opportunity. The translation to equal outcomes, if it was to be achieved, would clearly require vastly differing inputs to different groups of children. The program made provision for direct assistance to 'schools where students are not gaining the benefits of full participation in education because of the combined effects of cultural and social background and economic factors' (CSC, 1983, p. 2). The publicity at the launch of the program noted that a 'sustained national effort will be needed for this decade at least'.

The second important initiative included in the 1984 budget was funding designed to stimulate the development of computing in secondary schools. At that time there were major differences in the level to which an understanding of computing had been included in the programs of secondary schools in different states. Here again, the Commonwealth was using specific-purpose funding to achieve changes in the curriculum of schools over which they had no constitutional authority.

The third significant difference in the program announced for 1984 was a reduction in the level of funding for professional development. It would have been expected that, at a time when major changes in both the groups being targeted and the nature of the program provided at secondary level were being promoted, such funding would have been increased. The reason given for this decision was that maintenance of the professional skills of teachers was a joint responsibility of the professional and of employers. This decision was also significant because it demonstrated that special purpose programs, were not necessarily permanent features of the schools' financial landscape.

Other Commonwealth-funded Programs

As well as general recurrent grants, capital grants, and long-running programs such as those designed to assist disadvantaged schools, the Commonwealth through the Schools Commission funded many small innovative programs and some dealing with special projects. One major avenue for funds was through special projects of national significance. A wide range of topics which provided both information for other systems and exemplary programs were funded in this way. The list of such projects for 1984 included thirty-three separate projects, ranging from a $2464 grant to consider 'diabetic children in the school environment', through the development of a 'transition curriculum' program for refugee students ($46,640), to a national review of teacher education ($77,476).

As well as projects of national significance there was also funding, usually in programs lasting for only two to four years, to investigate, develop, and initiate programs which supported the directions in which the Schools Commission believed education should be progressing. Among the items funded in 1984 were programs designed to develop choice and diversity in government schools, to develop policies which would improve the outcomes of schooling for girls, to improve provision for gifted and talented children, to improve techniques of school evaluation, to promote closer and more effective relationships between school and community, to improve the education of Aboriginal children, to develop education in the arts, and so on. The breadth of programs being sponsored by the Schools Commission meant that its influence was pervasive throughout schooling in Australia even though the sums it was providing were relatively small.

One other significant change implemented in 1984 was to amend the Commonwealth Schools Commission Act to include, within the role of the Schools Commission, responsibility for the Curriculum Development Centre which had previously been independently responsible to the federal minister.

The Period 1985–1987

The federal government's 1984 program had to be put together in haste since the budget was due within three months of assuming office. If was to be expected that any major long-term changes in policy would be reflected in 1985. Simple comparisons of the budget provisions for 1984 and 1985 do not reflect the quite major changes which were taking place since the amounts provided did not vary greatly and the only new program introduced was designed to focus attention on basic learning in primary schools. There were, however, massive changes in program management. The first of these was the transfer of the administrative management of the 'general recurrent' and 'capital grants' programs from the relatively independent Schools Commission to the Commonwealth Department of Education. Additionally, following a major report *Quality of Education in Australia* (Quality of Education Review Committee, 1985) there was a change in the way in which recurrent grants would be made to states. The Quality of Education Review Committee (QERC) had been set up by the federal Minister for Education to 'develop strategies for the Commonwealth government in its involvement in primary and secondary education for raising the standards attained by students in communication, literacy and numeracy and for improving the relationship between secondary schooling and subsequent employment and education'. One of a number of significant recommendations was that there should be concentration on the outcomes of education rather than inputs. The committee proposed that there were general competencies required by all individuals and that Commonwealth funding should concentrate on assuring the acquisition of these. The five competencies considered essential were: acquiring information, conveying information, applying logical processes, undertaking tasks as an individual, and undertaking tasks as a member of a group. It was conceded by the committee that the attainment of these competencies depended upon teachers and that there should therefore be an emphasis on improving teacher quality through in-service development. Expenditure on this function was thus seen as a legitimate use of Commonwealth funding.

The committee also took the view that, in the past, too many objectives had been sought simultaneously through Commission programs, that short-term funding had prevented long-term planning, and that the existing financial arrangements between Commonwealth and states were too rigid. The recommendation made by the committee was that the Commonwealth should use four delivery mechanisms for its funding:

- Negotiated agreements under which general funding would be provided by the Commonwealth for the achievement of specified objectives;
- Long-term specific-purpose programs;
- Limited-life specific programs;
- Directly administered initiatives mounted by the Commonwealth.

Acting on this advice the Commonwealth announced an eight-year program of recurrent funding which would be the subject of negotiated resource agreements with states and would involve the states in providing outcome measures.

On the one hand states violently objected to the Commonwealth's demands for accountability in outcome terms. On the other hand the proposals gave stability to educational funding which would allow long-term planning and were designed over the eight-year period to increase the per-capita grant for each primary student by over 30 per cent per annum and for each secondary student by 74 per cent. With such significant sums involved, all but one state agreed to these proposals. Some changes in the capital grants for government schools were announced. These mainly related to shifting the balance between the provision of new places (which was seen as largely a state government responsibility) and refurbishment and upgrading of older schools.

The non-government sector was also faced with major changes in 1985. The first of these was in the categorization of schools according to their level of resources. Initially, there were three categories of non-government schools receiving respectively 20 per cent, 30 per cent, and 38 per cent of the cost of educating a child in a government school. Later this was increased to six categories. In 1985 this scheme was modified to reflect twelve categories of school. The level-1 schools had their allocations frozen. Level-12 schools, on the other hand, received increases on the order of 40 per cent over the maximums which had previously existed. This reflected the Commonwealth's concern that the relative position of the least wealthy schools was continuing to decline.

Non-government schools, like government schools, were also to receive guarantees of funding for the period 1985–94. At the lower levels of funding (levels 1 and 2) no increases in real terms would be provided. At the other end of the scale, however, increases of up to 32 per cent would be paid to the least wealthy primary schools and 24 per cent to secondary schools. Several conditions were attached to these grants. The first was that schools should maintain, in real terms, their level of per-student recurrent expenditure from private sources and that to maintain their present categories, a 3 per cent increase in income, raised by schools, would be required.

Changes were also made in the capital grants. Joint state-Commonwealth committees were set up to ensure that there would be no excess accommodation capacity. If a new non-government school was proposed it needed to be shown that it was justified and that existing schools, government or non-government, would not be adversely affected by the building of the new school. In addition, new schools must be of an economic size. This was done to provide some control over the rapidly increasing number of non-government schools.

In addition to the above changes which flowed largely from the Quality of Education Review Committee's report, another report *Quality and Equality* (Commonwealth Schools Commission, 1985) focused on specific purpose programs. The terms of reference required this committee to report on the effectiveness of existing programs, the relative roles of Commonwealth, state and community groups, and advise on accountability arrangements. The linking of these programs to the search for equality of educational outcomes was a clear recognition of the aims which the Schools Commission had for this group of programs. The report recommended the continued provision of equity-related programs and identified socio-economic, cultural, and gender-related factors contributing to inequality as well as the effects of isolation and physical and intellectual disabilities. This report was seen as an attempted rebuttal by the Schools Commission of the QERC report. It precipitated relatively little discussion.

The laying out of future directions by the Commonwealth during 1985 greatly reduced the uncertainties which had previously existed, particularly with respect to the two major elements of Commonwealth funding, i.e., general re-current funding and capital. However, there were major changes in 1986 and 1987, which caused grave concern at the state level. The first of these was an announcement at the commencement of 1986 that the 'participation and equity' program, which only two years before had been hailed as the centre-piece of the government's youth policy, would have its funding halved and be terminated in 1987. In equally spectacular fashion funding for the 'English as a second language' program was cut from $60.8 m to $35.1 m despite the continuing arrival of non-English-speaking migrants. In addition, the Commonwealth stopped its funding for the professional development of teachers. The decisions regarding these programs caused grave concern. All were important to all states and their termination or reduction was viewed with alarm. Clearly, the decision to reduce the language funding would have a profound effect on non-English-speaking migrants. Politically, states had no alternative but to continue these programs and much of the general recurrent grant increases were used to replace the language and teacher education program.

These decisions, made unilaterally by the Commonwealth, may have been economically essential but they left a legacy of suspicion in states about Commonwealth initiatives which allow the Commonwealth to achieve its short-term objectives but leave states with financial responsibility for programs which are worthy of funding but are not the state's own priorities. It was ironical that at a time when there was such suspicion and, indeed, antagonism between states and Commonwealth, the first nationally accepted policy statement was published: 'The National Policy for the Education of Girls in Australian Schools' (May 1987). It was the culmination of years of effort by Senator Ryan and the Schools Commission.

It was also to be one of the last actions of that body whose influence had been considerably reduced by the transfer of all but its policy advisory function to the Commonwealth Department of Education. In the fourteen years of its life great changes had taken place in Australian education, many resulting from the influence of the Schools Commission. A review of progress indicates that of the six 'values' expressed in its 1973 document, 1987 saw less central control over schools and far greater devolution of authority and responsibility to them than had existed. The Commission had pursued the equity goal with great determination. Its quest for greater equality of opportunity for girls appears to have had a significant effect not only in terms of changing their expectations of schooling but in sensitizing young people to the question of disadvantage generally. It may even be that a self-sustaining movement has been created. In other equity areas the success was more limited. Despite programs for economically and socially disadvantaged children, success measured by their retention into educational courses which give entry to the professions is still low as it is for children who live in the country. Education has contributed to a society which accepts and values multiculturalism more than did the society of 1973 but substantial work remains to be done. It is the area of Aboriginal education that least progress has been made despite continued and continuing efforts at state and federal levels. The Commission's support for diversity has been realized. The variety of courses available to students, particularly at the secondary level, multiplied and devolution, together with the abolition of school boundaries, allowed schools to take on quite distinctive personalities.

Perhaps the most successful area of the Commission's work had been in the expansion of the non-government sector. Strong financial support from both federal and state governments has seen both political and financial advantage in the support of non-government schools. It led to the emergence of many low-fee schools and made a 'private' school education affordable to a greatly increased percentage of children.

A fifth 'value' espoused by the Schools Commission in its 1973 statement had been promotion of community involvement in schooling. At that time there was little such involvement in most states. Today, parents or their representatives have a legislatively binding right to be involved in decision-making at the school level. Finally, in all states by 1987 the provision of relevant and appropriate education for a far larger percentage of students than could have been envisaged in 1973 had become a reality.

As early as 1978 the Commission was seen by Keeves and Mathews (1978) to have contributed to:

> general rejuvenation and improvement in the quality of the education debate; the vastly improved morale, enthusiasm and involvement of those concerned in the schooling process; the increased willingness to grapple with basic philosophical questions about the functions of schooling; and the more positive climate for education.

By 1987 the Commission had made a major contribution to Australian education but new agendas were about to dominate the Australian educational debate.

Towards the 1990s

In June 1987 the federal Labor government was re-elected for a third three-year term. The ensuing period brought major changes which could not have been envisaged when the federal Constitution was drafted. To understand these changes it is necessary to look beyond education.

In forming the ministry in June 1987, the Prime Minister (Bob Hawke) took a new approach, of the setting up of a small number of 'super ministries' in place of the twenty-seven which had previously existed. The 'super-ministry' which included education was the Department of Employment, Education and Training. Instead of being headed by a relatively junior senator, the new ministry was led by John Dawkins, a senior member of the House of Representatives. The grouping of employment with education and training reflected a belief that Australia's future prosperity was associated with the development of a highly educated and skilled workforce. The view that education and many other activities of government should contribute to Australia's increased competitiveness has been termed 'economic rationalism'. From the outset Dawkins made it clear that he proposed to bring about major changes in education generally in Australia and that he would use the federal Government's funding power to enforce these changes.

Changes in the School Sector

During the fifteen years of its existence the Schools Commission had used a highly consultative approach and much of the dialogue between state systems and the Commonwealth took place under the Commission's general sponsorship.

Another forum for discussion across the whole education spectrum was the Australian Education Council. This Council was set up in 1936 to 'provide a basis of continuous consultation among Australian Governments on aspects of education, particularly in relation to the responsibility of the States and Commonwealth' (Spaull, 1978, p. 14). The body was to consist of both Commonwealth and state ministers. It was to have a 'Standing Committee on Education' comprising the permanent heads of state Departments of Education, superintendents of technical education and Commonwealth representatives. The Australian Education Council has been a steady contributor to dialogue between the state systems and between these systems and the Commonwealth. It has been involved in managing working parties which have led to cooperative decisions by states. It has set up a business enterprise to produce school library catalogue information, developed the Australian curriculum-information network, the Australian 'cooperative assessment' program, has contributed to national policy statements in areas such as equal opportunity and the education of girls and has produced agreements between states e.g., in respect of a common convention for spelling and punctuation.

In the 1980s the ambit of the Australian Education Council increased significantly. It established links with the Education Commission of the United States and was involved in the OECD (The Organization for Economic Cooperation and Development) initiatives in regard to performance indicators. It was to this increasingly important body that in 1988 the federal Minister for Education brought a number of proposals concerning schooling in Australia.

Proposals for Schooling, 1988 and Beyond

Changes to the recurrent funding of schooling involving resource agreements between states had commenced in 1985 and guarantees concerning funding had been given for four years. These guarantees expired at the end of 1988. At the June 1988 meeting of the Australian Education Council in Darwin, the federal minister tabled a paper entitled 'Strengthening Australia's Schools: A Consideration of the Focus and Content of Schooling' (Dawkins, 1988). The paper noted: 'Schools play a critical and central role in the nature of our society and economy . . . There is little to be gained from adjustment to the structure of our nation and the way we live and work if the central position of the school is ignored. That would be self-defeating'. The view was clear, the nation's future depended upon the nation's schools. The federal minister was calling for a national effort to strengthen the nation by strengthening Australia's schools.

In the document the federal minister stated, 'The Australian States have had and will continue to have primary responsibility for the education of our young people.' He further noted, 'the Commonwealth recognizes . . . it is not the primary policy maker in schools. But the Commonwealth will not ignore the very real responsibility it has to provide national leadership.' In calling for a national effort for schools the minister noted, 'Accordingly we have decided to invite the cooperation of the States to develop and implement a national effort to strengthen the capacity of our schools to meet the challenges they face'.

The actions proposed to this end were:

1 Development of a clear statement of the fundamental purposes of schools;

2 Preparation of a common curriculum framework for use throughout the nation but within which the needs of different parts of Australia could be accommodated;

3 Criteria for methods of assessing the achievement of curriculum objectives would cooperatively be developed;

4 A common national approach to assessment and reporting to parents and the community would be negotiated;

5 Improvement in the quality of training of teachers and perhaps their registration would be pursued;

6 An increase in the retention of students to year 12 to 65 per cent by the early 1990s would be sought;

7 The targeting of presently under-represented groups in the quest for greater equity of opportunity would be continued and expanded.

It was to be expected that in a federal–state relationship any proposal which has the effect of changing the powers of one partner at the expense of the others would be met with opposition, if not hostility. This was the initial reaction, particularly from the newly elected Liberal government of New South Wales.

Despite its lack of constitutional powers, the federal government had some incentives at its disposal which could be used. Among these were:

1 Three of the states were governed by Labor from whom the federal government could expect some support;

2 1988 was the bicentenary of Australia and a strong nationalistic spirit was evident in the country;

3 There was a strong lobby group among people who were mobile between states. Most important among these were armed-services families but the is a high level of interstate migration caused consequent pressure for uniformity of education provision;

4 Probably much more importantly, the resource agreements for the next four years needed to be endorsed and these were highly significant to the states;

5 The previous resource agreements were administratively awkward, requiring separate negotiation of priorities, outcome indicators and financial arrangements. Much simpler arrangements were offered if there was acceptance of the Commonwealth's proposals.

As a result of these offers the expected outright rejection of the proposal did not eventuate. This was perhaps because states had observed Dawkins' handling of equally radical changes in tertiary education, which had been implemented in spite of strong opposition and they recognized his determination. Whatever the reasons it was agreed that the feasibility of the proposal would be investigated and discussed at a special meeting in October.

To determine the feasibility of these proposals several working parties were set up. One of these produced a series of options concerning the conditions under which federal financial grants would be made available, ranging from untied grants to a system based on agreed national priorities, national testing, and publication of state and system results. The latter was the Commonwealth's preferred position. A second group consisting of the directors of curriculum undertook an overview of the curriculum across the states, which confirmed that there was a good deal of commonality of content and a much greater similarity in the broad general objectives of education in the states. A national curriculum was thus a possibility. A third group met to review a Commonwealth-produced paper on goals of schooling. A statement in terms sufficiently general to allow for states to pursue specific objectives while providing a basis for national reporting was produced. A further existing working party provided options in which evaluation could be undertaken at the national level.

The final working party was asked to consider how existing organizations which provided educational services to schools might be more effectively organized. States and the Commonwealth were already jointly engaged in groups concerned with educational research, curriculum construction, library and information services but in addition had similar functions being performed within states. Adoption of a more cooperative approach had the potential to reduce overall outlays on education.

At the special October 1988 meeting of the Australian Education Council reports from all groups were tabled. The reports could be classified into three categories: those on which further work was required (curriculum review and agency cooperation), those on which there was substantial agreement (goals of schooling), and those where there was strong disagreement from one or more states (funding options and national reporting). In view of these findings the Commonwealth agreed to interim arrangements covering the 1989 school year, based on bilateral discussion. The Commonwealth's overall determination that continued Commonwealth participation in the funding of government schools would be on the basis of agreed national objectives, outcome-oriented performance indicators, and national reporting was made clear.

Consideration of these Trends in the Context of Changing Social Goals: Federal–State Relations

In the necessarily short account of developments in Australian education in recent years a number of different periods can be identified, related to the social climate of the times. The setting up of the Schools Commission in 1973 reflected the belief of a government (with Labor being returned to office after twenty-four years) that society could be changed through changing the education system and by ensuring equal opportunity for all students. To this end substantial funding of education at the federal level was willingly made available. Schools and the conditions of those who studied and worked in them were improved but the attempts to bring about major changes in society through this avenue were disappointing.

The late 1970s with the onset of double-digit unemployment and double-digit inflation brought about a realization that Australia was no longer 'the lucky country' and that economic survival depended upon major changes being made. The rhetoric of the Conservative government was that it was not the economy which was in need of overhaul but that schools had failed to provide a workforce with the necessary skills. This view was promoted by the media and the blame was attached mostly to government schools. This was reflected in reduced expenditure and an emphasis on vocational training.

From 1983 a Labor government held office. When it assumed government, Australia's financial situation was critical and, as a result, the government placed major emphasis on improving this position.

Economic Concerns in the 1980s

There are particular problems for governments faced with severe economic problems if their power base rests principally on the less well-off. The 'softest' areas of government expenditure are concerned with the provision of what might be described as social services and yet Labor's supporters tend to be the main beneficiaries of such services.

This dilemma has been expressed by Costello and Dawkins in the following terms:

> The need to take control of our economic life in the 1980s intersects with another great need of the 1980s. This is to give effect to Labor's vision of Australia as a just and equal society. These two great tasks are so intimately connected that progress in one is impossible without progress in the other. (Costello and Dawkins 1983, p. 68)

The approach used by the federal government had three main features. The first was to reduce public expenditure partly by improving the efficiency of the public sector but largely through applying a 'user-pays' principle to many services. The second strategy was to negotiate with the trade-union movement to enter into an 'accord' based upon community acceptance that Australia was living beyond its means. In Australia most wages and salaries in both the private and public sector are fixed by state and federal arbitration courts. Under the accord unions accepted that real wages had to be reduced in an orderly way through the courts. Finally, but most importantly in the longer term, attention was focused on improving Australia's competitive position. Financial inducements were offered to industry to invest in the most modern plant and equipment. Efforts were made through education to improve the skills and knowledge of the workforce. At the tertiary level this involved application of the user-pays principle. In the government's view, however, a critical element was 'industry restructuring', consisting of removing all work practices which inhibit effective operation and reshaping the manner in which occupations operate. As part of the wage-fixing process any union seeking any increase in the remuneration of its members was required to enter into an agreement to investigate industry restructuring.

The Dawkins' Proposals for Schooling in Australia

In attempting to forecast whether changes are likely to be implemented, three questions need to be answered. The first such question is: Is a change, which will be bitterly opposed and extremely difficult to bring about, sufficiently important to the federal government to make it worthwhile? Given the need to increase competitiveness and given the centrality the government placed on the development of human resources, the answer to this question is probably yes!

The second question is: Can the federal government influence state governments to adopt voluntarily the changes which it proposes or require the changes through the constitution? Throughout this chapter it has been emphasized that the federal government's direct contribution to state-education systems is only of the order of 10 per cent. However, the importance of this 10 per cent has also been emphasized. The position of the federal government as the principal tax collector gives it additional influence. Unlike the United States and the Canadian state and provincial governments, state governments in Australia do not levy direct income tax, though they have the power to do so. The power of the federal government to vary 'grants' to the states and to make special grants through the Grants Commission, however, gives the federal government very significant financial power if it chooses to exercise it. It is doubtful, however, that states would agree to the continuance of the present taxation system if the federal government applied increased financial pressure to increase federal powers. The constitution gives the federal government no direct control of education, and such control Australians have been reluctant to amend the constitution to allow the transfer of this power to the federal government through referendum.

The final question which requires an answer is: Is it practically feasible for the federal government to bring about the changes which it has proposed? In answering this question, it must be remembered that the federal government does not seek operational control over the nation's schools and at no time has this been proposed. What it has sought to do to influence what happens within the schools. It is of interest to note that this has been the process used by states in their devolution of authority to their own schools. The linchpin of this influence is the federal government's insistence on national reporting. Any educator who has been involved in syllabus development will know that whatever the philosophic intention of the syllabus, this will only be realized if the examination reflects this philosophy. It is the nature of the report card which influences teaching/learning within schools. The Commonwealth in 'selling' national reporting has described the sorts of performance measures which might form the basis of the report to the nation. It focused on relatively non-contentious indicators of various types. There has been no reference to a national scorecard or a 'league table' of systems or schools. However, if national testing was to be part of the framework, there is little doubt that considerable influence could be exerted on what happens in Australia's schools.

Pressure Groups

Attempts to influence what happens in government schools in Australia come from many quarters. Perhaps the most important of these are parents, teachers' unions, and social-welfare agencies, both public and private. In the past parents had relatively little influence in government schools. Teachers were regarded as 'experts' and apart from some fund-raising, parents accepted what happened in schools. Increasing levels of citizen education, changes in the perception of human-service organizations by tax-payers, the increasing importance of qualifications in securing a desirable occupation, and legislative changes which have given parents formal involvement in decision-making at the local school level have radically altered parental involvement in schools. It may be too early to interpret accurately what the effect of these changes will be. Initial observation, however, indicates that it has led to greater acceptance by parents of what schools are doing, increased support for the work of schools and the realization by governments that education is an increasingly important political issue.

The influence of teachers' unions on education in Australia is highly significant. In the past, teaching was regarded as a profession and teachers were both independent within their classrooms and their workloads were a matter of individual negotiation at the school level. More recently, individual state teachers' unions have become members of state councils of trade unions. The result has been insistence by unions on specification of the roles and responsibilities of teachers, hours of class contact, size of classes and so on. In addition, an Australia-wide federation of teachers' unions has been set up and the intention to seek a federal salary and conditions award has been announced. Such a body represents all teachers in the negotiations about industry restructuring.

Thirdly, there is increasing pressure for schools to take over roles previously occupied by parents, the extended family, churches, and youth clubs. In many ways these forces are mutually cancelling but an amalgamation of any two of these groups would be powerful in achieving policy changes.

Accountability

The concept of accountability has flourished in Australia in the 1980s, nowhere more strongly evident than in the public sector where the need to provide more services with static or declining budgets has brought from governments a quest for efficiency and effectiveness which rivals the most entrepreneurial organizations in the private sector.

The chief executives of government enterprises have been given wider powers to manage but this increased authority has been matched by increased accountability, which takes a variety of forms. Government enterprises in most states are required to prepare corporate plans which specify their intentions. Performance indicators must be provided and the auditor-general in his annual report to Parliament is required to comment on the suitability of the indicators and the extent to which they have been achieved. In addition, in some states performance agreements which specify that chief executive officers will achieve agreed objectives or be personally responsible are commonly used. In the specific area of schooling, in addition to these state-mandated accountability measures, the federal government through negotiated resource agreements requires outcome-oriented performance indicators to be specified and met.

In an attempt to ensure discharge of their responsibilities, senior bureaucrats have initiated procedures which impose on schools accountability for both efficiency and effectiveness. There are many who claim that the devolution process is a way of forcing financial accountability on schools. There is also pressure for regular teaching-performance review, a procedure which has not been used in Australian schools for twenty years. In a climate where restructuring is accepted as an economic necessity, teachers' unions are showing little opposition to a practice which in the past they would have bitterly resisted.

In a number of states, governments have indicated their intention to introduce mandatory system-wide testing of whole cohorts of students. Teachers' unions in Australia have always totally rejected plans to do this, believing that to do so exerts a narrowing influence on the curriculum and that such testing encourages comparisons between schools which are totally different in their intakes.

Non-government Schools

The growth of government aid to non-government schools has been paralleled by growth in enrolments in non-government schools. Since the number of children in Australia is declining overall and non-government schools are increasing, a significant reduction in the number of children attending government schools is occurring and in some states this decline is quite dramatic.

Many reasons are advanced for the growth of the non-government sector. Common among these are that such schools have a clearly espoused spiritual/ moral position, that because students have no right to entry, disciplinary standards can be set at a higher level, that there are future socio-economic benefits from membership of a prestigious school and so on. For their part, supporters of government schools claim that non-government schools are divisive and that they do not allow their students to gain a realistic appreciation of the diversity of Australian society. More commonly the criticism is made that government support for non-government schools together with tax concessions for parental contributions to such schools allow non-government schools to be better resourced than their government counterparts. Supporters point out that government schools are locked into a vicious circle in which increasing ease of access to non-government schools is leading to the flight from government schools of the children of the most influential and able parents. Such a trend, taken to an extreme, would see government schools as residual schools catering only for those disadvantaged by socio-economic status, disability, isolation and/or transiency. The need to revitalize government schools has been part of the reason for the devolution to schools of authority and responsibility. The finding of a balance between government and non-government education is one of the problems confronting education authorities throughout Australia.

Teacher Morale and Supply

The quality of education is closely related to the quality and enthusiasm of the teaching force. In Australia over the past ten years factors which have affected the supply of teachers of high quality, particularly those required to teach science, mathematics, business, and languages in secondary schools have coincided. Because of the need to reduce government expenditure in the light of Australia's economic crisis there was little improvement in pupil–teacher ratios and a diminishing demand for teachers. As an economy measure, too, bursaries which in the past had encouraged able but less financially well-off students to achieve a tertiary education by entering teaching were discontinued.

The accord mentioned previously has led to reduced living standards generally but the burden fell unequally upon those in the public sector who had professional or sub-professional qualifications, because some wage and salary increases were by fixed amounts, not by percentage increase as had been the case in the past. Teachers and academics were amongst those most affected by this 'plateau indexation' and the financial attraction of teaching declined. Students with the ability to undertake science and mathematics courses did not choose to do the extra education required to become a teacher. Shortages of teachers began to emerge in these areas. During the mid 1980s, attractive positions in private industry became available and some existing teachers, particularly of science and mathematics and those with accountancy qualifications, accepted these positions. Through the 1980s there was strong media criticism of teachers generally and some consequent reduction in the perception of both the importance of teaching and the desirability of being a teacher. As a result morale was affected. There is a need to restore both the financial attractiveness of teaching and the prestige which once was attached to the profession.

Lessons from the Australian Experience and Future Prospects

The predominating characteristic affecting all areas of education throughout the time period being considered is that of change. The pressures for reform are related to many factors. Some are external, such as the 'effects of social cultural and political changes, economic adjustments and industry developments ... in other parts of the world which have led to pressures for the education system to respond' (Dawkins, 1987). Some are internal such as granting more powers to schools, the clamour for curriculum to become more vocationally oriented, and implementing principles of social justice in the operation of school systems. However, while there have been many policy changes during the period under review, one commentator suggested that the schools have 'escaped relatively unscathed from the ten-year-long upheaval that disrupted the education bureaucracy. They have been, by and large, the static core in the cyclone of structural change' (Maslen, 1988).

The changes have included the structural reorganization of most state departments of education and the demise of the Schools Commission with its functions essentially being absorbed into an expanded federal department now called the Department of Employment, Education and Training.

One could catalogue many controversial features of school-related education-policy developments over recent years which include the lack of planning for future directions, the continuing challenge for more decentralization in the running of schools, the capitulation to the so-called economic imperative with its instrumental, philosophical base dominating the thinking of senior policy makers, the significant decrease in support for teachers' professional development and the continuing lack of a curriculum perspective focusing on Australia's place in the world community (evident, for example, in the relative neglect in the teaching of languages other than English). Among the positive gains over the decade have been that education has a higher profile, there are improved access for disadvantaged groups, gains in equal opportunity policies for women and girls, and an upsurge of interest in developing a national approach to the goals of schooling, to curriculum issues and to assessment.

In respect to federal–state relations in education through the 1990s, three scenarios are possible: an expanding federal role, a contracting federal role, or maintaining the *status quo* into the future. It is not possible to gauge which one will eventuate, and, two or all three could prevail at various stages. Some tentative propositions, however, can be advanced. The first is that the future patterns of federal-state relations are best anticipated by considering several lead indicators, namely:

- Decisions of the High court which result in constitutional interpretations affecting education;
- The political complexion of federal and state governments and their respective educational platforms;
- The future role and decisions of consultative bodies which are specifically set up to facilitate federal–state cooperation;
- The objectives and effectiveness of mega pressure groups, particularly teachers' unions and parent councils.

It seems likely that at least in the short term there will be a movement towards greater similarities of schooling provision among states than is presently the case.

A second proposition is that, in the short term, the decision-making capacity of the federal government will be cooperatively decided by the states and the federal government. We anticipate a trend to new centralism, greater devolution of management responsibility to schools accompanied by strengthened centralizing of policy generation, goal setting, and performance monitoring. There will be continuing tension between federal and state authorities in formulating education policies with the former being interested in central planning with the nation's economic well-being the central concern, and the latter emphasizing devolution and grass-roots considerations.

Thirdly, pressure groups and individuals will become more prominent at all levels of policy determination; at the federal level they will challenge federal programs and policies and at the local level they will attempt to be increasingly involved in the planning of curricula and in the operation of schools.

In his book on public-policy analysis Dunn (1981) indicates that the public-policy evaluation can be seen in terms of adjustment cycles, continuation cycles, termination cycles, and restructuring cycles, and that the essence of policy evaluation is to ask the key question of policies: What difference do they make?

This vision of education was advocated in earlier decades by Newman who described an adequate education as follows:

It aims at raising the intellectual tone of society, at cultivating the public mind, at purifying the public taste, at supplying true principles to popular enthusiasm and fixed aims to popular aspiration, at giving enlargement and sobriety to the ideas of the age, at facilitating the exercise of political power and refining the intercourse of private life. It is education which gives man (sic) a clear conscious view of his opinions and judgements, a truth in developing them, an eloquence in expressing them and a force in urging them. (Bassett, 1987, p. 53)

Educators, to their professional discomfort, have experienced through the 1980s the tyranny of economic rationalism. It has partly sapped their commitment. Perhaps those with imaginings of a more inclusive world view will now begin to emerge.

References

AUSTRALIAN SCHOOLS COMMISSION (1973) *Schools in Australia*, Australian Government Publishing Service, Canberra.

AUSTRALIAN SCHOOLS COMMISSION (1979) *Annual Report 1979*, Australian Government Publishing Service, Canberra.

BASSETT, G.W. (1987) *Postscript on my fifty years in education*, Queensland Institute for Educational Administration Inc.

BIRCH, I.F.K. (1983) 'Education and the External Affairs Power: Implications for the Governance of Australian Schools; *The Australian Journal of Education*, 27, 3.

COMMONWEALTH DEPARTMENT OF EDUCATION (1967) *Annual Report of the Commonwealth Department of Education*, Australian Government Publishing Service, Canberra.

COMMONWEALTH SCHOOLS COMMISSION (1983) *Participation and Equity in Australian Schools*, Australian Government Printing Service, Canberra.

COMMONWEALTH SCHOOLS COMMISSION (1984) *Funding Policies for Australian Schools*, Commonwealth Schools Commission, Canberra.

COMMONWEALTH SCHOOLS COMMISSION (1985) *Quality and Equality*, Australian Government Publishing Service, Canberra.

COSTELLO, R. and DAWKINS, J. (1983) 'Education: Progress and Equality', in REEVES, J. and THOMSON, K. (Eds) *Labor essays 1983*, Melbourne, Dove.

DAWKINS, J. (1987) *Higher education: A policy discussion paper*, Canberra, AGPS, December.

DAWKINS, J. (1988) *Strengthening Australia's Schools: A Consideration of the Focus and Content of Schooling*, Canberra, Department of Employment, Education and Training.

DUNN, W.N. (1981) 'Glossary', *Public policy analysis: An introduction.* Englewood Cliffs, NJ, Prentice-Hall.

ELAZAR, D.J. (1968) 'Federalism', in SELLS, D.L. (Ed.) *International Encyclopedia of the Social Services*, London, Collier-MacMillan, 5.

HORNE, D. (1988) 'Think or perish!: Towards a Confident and Productive Australia', *Future*, 8 September.

KEEVES, J.P. and MATHEWS, J.K. (1978) 'Renewal in Australian Education — a changing prospect', in D'CRUZ, J.V. and SHEEHAN, P.J. (Eds) (1978) *The Renewal of Australian Schools*, Hawthorn, Victoria, Australian Council for Educational Research.

KEMMIS, S. and RIZVI, F. (1987) 'Issues and conclusions: Dilemmas of Reform', *Dilemmas of Reform*, Geelong, Victoria, Deakin University.

MASLEN, G. (1988) 'Signs of improvement but so much to be done', *The Age*, 15 November.

MORAN, B. (1980) *The Establishment of a National Curriculum Development Centre*, Canberra, Curriculum Development Centre.

POPEWITZ, T.S., TABACHNICK, B.R. and WHELAGE, G. (1982) 'Social Reform and institutional life, *The Myth of Educational Reform: A study of school responses to a program of change*, Madison, WI, University of Wisconsin Press.

QUALITY OF EDUCATION REVIEW COMMITTEE (1985) *Quality of Education in Australia*, Report of the Review Committee, Canberra, Australian Government Publishing Service.

SCHOOLS COMMISSION (1979) *Schools Commission Report for 1980*, Canberra, Australian Government Printing Service.
SCHOOLS COMMISSION (1981) *Schools Commission Report for 1980*, Canberra, Australian Government Printing Service.
COMMONWEALTH SCHOOLS COMMISSION (1985) *Report for the Triennium 1982–1984*, Canberra, Commonwealth Schools Commission.
SPAULL, A. (1987) *A History of the Australian Education Council 1936–1986*, Sydney, Allen and Unwin.
STEPHEN, N. (1989) 'On Being an Australian', Address to National Press Club, Canberra, 25 January.

Chapter 8

Educational Reform in Japan Since 1984

T. Sasamori

Historical Background of Education in Japan

The educational reform which took place immediately after World War II was designed to eliminate militarism and ultra-nationalism, to help create a peaceful and cultural nation, and to realize the ideals of democracy, freedom, and equality. The basic principles for education are provided for in the Constitution of Japan (enacted in 1946) and the Fundamental Law of Education (enacted in 1947). The Constitution provides the basic right and duty of the people to receive education:

> All people shall have the right to receive an equal education corresponding to their abilities, as provided for by law. The people shall be obligated to have all boys and girls under their protection receive general education as provided for by law. Such compulsory education shall be free. (Article 26)

The Fundamental Law of Education sets out the basic national aims and principles of education in accordance with the spirit of the Constitution. To achieve the aims, the law provides for such national principles as equal opportunity for education, nine years of compulsory education, co-education, and prohibition against partisan political education.

In the same year (1947) the School Education Law was also enacted providing for a 6–3–3 school system. The post-war educational system in Japan can be said to have been established in the latter half of the 1940s, according to the recommendations submitted to the Prime Minister by the Education Reform Committee set up in 1946, which played a large role in establishing the whole field of a new educational system after the war. This new system achieved a quantitative expansion through the years of rapid economic growth in the 1950s, ensuring also equal educational opportunity for all and improving educational standards throughout the country. As a result, in the 1960s and 1970s Japan succeeded in catching up with western industrialized nations and its share of the world's GNP reached the level of nearly 10 per cent of the national products of all nations in the world in 1980 (See Table 8.1). On the basis of this material prosperity, the proportion of the age group going on to upper secondary

Table 8.1:   *Changes in the Share of GNP in the World*

	USA	EC	JAPAN	USSR	CHINA	Miscellaneous
1955	36.3	17.5	2.2	13.9	4.4	25.7
1960	33.7	17.5	2.9	15.2	4.7	26.0
1965	31.3	18.7	4.0	15.0	4.4	26.6
1970	30.2	19.3	6.0	15.9	4.9	23.7
1975	24.5	22.1	7.9	14.0	4.9	26.6
1980	21.5	22.4	9.0	11.6	4.7	30.8

Notes: Based on the 'Annual Report on the National Accounts' by the Economic Planning
Agency.

Table 8.2:   *Historical Trends in the Proportion of Students Going to Senior-level Institutions*

	Percent of Students going on to Upper Secondary Schools			Percent of the age group going on to Higher Education		
	Total	Male	Female	Total	Male	Female
1955	51.5%	55.5%	47.4%	10.1%	15.0%	5.0%
1960	57.7	59.6	55.9	10.3	14.9	5.5
1965	70.7	71.7	69.6	17.0	22.4	11.3
1970	82.1	81.6	82.7	23.6	29.2	17.7
1975	91.9	91.0	93.0	37.8	43.0	32.4
1980	94.2	93.1	95.4	37.4	41.3	33.3
1985	94.1	93.1	95.3	37.6	40.6	34.5
1987	94.3	93.2	95.4	36.1	37.1	35.1

Notes: 1. Based on the 'Basic Survey on Schools' by the Ministry of Education, Culture and
Science
2. The percentage represents the proportion of lower secondary school graduates in
March of each year going on to upper secondary schools and colleges of
technology
3. The percentage was calculated by dividing each year's number of entrants to
universities (degree-granting courses only) and junior colleges (regular courses
only)

schooling in 1987 has reached 94.3 per cent and the proportion of the age group
advancing to higher education 36.1 per cent (See Table 8.2)

Japan has succeeded in becoming an 'educated society' by providing its
people with equal educational opportunity and by maintaining and improving the
people's educational standards. On the other hand, Japan has neglected giving
genuine value to childrens' spiritual and cultural development. Japan has paid
attention only to those simple values which can be observed and measured, such
as national income, salaries and receipts of income, enrolment ratios and deviation values. Since the 1970s, therefore, serious problems have occurred in
education, such as children's suicide, children's refusal to attend school, violence
in school and at home, and insidious school bullying. The educational system in
Japan has been said to be in a grave 'state of desolation' (See Figure 8.1). With
respect to the factors contributing to the desolation in education, the second
report of the National Council of the Educational Reform (NCER) said:

Figure 8.1: Children's Problematic Behaviour

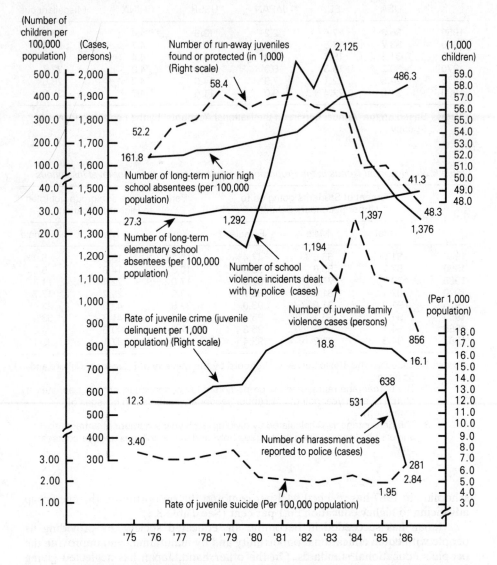

Notes: 1. Based on the 'Basic Survey on Schools' by the Ministry of Education, Culture and Science, 'Vital Statistics' by the Ministry of Health and Welfare, and data from the National Police Agency.
2. Rate of juvenile delinquency is a number of delinquent juveniles (14–19 years old) per 1,000 population.
3. Rate of juvenile suicide is a number of juvenile suicides (5–19 years old) per 100,000 population.
4. Number of long-term absentees is the number of children with absence of total of 50 days or longer in an acadamic year due to dislike of school per 100,000 children.
5. Number of school violence incidents is that of those in junior and senior high schools.

It can be considered that the various factors contributing to the patho-logical phenomena collectively referred to as desolation in education are inter-related in a complex way. They may be categorized into three problem areas: problems inherent in modern industrialized civilization; problems related to the basic character of, and recent changes in, Japanese society and culture; and problems related to the basic char-acter of, and recent changes in, formal education in Japan. (*The Third Report*, p. 19)

Thus during recent years there has been increasing public criticism express-ing distrust of the schools, teachers, and the education sector as a whole. Japan has been confronted with the harsh reality of the problems in its schools and the serious state of dilapidation or desolation of its educational system. In these circumstances the central council for education submitted several recommendations to improve this grave situation. However they were not implemented in the decade because of the passive attitude of educators and administrators. As a result, most of the recent recommendations served to strengthen some sort of formalistic control, rather than to help children develop self-control and a normal sense for self. Accordingly, up to the present time there exists a deep-rooted distrust in every education sector: between teachers and parents, between educational administrators and teachers, and between the central and local government. This mutual distrust in the education sector is not unrelated to the desolation in both the adults' and the children's minds.

These educational circumstances were the major reasons which led to the call for educational reform. Table 8.3 shows the number of educational institutions and the enrolments at different school levels as of May 1988. As indicated in this table, the total enrolment in schools and universities in Japan reached approximately 27.1 million.

Establishment of the National Council on Educational Reform

Strategies Toward the Establishment

The National Council on Educational Reform (NCER) was set up on 21 August 1984, as an *ad hoc* advisory committee to the Prime Minister, Mr Yasuhiro Nakasone, who held the post from 27 November 1982 to 5 November 1987. To explain the setting up of this Council, it is necessary to have some knowledge of Mr Nakasone's ideals and his political background.

He was first elected to the Diet (or Parliament) at the age of twenty-eight. Since then he has belonged to the conservative (Liberal-Democratic) party although he has not kept his position in the mainstream faction of that party. He formed a 'group for asserting the defence of Japan', which was reorganized as a 'national conference relevant to the defence of Japan' on 27 October 1981. This conference, at which he was a representative, aimed to promote the re-vision of the present peace Constitution. Prior to this in 1947 he had set up a 'group for youth' (*Seiun Juku*), as an attempt to inspire young people to develop a pioneer spirit for rebuilding Japan. From this evidence he seems to emerge as an ultra-racialist or a nationalist. He is one of the most remarkable politicians,

Table 8.3: School Institutions: Survey of Number and Attendance

Type of Institution	Number of Institutions	Number of students
Kindergartens	15,115	2,041,820
Primary schools	24,901	9,872,520
Junior high schools	11,266	5,896,080
Senior high schools	5512	5,533,393
Special schools for the Handicapped	931	95,825
Technical colleges	62	50,934
Junior colleges	571	450,436
Universities	490	1,994,616
Special training schools	3191	699,534
Miscellaneous	3685	451,988
Total	65,724	27,087,146

Notes: Based on the 'Basic Survey on Schools' by the Ministry of Education, Culture and Science, as of May 1988.

but he has been criticized for his political style because of the way he established various kinds of private and official advisory groups or councils to be responsible for decisions in important areas of policy. His value as a politician has been differently reported on in a variety of papers.

At the time the Diet appointed him to the premiership, there was an urgent need for administrative as well as fiscal reform. In education, with juvenile groups prone to violence and delinquency, Nakasone adopted the following two measures. First, he required the Ministry of Education, Science and Culture to hold a meeting on 21 February 1983 with scholars and experts on education problems to exchange views on what measures the ministry should take to cope with juvenile delinquency (*The Japan Times* 1983, 22 February, p. 2). Second, the government also convened on 4 March 1983 a meeting of the Liaison Council to promote anti-delinquency measures, comprising the Prime Minister's office, the Ministry of Education, and other ministers and government agencies (*The Japan Times*, 1983, 5 March, p. 2). After the meeting, the director-general of the Prime Minister's office asked government organizations concerned with young people to cooperate in fighting juvenile delinquency. This meeting was called because of a spate of violent incidents involving junior high-school students. As a result the government decided on a national public relations campaign against juvenile delinquency. Mr Nakasone was able to use these serious situations to stir up public opinion for educational reform.

Three months, later, on 14 June 1983, Nakasone set up the 'forum on culture and education', a private advisory group, and called for a review of the nation's post-war education system. At the session of the forum he said:

> Education played a key role in developing Japan's economy and raising the standard of living. The period of catching up with advanced Western nations, or the period of modernization, is over. From now on we must build a new state, a new society through our own wisdom and effort. (*The Japan Times*, 1983, 15 June, p. 1)

On 22 March 1984 the forum submitted a report to him, recommending that the government should re-examine the present education system by seeking 'diversification' of education and providing 'more options' for students. The forum pointed out that the recent problems of juvenile delinquency, of school violence and of students being incapable of coping with their studies showed the need for educational reform. The proposals of the Kyoto forum for 'thinking about the world', published on 17 March 1984, also encouraged him in his drive towards educational reform. This forum consisted of twelve, well-qualified persons including the president of Matsushita Electric Industrial Co. Ltd. and some well-known university professors. The forum submitted seven proposals to the Prime Minister, most of them similar to those in the report of the forum on 'culture and education' (Gyosei, 1985, p. 214).

Everything went as Nakasone intended. Using these reports and proposals, he planned to stir up public opinion about the need for educational reform; and he promoted the reform directly from the Prime Minister's office, not from the Ministry of Education, Science and Culture. However, in the first instance, it is clear that he wanted to support the measures designed by the Ministry of Education, Science and Culture. For example, in a press conference in 10 December 1983 during a pre-election tour, Mr Nakasone said that he had instructed the Minister of Education earlier in the day to ask for recommendations from a ministry advisory panel on educational reform. He had also suggested to the Minister of Education on the same day that he should implement a report prepared by the Central Council for Education. As a result the Ministry of Education, Science and Culture itself immediately decided that it would study the requests put forward by the Central Council.

Nevertheless on 4 February 1984, Nakasone told a press conference that an *ad hoc* commission to review the nation's education system would be created in the Prime Minister's office (*The Japan Times*, 1984, 5 February, p. 1). He officially conveyed his view to the Ministry of Education, Science and Culture. Why did Nakasone want to create the commission in the Prime Minister's office? It is worth noting that he earlier had revealed his intention to set up a panel to advise him on ways to reform the education system and to function separately from the Central Council for Education, an advisory body to the Minister of Education. Firstly, then, Nakasone was dissatisfied with the recommendations submitted to the Minister of Education by the Central Council for Education. On 27 July 1981, at the meeting of the study group for national policies, he had stated that large-scale educational reform concerned with the basics of the education system should be promoted by an authorized advisory body, rather than small-scale reform through the Central Council for Education (Hara, M. and Kawabe, M. 1984, p. 21). His attitude to the Central Council for Education seems to be clear in this statement. Secondly, he promoted political issues by means of his powerful political position. The time when he was appointed to the premiership was an important period for implementation of administrative and fiscal reform. At the ruling Liberal-Democratic party's convention held in January 1984, Nakasone said he was determined to carry out administrative, fiscal, and educational reforms as the three priority policy targets for the party as Japan headed toward the 21st century. To achieve these reforms in a short period, it was necessary to have a strong will to bring them about. As a result, he seems to have won support to create an *ad hoc* commission in the Prime Minister's office.

Establishment of the Council

On 20 August 1984, the government submitted to the Diet a list of twenty-five members to form the *ad hoc* Council of Educational Reform, and its first formal meeting was held on 5 September 1984. The membership of the National Council of Educational Reform consisted of people like the president of a supermarket chain, the chairman of the Japanese federation of iron and steel workers' unions, a senior adviser of the Industrial Bank of Japan, and the president of the overseas economic-cooperation fund (The Ministry of Finance, 1988, p. 319).

However, there were noteworthy omissions. Firstly, it did not include any member of the nation's biggest teacher organization, the Japan teachers' union (*Nikkyoso*). The union boycotted the Council on the ground that the panel, most of whose members were former bureaucrats, businessmen and Mr Nakasone's advisers, could not bring about any 'national consensus' on reforms. It was certainly true that there were a number of criticisms on that point soon after the list of members was submitted to the Diet. A professor of Tokyo Metropolitan University criticized the composition of the Council, comparing it with the membership of the Education Reform Committee set up in 1946.

> The composition of the membership of the National Council on Education Reform is quite different from the one of the Education Reform Committee. The former consisting of 25 members is the so-called 'child' of Mr Nakasone, the latter consisted of 50 members who were all authorities on pedagogy, not bureaucrats or businessmen. (*The Yomiuri*, 1984, 23 August)

Secondly, it did not include any representatives from high schools where the educational problems were said to occur. Most serious of all, only one primary school teacher and one principal of a junior high school were included on the panel. Thirdly, except for one member, no other authorities on pedagogy were included on the Council, although there were several representatives from universities and colleges.

From these points of view the opposition parties (the Socialists and the Communists) strongly criticized the Prime Minister for inaugurating the panel, claiming that he was trying to tighten state control on education. Accordingly it is undeniable that the NCER was set up as a political group. The Council was expected to discuss a wide range of educational issues and to submit recommendations to the Prime Minister within three years.

The Contents of Educational Reform

The NCER, created on 21 August 1984, submitted four reports to the Prime Minister before the termination of its tenure on 20 August 1987. The reports were framed in accordance with the spirit of the Fundamental Law of Education. The Council identified the following basic concepts as the most important to be emphasized through all the aspects of the coming educational reform (NCER, 1985, *The First Report*, pp. 13–18):

1 The principle of putting emphasis on individuality;
2 Putting emphasis on fundamentals;
3 The cultivation of creativity, thinking ability, and power of expression;
4 The expansion of opportunities for choices;
5 The humanization of the educational environment;
6 The transition to lifelong learning;
7 Coping with internationalization;
8 Coping with the Information Age.

Based on these principles, the Council identified the following major issues to be considered (*ibid*, pp. 19–28):

1 The basic requirements for an education relevant to the twenty-first century;
2 The organization and systematization of lifelong learning and the correction of the adverse effects of undue emphasis on the educational background of individuals;
3 The enhancement of higher education and the individualization of higher-education institutions;
4 The enrichment and diversification of primary and secondary education;
5 Improvement in the quality of teachers;
6 Coping with internationalization;
7 Coping with the Information Age;
8 A review of educational administration and finance.

The National Council on Educational Reform deliberated on these issues, keeping in mind the necessity of securing an educational system which could cope with the changes of the times. After energetic deliberation on these different issues and problems in the present state of education, each report was submitted to the Prime Minister, including a wide range of recommendations on the major issues mentioned above.

The main characteristics of each report can be described as follows. *The First Report*, submitted on 26 June 1985, comprised three parts. It set out the fundamental task of the National Council on Educational Reform, that is, to show the basic direction for educational reform, to list the major issues to be considered by the Council, and to bring forward specific proposals for reform. Especially in Part 3, the Council dealt with the issue of rectifying the adverse effects of the undue emphasis on the educational background of individuals, recognizing that one of the underlying factors affecting the excessive competition in entrance examinations and the so-called state of 'desolation' in education is a social climate which attaches too much importance to the educational background of individuals. Three concrete proposals were put forward. The first was to create, as a long-term objective, a lifelong learning society relevant to the twenty-first century. The second was to reform formal education in schools and universities, including the establishment of a new type of six-year secondary school and a 'credit-system' senior high school, as well as liberalization of and more flexibility over the qualifications for university entrance. The third asked both industrial firms and government offices to make further positive efforts to value the diverse abilities of individuals in the process of personnel management.

The Second Report, submitted on 23 April 1986, is the most voluminous of the four, and consists of four parts. In this report the Council made fundamental and comprehensive recommendations for educational reform regarding families, schools, and society as a whole. In Part 1 the Council analyzed the causes of the state of desolation in education and offered an overview of both the basic changes in society and in educational tasks which the country would face in the rest of this century and in the next. Moreover the Council offered guidelines for the reorganization of the educational system, with the transition to a lifelong learning system as the key element. In Part 2 the Council set out a basic strategy for education in the home, school, and community, which would ensure the transition to a lifelong learning system. From this point of view the Council recommended with reference to the following aspects: recovery of the educational influence of the home; reform of primary and secondary education; reform of higher education and the promotion of scientific research; and the activation of non-formal education (NCER, 1986, *The Second Report*, pp. 68–147). In Part 3 a number of recommendations address specific issues about coping with the changes anticipated in the rest of the present century and in the next. In Part 4 the council proposed basic reforms in educational administration and finance with the twenty-first century in view. As the basic direction for the reform, it emphasized diversity rather than uniformity, flexibility rather than rigidity, decentralization rather than centralization, and freedom and self-determination rather than control and regulation.

The Third Report, submitted on 1 April 1987, is the second most voluminous, consisting of six chapters and almost the same number of pages as *The Second Report*. In this report the Council offered a number of concrete proposals for educational reform with regard to those important issues which could not be adequately dealt with in the preceding reports, like a lifelong learning system; reforms in primary and secondary education; reform in the organization and management of institutions of higher education; sports and education; and educational finance. This report, together with the second, can be said to be the main portion of the Council's reports. With respect to the reforms in primary and secondary education, for example, the Council recommended: reform to the text-book system; diversification of senior high school; promotion of pre-school education; promotion of education for the handicapped; opening schools to the community and ensuring appropriate administration and management of schools; school attendance districts; and cooperation with other private education industries.

The Fourth (and final) Report, submitted on 7 August 1987, consists of five chapters. The Council offered specific recommendations on the public administration in education, science, and culture and on the beginning of the school year. In addition, specific strategies for implementing educational reform for the future are also suggested in this report. The report had two major characteristics. First, the Council gave careful consideration to the demands of the present times for education and to the current state of affairs in education, and suggested basic requirements for education in the future. Second, the Council suggested specific proposals for reform, arranging the eight basic concepts mentioned above into three points, namely 'principle of putting emphasis on individuality', 'transition to a lifelong learning system', and 'coping with change' (NCER, 1987, *The Fourth Report*, pp. 19–25).

Throughout its deliberations over three years, therefore, the Council always envisaged that an educational system would be secured, which could cope with the social changes as well as the cultural developments likely to occur in the rest of the present century and the twenty-first century. It also aimed at overcoming the problems and difficulties with which the present educational system was confronted.

Implementation of Educational Reform

Establishment of Governmental Organs and Publication of the Policy Guidelines

Whether educational reform is successfully brought about or not will affect the future of Japan. It was therefore important that the Council's recommendations should be immediately implemented, and that the Japanese government should tackle educational reform as a national task, since it is so closely related to the lifestyle of people in Japan. Indeed, the implementation touches on policies and measures not only of the Ministry of Education, Science and Culture, but also of other government departments both national and local.

Because of this, the government was forced to establish a system for implementing the reform. On receiving the first report in June 1985, the government created a 'ministerial conference for the implementation of educational reform', comprising all members of the Cabinet, since it was seen as a responsibility of the entire government. In July 1985, the Ministry of Education, Science and Culture set up 'headquarters for the implementation of educational reform' (chairman: the permanent vice-minister) as a key government department to carry out educational reform. Soon after the publication of the fourth (final) report of the Council, the headquarters were dissolved and a 'Ministry of Education, Science and Culture headquarters for the implementation of educational reform' (chairman: the minister) was created on 18 August 1987.

However to implement educational reform, it is necessary to set policies in sequence, paying due attention to the inter-relationships among the various recommendations. From this point of view, the government published a paper entitled 'Immediate Policies for the Implementation of Educational Reform' on 6 October 1987. In this policy statement the government showed its strategies for confronting the urgent policy issues raised in the Council's recommendations. The strategies consist of the following seven items (MESC, 1989, pp. 81–2):

1 To promote a variety of learning activities for people throughout their lives, including opportunities for various sport activities and for developing vocational capabilities;
2 To reform primary and secondary education, by enhancing moral education and improving the content of teaching in general at these schools, as well as upgrading the quality of teachers by introducing a new system of induction training for beginner teachers;
3 To promote reforms in higher education by helping universities to individualize, invigorate, and deepen their programs;

4 To promote academic research by encouraging the most advanced basic research;
5 To introduce reforms to cope with international trends and with the spread of information technologies;
6 To reform educational administration and financing;
7 To set up an agency to advise on the implementation of educational reform.

Amendment to Laws and Regulations

The Ministry of Education, Science and Culture made every effort to implement reform measures. As a result since 1987, the Ministry has submitted to the National Diet the following seven bills related to educational reform:

1 Bill for partial amendments of the School Education Law (passed in September 1987). Main aim: to create a university council, which is an advisory organ to the minister;
2 Bill for partial amendments of the National School Establishment Law (passed in May 1988). Main aim: to change the functions of the national centre for university entrance examination, and to create an independent multi-disciplinary graduate school;
3 Bill for partial amendments of the law governing special regulations concerning educational public-service personnel, and the law concerning the organization and functions of local educational administration (passed in May 1988). Main aim: to create a new system of one-year, induction training for new teachers;
4 Bill for partial amendments of the School Education Law (passed in November 1988). Main aim: to introduce flexible provisions relating to the duration of part-time and correspondence courses in senior high schools;
5 Bill for partial amendments of the Teacher Certification Law (carried over to the next session of the Diet). Main aim: to review the existing categories and standards of teacher certificates and to enable people working in other sectors to be employed as teachers;
6 Bill for partial amendments of the law concerning the organization and function of local educational administration (carried over to the next session of the Diet). Main aim: to make the municipal superintendency of education a full-time position, and to introduce a specific term of office for the superintendent;
7 Bill for establishing an *ad hoc* commission for the implementation of educational reform (rejected in June 1989). Main aim: to establish the commission as an advisory body to the Prime Minister.

In addition the Ministry of Education, Science and Culture made every effort to take appropriate action over the Council's recommendations which demand amendments to Cabinet orders or Ministry regulations. As a result the ministry proposed several amendments related to the Council's recommendations, including two remarkable measures. The first was the amendments of the enforcement regulations for the School Education Law, and the second amendments of the Cabinet order on the organization of the Ministry of Education, Science and Culture. The aim of the former was to create a new system of 'credit-system' senior high school, the purpose of which was to expand the opportunities by providing for a wider range of students in response to their growing needs. The aim of the latter was to reorganize the structure of the ministry, abolishing the 'social education' bureau to create a 'lifelong learning' bureau, and dividing the sports division into a sports-for-all division and an athletic sports division. Even so, it must be said that merely amending Cabinet orders and ministry regulations does not come to terms with the current grave educational situation. That needs to be confronted directly.

Deliberations by Various Advisory Committees

The Ministry of Education, Science and Culture asked its relevant advisory councils to consider how to respond to the specific NCER recommendations. The curriculum council in December 1987 submitted to the Minister of Education a report on how to improve national standards for the curriculum by enriching and diversifying of primary and secondary education. In the process of its deliberations, the curriculum council highlighted the references in the fourth NCER report to the enrichment of moral education, the full acquisition of basic knowledge and skills, and the development of personality. The educational personnel-training council also submitted to the Minister of Education a report aimed at the improvement of the teacher-training system, including in-service training programs. Its report, published in December 1987, recommended the creation of a new system of induction training for newly employed teachers. In addition to the deliberations by these councils, the Ministry of Education, Science and Culture itself sponsored studies with the cooperation of scholars and experienced educators on issues raised in the NCER reports, especially the promotion of lifelong learning, the improvement of teaching methods in primary and secondary schools, the promotion of individualized teaching, and the promotion of educational programs for Japanese children living abroad.

Educational Policies Enforced Since the NCER Reports

In the two years after the NCER submitted *The Fourth* (final) *Report* to the Prime Minister, the government submitted to the national Diet seven bills related to educational reform, and the ministry made several amendments to cabinet orders and ministry regulations. The policies the ministry actually enforced were the creation of one-year induction training for beginning teachers, the improvement of the national standards for the curriculum for schools, and the reorganization of the ministry.

With regard to the new system of induction training for beginning teachers, the ministry submitted to the Diet in February 1988 a bill to create this new system and it was passed on 25 May 1988. Under this amended law, one year of induction training for beginning teachers employed at public primary and secondary schools was made compulsory for the administrative authority employing them. At the same time, the probationary period for teachers was extended from six months to one year. To be precise a beginning teacher must now be put under the guidance of an experienced teacher nominated by the headmaster for one year in order to learn how to use teaching materials and how to manage his or her class.

As regards the improvement of the national standards for the curriculum for schools, the Ministry of Education, Science and Culture, after receiving the report from the curriculum council, issued in December 1988 a revised course of study for kindergartens, primary and junior high schools. The course of study for senior high schools was revised in March 1989. The basic objectives of the revisions were to cultivate people who have rich and strong hearts and minds; to nurture in children the ability to cope positively with changes in society; to place more emphasis on basic knowledge and skills; and to promote such educational programs as will help students fully develop their individuality. These revisions were clearly influenced by NCER concepts. However, it is worth noting that the courses of study had been published in 1947, and that the last revision took place in 1977. The new revisions were long overdue.

The reorganization of the Ministry of Education, Science and Culture was enforced by the June 1988 amendments of Cabinet orders. As a result the ministry reorganized its own structure in July 1988 in the light of the NCER recommendations, its basic aims being to cope with the transition to a lifelong learning system; to give greater weight to the ministry's policy-making functions; to promote physical education and sports; and to promote educational programs for coping with internationalization and other changes in contemporary society.

The major structural changes were the establishment of a 'lifelong learning' bureau in place of a 'social education' bureau; reorganization of the minister's secretariat into a 'research, statistics and planning' division; setting up an 'overseas children education' division in the 'educational assistance and administration' bureau; and dividing the sports division into a sports-for-all division and an athletic sports division. Thus although the NCER had submitted to the Prime Minister recommendations across the whole field of educational reform, by 1989 only the issues mentioned above had been taken up, and it was doubtful whether other bills and amendments would now be enforced by the ministry.

Why, then, was educational reform not being given impetus by the government? Several reasons can be cited. First, the resignation of the Nakasone Cabinet came too early to allow the NCER reforms to be implemented. Because the Cabinet resigned on 5 November 1987, soon after the NCER's final report came down, Nakasone did not have enough time to enforce many reforms. In addition to that, the ignominious 'Recruit scandal' was brought to light just after the resignation of his Cabinet, and he lost his nation-wide credibility. Second, the Cabinets which followed, including those of both Prime Ministers, Mr Takeshita and Mr Uno, did not given much attention to the implementation of the NCER reforms; indeed they did not have much time to do so because of the disposal of the 'Recruit scandal' and of the consumer tax. Third, as the NCER empowered by Prime Minister Nakasone was set up in the Prime Minister's office, some staff working in the Ministry of Education, Science and Culture in the first instance were not willing to work together to promote the reforms. As a result the political climate was not conducive for the government to push through its reforms. In these circumstances, the bill for establishing an *ad hoc* commission for the implementation of educational reform became null and void in the last session of the Diet in June 1989.

The *Asahi Shimbun*, one of the major newspapers in Japan, noted:

A senior staff member of the Liberal-Democratic Party revealed that we gradually made the Bill for Establishing An *Ad Hoc* Commission for the Implementation of Educational Reform null and void. The Ministry of Education, Science and Culture itself seems to be (now) released from the restriction of the National Council on Educational Reform.

Nevertheless, the basic concepts for the reforms outlined in the NCER reports will influence the future of Japanese education, even though only a few of its recommendations have been acted on up to the present time.

Restructuring Schools in Japan

Despite the passive attitude by the government towards the enforcement of educational reform, the basic concepts in the NCER reports are important for Japanese concerned in educational administration. Contemporary Japan is defined in terms of a 'highly information-intensive society', an 'internationalized society', or an 'aging society'. Every Japanese is keenly encouraged to live an enriched life, aiming to develop his or her personality to the full and striving to achieve self-fulfilment, as well as making active contributions to the international community. However, in its education provisions the formation and development of personality, respect for individuality and the concept of freedom have not been fully established. Japanese education has become uniform; it tends to stress rigid, formal equality, and too much emphasis placed on academic-background results in heated competition for entrance to prestigious schools and corporations negatively influences education.

In these circumstances, the reports of the NCER give useful guiding principles on what is needed to create an appropriate educational system. The three most fundamental ideas emphasized in the reports are to introduce the transition to a system of lifelong learning; to develop educational programs in which emphasis is placed on each student's individuality; and to make the education system adapt to changes of the times, such as internationalization. These three ideas ought to be the basis for reform, but plans are inhibited by a number of barriers, chief among which are the increasing cost of education paid by parents, the declining educational function of the family, and severe competition for entrance examinations.

With respect to the educational costs of education paid by parents, the proportion of those costs paid by parents in terms of total consumer spending declined from 3.9 per cent in 1965 to 2.5 per cent in 1973, but they have been rising constantly since 1974, reaching 4.5 per cent in 1986 (EPA, 1988, p. 108) This growth is due to a higher growth rate in education costs than in gross income (see Figure 8.2). The patterns demonstrate the growing burden of education costs. In addition, because of high school expenses, students' living expenses are high. Tuition and cost of living are mostly financed by parents; some 80 per cent are met with allowances from family and the rest is covered

Figure 8.2: *Growing Burden of Educational Costs on Parents*

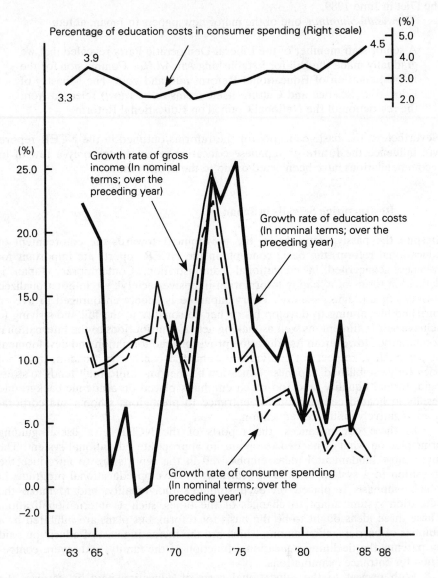

Note: Based on the 'Family Income and Expenditure Survey' by the Management and Coordination Agency.

by students' income from part-time jobs and scholarships. Comparative studies among major industrialized countries about who bears college expenses (tuition and cost of living) show that whereas 50 per cent of respondents in Great Britain and 40 per cent in the US financed college educations without parents' help, in Japan 80 per cent said their parents paid for most of the expenses.

150

The declining educational function of the family does break students' tranquility of mind at home. The public-opinion survey on family and home (1986) conducted by the Prime Minister's office found concerning the relationship between the causes of juvenile delinquency (such as violence and harassment) and home life that 37.1 per cent of respondents said the causes of delinquency were 'mostly home', 34.4 per cent replied 'complicatedly interwoven problems of juveniles themselves, home, school, society, etc.', followed by 'mainly social circumstances and social trends' (11.5 per cent), 'mostly juveniles themselves' (9.6 per cent) and 'mostly school' (2.5 per cent) (EPA, 1988, p. 116). The educational function of the family, particularly the development of a basic trust with the family members, was therefore considered very important for students.

Competition in entrance examinations had become extreme in the 1980s, due in part to employment systems and to the general social tendency to value higher educational achievement. Regarding the highly competitive entrance examinations, many students have been forced to go to cram schools or preparatory schools, and in consequence the expenses paid by parents for these schools has also been growing (see: Figure 8.3). As for teachers and students, they have been laying heavy stress on acquiring knowledge, and ignoring the development of the students' personality.

The following measures seem to be necessary to break these barriers and to create an appropriate educational system. The first is to establish a schooling based on respect for individuality, doing away with the uniformity, inflexibility, and exclusivity of current education. It is very important for schools to respect the dignity, freedom, and self-responsibility of individuals. In order to deal with social change positively and flexibly, schools must foster creativity, the ability to think, and the ability to express oneself. It was concern for this point which led the Ministry of Education, Science and Culture to revise the course of study for school from kindergarten to senior high school in 1988 and 1989. Its stated purpose was to help students fully develop their individualities, to cultivate students who have rich and strong hearts and minds, and to place more emphasis on basic knowledge and skills.

A second measure is to establish a schooling which emphasizes the enrichment of moral education. Moral education has an important role to play in the development of a sound character. A number of problems in schools, especially in junior high schools (such as harassment, school violence, and family violence) must be considered as one kind of social problem. To correct this undesirable situation, emphasis should be placed on teaching basic manners of living, the development of both self-control and a willingness to follow social norms in daily life, and the development of a good attitude towards life. In other words, moral education must be enriched by primary and secondary schools.

A third measure is to establish an institution which provides diverse educational opportunities for students, especially in secondary and higher education levels. At the present time, most junior high-school students proceed to senior high school, and nearly one-third of the senior high-school graduates go on to universities or junior colleges (see Table 8.2). This means that many students have already experienced diversity, but it is very important to make the structure of their educational programs as flexible as possible. In order to cope with needs for diversification, the NCER recommended:

Figure 8.3:   Increase in the Number of Students Attending Cram or Preparatory Schools

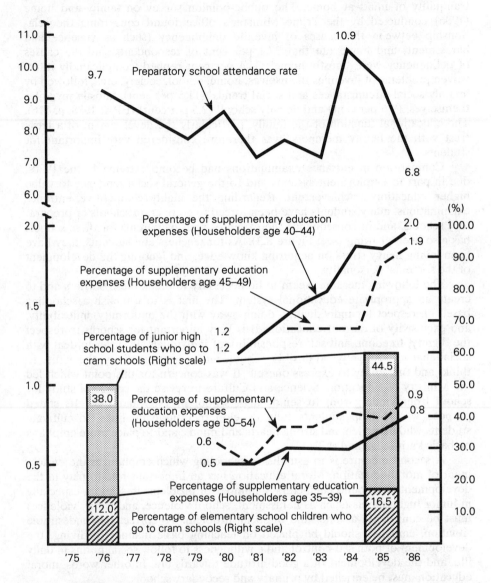

Note: 1.   Based on the 'Basic Survey on Schools' and the 'Survey on Children's Study Outside the School' by the Ministry of Education, Culture and Science, and the 'Family Income and Expenditure Survey' by the Management and Coordination Agency.

With regard to policies for the diversificaton of upper secondary education, further examination needs to be made of various issues, including the feasibility and necessity of restructuring upper secondary schools. (NCER, 1987, *The Third Report*, p. 51)

With respect to higher education, the Council went on:

> Institutions of higher education should be encouraged to develop in diverse ways, and mutual cooperation and exchange should be promoted among institutions. With these as aims, the government should study the following measures: diversifying the departments and curricula in junior colleges and giving more flexibility to the content of education in these colleges. (NCER, 1987, *The Fourth Report*, p. 40)

Although no concrete measures were promoted by the government up to 1990, some policies for educational diversification at all levels need to be enforced as soon as possible.

A fourth measure is to re-examine the existing system of entrance examinations. During the period of high economic growth, a number of educational institutions grew up to meet the people's demand for equal opportunity in education. However, in the course of this process, the competition for entrance examinations had become severe even from the level of primary school. Many parents want to give more and higher education to their children because most Japanese people believe that educational achievements are highly valued in getting good jobs, but too much emphasis on educational achievements has negative effects, as was mentioned above. With respect to this issue, the National Council on Educational Reform recommended:

> With regard to the procedures for selecting entrants to upper secondary school, each school should strive to secure more diversified and more distinctive selection methods and criteria in accordance with the real circumstances in each prefecture. (NCER, 1987, *The Third Report*, p. 43)

Further, regarding the procedures for selecting university entrants, *The Fourth Report* said:

> In order to help remedy the evil effects of competition for university admission which are characterized by an excessive emphasis on applicants' standard scores on achievement tests, the Council requests every university to attempt to reform the content and methods of its entrance examination with the aim of ensuring an independent and distinctive selection process. (NCER, 1987, *The Fourth Report*, p. 41)

The reform of the existing system of entrance examinations must be one of the most urgent necessities in Japan. Although there have been several attempts to reform the system, it is a matter of regret that no effective system has been found up to the present time. Although a new 'common test' was to replace the nationwide standardized test in 1990, it is questionable whether the new test could solve the inconsistencies and ensure equal opportunity among those who take the entrance examinations.

A fifth measure is to establish a school open to the community, and which ensures cooperation with the parents. It is important to open both the facilities and the functions of schools to the community. Schools, families, and the commuity must mutually cooperate if they are to carry out their own roles and responsibilities to school children. Schools, home, and community are places of human-assets development and bear responsibility for the formation of basic character traits. However, schools set up by national or municipal governments have been strictly administered by the authorities, and have not been opened to the community. The NCER recommended that the government break down this situation:

> The roles of schools should be reviewed with the perception that schools are common properties of community people, and a relationship of mutual collaboration should be established among schools, families and the community. (NCER, 1987, *The Third Report*, p. 69)

Establishing schools open to the community and to families is an urgent demand on governments, both national and local.

Conclusion

After World War II, Japanese education spread dramatically, based on the principle of equal educational opportunity. Such progress came about mainly because Japanese people put emphasis on education and because of the improved living standards resulting from the high post-war growth of the Japanese economy. But with time, the education system became a target of criticism. The National Council on Educational Reform was established to overcome these difficulties, yet in spite of submitting four reports relevant to all aspects of the future of education, only a few of its recommendations were enforced, mainly because the Council itself has a strong tinge of politics. The rejection of the bill for establishing an *ad hoc* commission for the implementation of educational reform was a symbolic response to the political character of the Council.

Nevertheless, Japanese education still seems to be in 'a grave state of desolation'. The basic concepts for reform outlined by the NCER remain absolutely necessary for the near future. Doing away with uniformity, inflexibility and exclusivity are the most urgent problems in Japanese education. The basic mission of education lies in conveying to the next generation the cultural assets developed by their ancestors, and also in bringing up young people who can carry the future of the nation on their shoulders. In order to realize this mission, education must aim at the full development of personality, striving to rear a people sound in mind and body. An ultimate goal of all educational efforts must be to develop good harmony among the moral, intellectual, and physical elements affected by restructuring schools. Educational reform from this point of view is absolutely necessary in Japan.

An objective evaluation of the NCER reports is impossible so soon after the Council submitted its final report. However, it goes without saying that educational reform based on individuality, flexibility, and the full development of the personality is not only urgently needed, but that restructuring schools along these lines should have begun as soon as possible.

References

Amano, I. (1985) *Kyoiku Kaikaku O Kangaeru* (Checking up the Educational Reform), Tokyo University Press.

Ebihara, H. (1984) *Shiyoshu: Rikyoshin.* (Materials: National Council on Educational Reform), Eidel Kenkyujo.

Ebihara, H. (1986) *Gendai Nihon No Kyoikuseisaku To Kyoikukaikaku* (Educational Policies and Reform in Modern Japan), Eidel Kenkyujo.

(EPA) Economic Planning Agency (1988) *Annual Report on the National Life for Fiscal 1987*, Tokyo, Economic Planning Agency.

Fujii, H. (1986) *Haha To Kyoushi No Kyoikukaikaku* (Educational Reform by Mothers and Teachers), Rodo Kyoiku Senta.

Fukayama, M. (1985) *Rikyoshin Toshin O Do Yomuka* (How to Read the Reports of NCER), Rodo Junposha.

Kukayama, M. (1986) *Rinkyoshin De Kyoiku Wa Do Kawaru* (What Changes Can be Expected by NCER?), Rodo Junposha.

Fukuda, N. (1985) *Kyoikukaiku-Miraishakai Eno Chosen* (Educational Reform — Challenge to the Future Society), Zenponsha.

Fukuda, N. (1986) *Kyoikukaikaku-Watashi No Teigen* (Educational Reform — My Proposals), Tairyusha.

Gyosei (1985) *Rinkyoshin To Kyoikukaikaku* (NCER and Educational Reform), Gyosei Ltd, 1, 5.

Hara, M. and Kawabe, M. (1984) *Rinkyoshin* (National Council on Education Reform), Token Shuppan.

Harada, S. (1988) *Rinkyoshin To Kyoikukaikaku* (NCER and Educational Reform), Sanichi Shobl.

Hamabayashi, M. (1987) *Sokatsu Hihan Rinkyoshin* (All-inclusive Criticism: NCER), Gakushu No Tomo Sha.

Kyoikuseisaku, K. (1987) *Rinkyoshin Soran* (Conspectus NCER), Daiichi Hoki.

Kurohane, R. (1984) *Kyoiku Kaikaku* (Education Reform), Kokudo Sha.

Kurohane, R. (1985) *Rinkyoushin* (NCER), Nihon Keizai Shimbunsha.

Kyoikumondai, K. (1987) *Kyoikukaikaku No Gensoku* (Principles for Educational Reform), lwanami Shoten.

Kyoikuho, H. (1985) *Rinkyoushin No Subete* (All of NCER) Eidel Kenkyujo.

Koyama, K. (1987) *Jiyu No Tameno Kyoikukaikaku* (Educational Reform for Freedom), Php Kenkyujo.

(Mesc) Ministry of Education Science and Culture (1987) *Kyoikukaikaku No Shishin* (The Promotion of the Educational Reform), Tokyo, Ministry of Education, Science and Culture.

(Mesc) Ministry of Education, Science and Culture (1989) *Outline of Education in Japan*, Tokyo, Ministry of Education, Science and Culture.

Ministry of Finance (1988) *Kyoikukaikaku Ni Kansuru Toshin* (The Reports on Educational Reform), Tokyo, Ministry of Finance.

Japan Communist Party (1987) *Kokumin No Tameno Kyoikukaikaku* (Educational Reform for Japanese nation).

Namimoto, K. (1985) *Kyoshi To Kyoikukaikaku* (Teachers and Educational Reform), Eidel Kenkyujo.

Nakamata, Y. (1987) *Rinkyoushin To Kokuminkyoiku* (NCER and National Education), Shin Nihon Shuppan.

Ohmori, K. (1987) *Rinkyoushin Nenkan No Kiroku* (The Three Years' Records of NCER), Hakari Shobo.

Rinkyoushin (1984) *Rinkyoushin Shingikeika No Gaiyo* (The Summary on the Process of Deliberations of NCER), 1–4. Japan, NCER, 1, 4.

RODOSHA, K.K. (1983) *Kyoikurincho No Kozu* (The Composition of NCER), Gakushu No Tomo Sha.

SATO, E. (1987) *Nihon No Kindaika To Kyoikukaikaku* (Modernization of Japan and Educational Reform), Kanekoshobo.

TAKANASHI, A. (1987) *Rikyoushin To Shogaigakushu* (NCER and Lifelong Learning), Eidel Kenkyujo.

YAMASHINA, S. (1985) *Kyoikurincho To Gakko, Chiiki* (NCER and Schools, Community), Ayumi Shuppan.

YAMASAKI, M. (1986) *Jiminto To Kyoikuseisaku* (The Liberal-Democratic Party and Educational Policies), Iwanami Shoten.

(NCER) NATIONAL COUNCIL FOR EDUCATIONAL REFORM (1985) *The First Report.*

(NCER) NATIONAL COUNCIL FOR EDUCATIONAL REFORM (1986) *The Second Report.*

(NCER) NATIONAL COUNCIL FOR EDUCATION REFORM (1987) *The Third Report.*

(NCER) NATIONAL COUNCIL FOR EDUCATION REFORM (1987) *The Fourth Report.*

The Yomiori (1984) 23 August.

The Japan Times (1983) 22 February, 5 March, 23 March, 15 June, 16 November, 1 December.

The Japan Times (1984) 27 January, 5 February, 21 August.

The Asahi Shimbun (1989) 26 June.

Part 3

Issues in the School-reform Movement

Chapter 9

Paradox and Uncertainty in the Governance of Education

B.J. Caldwell

A Turbulent Environment

If account is taken of events throughout the western world we must now accept that change is a permanent condition in education. Indeed, the late 1980s and early 1990s may have seen the most significant changes in the governance of public education in this century and we are now in a period of transition marked by paradox, uncertainty, and turbulence.

Writing in *Managing in Turbulent Times*, a book set in the business sector but which foreshadowed aspects of the changes now being experienced in public education, Peter Drucker (1981, p. 10) warned that 'the greatest and most dangerous turbulence . . . results from the collision between the delusions of the decision makers, whether in governments, in the top managements of businesses, or in union leadership, and the realities'. I believe we can gain some measure of stability in this period of transition by acknowledging the realities. I also share Drucker's optimism when he argues that 'a time for turbulence is also one of great opportunity for those who can understand, accept, and exploit the new realities. It is above all a time of opportunity for leadership'. I would like to take up this challenge, starting with a brief description of some of these 'new realities'.

The New Realities in a Shifting Pattern of Governance in Education

The following is a brief account of shifts in patterns of governance in public education across a number of western countries in the early 1990s:

- Britain embarked on the most comprehensive package of reforms of the century, with England and Wales to have a national curriculum and a national testing program, with all secondary and most elementary schools to have control of their own budgets, including staff, through a system of local management of schools (LMS), and with schools having the power to opt out of control by their local education authorities on the majority vote of parents;

- In the United States there were recommendations from influential organizations for the introduction of school-site management after several years of increasing control of curriculum and testing at the state level;
- In Australia, the foundations were laid for a national-curriculum framework and testing program, at the same time that state governments were, on the one hand, adopting a stronger role as far as goals, priorities and accountability are concerned and, on the other hand, shifting significant authority and responsibility to the school level;
- In Canada there was increased centralization in most provinces, especially in the areas of curriculum and testing, but also a trend to school-based planning and decision-making, with the evolution over ten years of a highly devolved system in the Edmonton public-school district which shaped a number of developments in the international setting;
- In a policy statement entitled *Tomorrow's Schools* issued by the Minister for Education, David Lange (1988), who was also the Prime Minister, the government of New Zealand accepted the major recommendations in the Picot report (Picot, 1988) which produced a virtual transfer of decision-making to schools within national guidelines.

These patterns were described in terms of their impact on elementary and secondary education, but similar patterns emerged in higher education, with developments in Australia and New Zealand among the more far-reaching. In each instance national governments were restructuring education but, more than ever before, were setting priorities for teaching and research and establishing a powerful framework of accountability, at the same time as they were encouraging a greater capacity at the institutional level for planning and resource allocation (Dawkins, 1988; Lange, 1989).

In general, governments in many countries adopted a more powerful and focused role in terms of setting goals, establishing priorities and building frameworks for accountability — all constituting a centralizing trend — at the same time as authority and responsibility for key functions were being shifted to the school level — a decentralizing trend in the centralization — decentralization continuum. Much uncertainty arises because these trends, almost paradoxically, were occurring simultaneously or in rapid succession.

The initial reaction in each nation or state was that these initiatives were capricious or arbitrary, being an ill-considered attempt to implement an ideological stance as far as education is concerned or an inappropriate application of economic or managerial values to a field of human service such as education. Strong union opposition was evident at the outset in each instance although, with time, the union position has been muted, if not supportive, as initial fears of a hidden agenda, harmful to the profession and to the quality of education, were not realized. Many academics adopted a strongly critical stance (see, for example, Bates, 1988, Codd, 1988 and Grace, 1988 in respect of changes for elementary and secondary education in New Zealand; Bessant, 1988, and Williams, 1988, in respect of changes for higher education in Australia).

While planning and implementation of change have left a lot to be desired, it is reassuring that governments are making similar responses to similar issues and that these responses seem to be independent of ideology. Drucker made this point in calling for acceptance of certain realities when managing in turbulent times:

> The new realities fit neither the assumptions of the Left nor those of the Right. They do not mesh at all with 'what everybody knows'. They differ even more from what everybody, regardless of political persuasion, still believes reality to be. 'What is' differs totally from what both Right and Left believe 'ought to be'. (Drucker 1981, p. 10)

Policy Issues for Governance in Public Education

Why are governments responding in similar fashion, regardless of ideology? What are the common issues? What are the underlying values? These questions are generally concerned with quality, effectiveness, equity, efficiency, accountability, and adaptability. Brief explanations are offered below, sufficient to suggest commonality across national or state settings and to highlight their interrelatedness in terms of the manner in which they are being addressed.

Quality

That there has been a central concern about quality is clear from recent OECD reports on education, including one devoted exclusively to the issue which states that concern for the quality of education in schools is today among the highest priorities in all OECD countries. It will remain so for the foreseeable future (OECD, 1987, p. 123). The report acknowledges different meanings of the term and differences in approach when efforts are made to effect improvement. It concludes that definitions of quality are determined by educational aims and that how the curriculum is defined, planned, implemented and evaluated ultimately determines the quality of education that is provided.

This concern underlies much of the interest in national or state curriculum and testing programs and the setting of priorities for teaching and research in higher education (centralizing trends). It also accounts for interest in an enhanced capacity at the school or institutional level to define, plan, implement, and evaluate within a centrally determined framework (decentralizing trends). That is, while measures are being taken to ensure that all schools address common aims through a common curriculum framework or a common set of priorities, there is recognition that quality in terms of learning at the most important level of all, the student, can only be achieved if schools and institutions have the capacity to deliver the curriculum in a way that satisfies the needs and interests of the particular mix of students in the local setting.

There is, however, a broader concern for quality having an impact on patterns of governance. This is the concern for quality in life which is determined by the capacity of a nation to perform well in an international economy. There is a sense in many nations that they are falling behind and that, to become more competitive, they must ensure a highly responsive economy which calls in turn for a highly responsive system of education which equips citizens with suitable knowledge, skills, and attitudes. This relationship between education and economic needs has, of course, always been there. Education has always made a significant contribution to the economic well-being of the nation. The rhetoric of governments has simply brought the relationship into sharp focus, and with a stridency and urgency that many find discomforting. It is likely that the relationship will become less prominent in public discourse. Nevertheless, it currently accounts in part for the stronger role governments are taking in many areas of educational policy.

School Effectiveness

While the issue of quality has ensured a continuing, strong role for government in setting goals and establishing priorities, recent research on school effectiveness and school improvement supports a shift in responsibility to the school level within a centrally determined framework. Much of the research has been carried out in the United States. A sample of findings and recommendations follows.

Purkey and Smith (1985) offered a model for 'creating an effective school' which drew from literature in four areas: classroom research on teacher effectiveness, research on the implementation of educational innovations and school organization which identify the role of school culture in school improvement, research in work places other than education, and consistency between effective schools research and the experience of practitioners. Their model contained thirteen characteristics, nine of which can be implemented relatively quickly, while four defining the school's culture take time because they require the development of an appropriate climate. In the first group they included an approach to the administration of schools wherein

> the staff of each school is given a considerable amount of responsibility and authority in determining the exact means by which they address the problem of increasing academic performance. This includes giving staffs more authority over curricular and instructional decisions and the allocation of building resources. (Purkey and Smith, 1985, p. 358)

Finn (1984) addressed another implication of the effective schools research when he called for 'strategic independence' for schools. He noted that 'the central problem faced by policy makers who attempt to transform the findings of "effective schools" research into improved educational practice at state or local level is the tension between school-level autonomy and system-wide uniformity' (p. 518). His nine commandments for strategic independence included recognition of the school as 'the key organizational unit in the public school system' (p. 520); the setting of 'rigorous educational standards for entire states and communities but [emphasising] broad goals and essential outcomes, not specific procedures, curricula, or timetables' (p. 521); encouraging 'schools to be different, except for the core of cognitive skills and knowledge that all students in a system or state should acquire' (ibid.); and devolving 'more budgetary authority . . . to the school level' (p. 523).

Drawing on a similar research base, the National Education Association (NEA) and the National Association of Secondary School Principals (NASSP) issued a joint report in 1986, in which it was stated that 'the NASSP and NEA remain committed to the principle that substantial decision-making authority at the school site is the essential pre-requisite for quality education' (NEA-NASSP, 1986, p. 13).

A degree of self-management at the school level within a centrally determined framework is also supported by recent research on school improvement, including that by Miles and his colleagues (Miles, 1987). Longitudinal studies in urban secondary schools in the United States revealed a cause-and-effect relationship between school improvement and some measure of school autonomy, especially in the area of resource allocation, with empowerment of staff in decision-making at the school level.

Recent research by James Coleman provides very powerful support for establishing the strongest possible linkages between school and community. Coleman and Hoffer (1987) examined the performance of public and private schools on key indicators and highlighted the importance of what they termed 'social capital' as a key determinant of success. Social capital is the network of mutual support involving the family, the student, the school, and (where appropriate) the church.

The findings from such research have been explicitly used in the formulation of policy on decentralization, especially in the United States. The report of the National Governors' Association (1986) and of the Carnegie Taskforce on Teaching as a Profession (1986) are examples of reports which have influenced new patterns of governance in several states. The relationship between research and policy is not immediately evident in the reports which have led to the new patterns of governance in the other countries under consideration in this chapter.

Equity

There has been a merging of two values, equity and excellence, which in the past have shaped policy in different ways. There has been a shift in focus concerning equity in recent years. Initially the goal in public policy was to ensure that every student could attend a place of learning ('equity in access'). The goal then shifted to ensuring that each place of learning received a fair share of resources to enable it to meet in broad terms the educational needs of all of its students ('equity in resource allocation'). In Australia, for example, this goal was evident in the late 1960s and 1970s when the Commonwealth Schools Commission established a complex series of grants designed to achieve a large measure of equity in resource allocation among schools and to meet the educational needs of particular populations of students.

But the focus concerning excellence has also shifted. Whereas excellence has traditionally implied superior achievement by a few, recent usage brings a meaning which comes close to the emerging view of equity. An illustration is the definition of excellence offered by the National Commission on Excellence in Education in the United States; it was really an eloquent call for equity:

> We define 'excellence' to mean several related things. At the level of the individual learner, it means performing at the boundary of individual ability in ways that test and push back personal limits, in school and in the work place. Excellence characterizes a school or college that sets

high expectations and goals for all learners, then tries in every way possible to help students reach them. Excellence characterizes a society that has adopted these policies, for it will then be prepared through the education and skill of its people to respond to the challenges of a rapidly changing world. (National Commission on Excellence in Education, 1983, p. 12)

In policy terms, the outcome in the United States was the aforementioned centrally determined curriculum and testing programs, reflecting a continuing concern for quality, in the so-called first wave of reform. The second wave, influenced more by findings from research on school effectiveness and school improvement, was marked by an interest in decentralization and school-site management.

The emerging view of equity and excellence suggests an emphasis on ensuring that each individual student has access to the particular mix of resources in order to best meet the needs and interests of that student, with resources in this mix being considered broadly to include school, curriculum, learning experience, teachers, supplies, equipment, and services. Greater attention is being given to each student, a strategy reinforced by advances in knowledge about developmental and learning processes. Advances in technology have also made possible a variety of highly individualized approaches. In terms of administrative processes to support learning and teaching, it seems that determining what the particular mix of resources should be for each student is a decision which may be made at the school level to a greater extent than has traditionally been the case. Expressed another way, the merging of equity and excellence may involve, among other things, a shift from uniformity in resource allocation, with all decisions at the centre, to different patterns of resource allocation according to the particular mix of student needs at the school level; with more decisions at the school level in determining these patterns (see Garms, Guthrie, and Pierce, 1978, for a similar line of argument).

The issue of equity thus has implications at all levels of education, reinforcing the need for a high level of centralization in some matters but raising the possibility of some measure of decentralization for others.

Efficiency

Only through the efficient allocation of resources can the three values previously explored — quality, effectiveness and equity — be optimally achieved. Governments at all levels are rightly concerned about efficiency. If anything, the need for efficiency is escalating as governments everywhere are faced with an increasingly complex and ever-changing set of demands for public services. And these demands are parallel demands made at a time when, in many countries, there are parallel demands for a reduction in the level of taxation and when resources are scarce, whatever their source. Governments can only respond with an approach to policy-making and resource allocation which takes account of costs and outcomes so that priorities can be set and reset. The aim at any one point in time is to ensure an optimal match of scarce resources to a complex, ever-changing mix of needs, wants, and demands.

Efficiency thus becomes a key consideration at all levels of education: the capacity to set and reset priorities; to monitor inputs, processes and outcomes; to tailor resources and programs in the face of shifting priorities and continuous monitoring calls for high levels of skill in administration. Expressed bluntly, every instance of duplicated or wasted expenditure or every instance where resources continue to be allocated to areas of low priority (although they may have been high in the past) means that the needs of some students will not be met. If we are concerned about equity, effectiveness, and quality, then we must strive for greater efficiency.

Accountability

Implied in the foregoing is acceptance of a framework for accountability and the selection of appropriate indicators, defined here as attributes of an educational program, measures of which are used to make judgments about the worth of the program.

The following questions are appropriate in the current environment:

- What are the indicators related to inputs, processes, and outcomes which will assist governments in setting priorities and allocating resources in their continuing drive to achieve quality, effectiveness, and equity through efficiency?
- Who shall determine these indicators and how shall information be gathered and aggregated to facilitate the decision-making process at the system level?
- What indicators can be used at the school or institutional level to meet school needs?
- Who shall determine the indicators at the school or institutional level and how shall information be gathered and aggregated to meet needs at the system level as well as at the school or institutional level?
- How can tensions be resolved between system and school needs in the use of indicators?

Determining answers to these questions is proving difficult. But to refrain from addressing them, or to deny the realities of the environment in which they are being asked, only contributes to a sense of uncertainty and an undue level of turbulence.

Adaptability

A capacity at all levels to adapt is evident in much of this analysis. Setting and resetting priorities; monitoring and tailoring; ensuring, particularly at the school or institutional level, that the program of learning and teaching matches as far as possible the needs and interests of students, and that valued outcomes are achieved, demand a high level of adaptability.

A further stimulus is the increasing interest in the community in the exercise of choice. For a variety of reasons, including greater affluence, access to a wider range of information about schools, limited employment opportunities for the young and higher levels of education in the community, parents and students are making choices among schools in the pursuit of what is perceived as higher quality in education. There is the analogy if not the reality of 'a market' in education, with parents and students seen as clients or consumers and with school systems and schools called out to be more sensitive to market needs. The response has generally been in the direction of decentralization, encouraging greater diversity among schools, a measure of 'deregulation' through the abandonment of attendance zones and, in the case of England and Wales, the 'opt-out' provision of the 1988 Education Act, which allows schools to leave their local education authorities on the majority vote of parents, and to receive their funds directly from the national government.

Tensions in New Patterns of Governance

Several tensions are evident in the new patterns of governance. Considered here are tensions at the centre and tensions between the centre and the institution. The focus here, as in the remaining sections of this chapter, is largely on governance in the elementary and secondary sectors.

Tensions at the Centre

Wirt (1988) offered a comparative perspective on the role of the Chief Executive Officer (CEO) in Australia, Britain, and the United States, noting that 'at different times and with different speeds, these CEOs have undergone successive stages of challenge from citizens and their elected parliaments, authorities and boards' (p. 43). These challenges have occurred across a range of areas traditionally regarded as 'professional': pedagogy, curriculum, finance, personnel, and student testing. They are most evident in the initiatives described earlier — in national or state curriculum and in testing programs. These are areas where, according to Wirt, the CEO and other senior professionals have traditionally and almost exclusively exercised power. Of particular interest, for example, was the short-term contract appointment of Dr Russell Ballard as Director-General of Education in New Zealand. Ballard, who came from the field of forestry, had a one-year brief to effect change in New Zealand by 1 October 1989.

Wirt believes 'there is clear evidence' of a shift in the role of the CEO 'from technical emphasis and value neutrality to a more political effort to promote professional goals' (Wirt, 1988, p. 47). He offered several explanations, including political impatience at an apparent lack of responsiveness among senior officers, especially in the face of declining resources; ideological shifts which have promoted a distrust of public officials; and a more highly educated citizenry with relatively youthful political leadership that demands solutions to difficult problems. This shift from the 'neutral technical' to the 'political professional' role calls for new skills in mobilizing support, new sensitivities to the needs of the community, and new approaches to formal training and career development. Wirt is optimistic that deeper understanding can 'provide a CEO with more effective leadership amid a power-sharing and elite challenging context' (p. 57).

His observations on the role of the CEO do not apply to all countries. In France, for example, what Wirt describes as a 'political professional' role has, in fact, been evident for more than a century. Indeed, one might argue that it prevailed in former times in other countries at least to the extent that the CEO was traditionally expected to respond to shifts in political ideology as governments changed. Perhaps the political dimension has broadened as governments and government agencies alike have had to respond to the wider range of powerfully articulated views of an increasing number of interest groups. Or again, given the greater complexity in the demand for service by government agencies, the shift may well be within a range of 'political professional' roles and toward 'powerlessness'.

Tension Between Centre and Schools

Tension between the centre and schools may be described in a number of ways. For example, central constraints on decision-making at the school level emerge as an issue in recent studies of school improvement. Miles and his colleagues found that relatively high levels of school autonomy, especially in planning and resource allocation, are important factors in improvement in urban high schools in the United States. Farrar described these findings in the light of constraints on school decision-making:

> I think there is a paradox in this situation, one that has serious implications for the prospect of improving urban high schools through school-based planning models. These approaches aim to decentralize authority, to shift responsibility for improvement needs, plans and strategies from the district to the school, where ownership and collegiality foster faculty commitment to improvement. Yet groups outside the school make a number of education decisions that seriously hamper the school's efforts. Some decisions ... have the effect of maintaining or recentralizing responsibility to the district or state over critical school functions and policies. This leaves building administrators and faculties with decision-making responsibility only along the periphery of school affairs. (Farrar, 1987, p. 8)

This tension was palpable in Britain as the government implemented the 1988 Education Act which sponsored a high degree of centralization in curriculum and testing but also a high degree of decentralization through the local management of schools. Participants in public and legislative debates fiercely contested the issue of curriculum control, with the government's initial rather detailed and prescriptive approach (Department of Education and Science, 1987) coming under heavy fire. Those advocating that the values of choice should prevail called for the government to drop this aspect of policy altogether (see, for example, O'Keeffe, 1987; Sexton, 1987; Sexton, 1988).

With research on school effectiveness and school improvement so consistently supportive of a relatively high degree of autonomy at the school level, a reduction of tension seems dependent on minimizing the number of constraining rules and regulations. A strong central role is important but should be limited to establishing a vision for the system as a whole, setting expectations and standards for student learning and providing strong support for schools.

The position of Albert Shanker, president of the American Federation of Teachers, is interesting in regard to this issue. While Purkey and Smith (1985) anticipated union resistance to school-site management, Shanker has given strong support to decentralization, believing that unity can be better attained through commitment to a shared vision than through extensive rules and regulations:

> How would the school reform movement have developed if these principles of management [decentralization] had been followed? For one thing, we would have looked for ways to encourage more decision-making by teachers in classrooms and principals in schools, rather than bind them by rules and regulations set down by legislatures and state education departments. . . . And perhaps most important of all . . . our education leadership would have risen above the petty squabbles about merit pay, the length of the school day and school year, and created a vision of our public school system, what it has meant to our country, why it succeeded in the past and what challenges lie ahead, and shared that vision with (teachers, board members and parents) without whom our goals will not be accomplished. (Shanker, 1987)

It should be noted, however, that Shanker's stance placed him at the cutting edge of union opinion. The union resistance anticipated by Purkey and Smith may still be a factor in the United States, as it is in Britain, Australia, and New Zealand.

Role Conflict Uncertainty and Ambiguity: Resolving the Tension

An initial reaction of those at the centre when responsibility has been decentralized to the school level has been a perceived loss of power. This has been the case in instances where, for example, decisions on the allocation of resources have been decentralized. Those who previously determined budgets for each school in more or less precise terms may no longer do so; those who formerly allocated staff to schools in precise categories according to centrally determined system-wide formulae may no longer have this responsibility; supervisors in subject disciplines and staff-development programs, whose responsibilities have been to allocate resources for particular programs on the basis of their personal judgments or according to some policy that applies to all schools, may find that schools no longer need or seek their services. Yet they know that their work was previously valued and that the same decisions must continue to be made at some level.

The key to resolving this tension seems to be a smooth transition to a new set of roles and responsibilities for those people employed at the system level so that, instead of a loss of power in regard to old tasks, they acquire power in a new set of tasks through a transition process which is well understood. What is involved becomes apparent if the responsibility of the centre in new arrangements is examined. The central authority now has a more sharply focused responsibility in formulating policy, setting priorities, establishing frameworks for accountability, allocating resources to schools in equitable fashion, providing support to schools and monitoring the quality of education (however defined).

Within this still powerful but focused framework, a person who was formerly, for example, a supervisor in a subject discipline, rather than exercising a direct oversight of people at the school level, now has the responsibility of making a contribution to the formulation of policy and the setting of priorities in their areas of interest and expertise. Such a person will also be involved in the selection of indicators, measures and standards and then in determining from time to time a target level of performance upon which judgments about effectiveness and efficiency might be made. Ensuring that support is provided for schools will also be an important responsibility, with ongoing monitoring of the various indicators an important, indeed necessary, task. A smooth transition and commitment to these new roles is aided, as it is in all fields of endeavor, by leaders who provide from the outset a vision of what is intended and then successfully communicate and gain commitment to that vision. That vision usually includes a vision of the process of change.

An example of successful transition is offered in the Edmonton public school district in Alberta, Canada. This system is selected because that pattern of decision-making featuring a high level of decentralization has been in place for a decade. It offers a model for many matters under consideration in this chapter. It is acknowledged that this setting is unique (like any other) but the general principles of action illustrated in Edmonton seem widely applicable.

After a three-year trial of school-based budgeting, system-wide implementation in Edmonton proceeded in almost 200 schools with a minimum of prior staff development but with many concerns among staff at the system level. Successful adoption of new roles then evolved over the next seven years or so. The system had the benefit of the same person occupying the superintendency throughout the change, with this person offering a clearly articulated vision from the outset. He fits the 'politically professional' rather than 'technically neutral' image (Wirt, 1988). A process is now institutionalized wherein the elected school board each year sets priorities which must be addressed in all schools. Budget preparation and staff selection are wholly decentralized to schools. Accountability in an educational sense is addressed through a system-wide set of standardized tests in language, mathematics, science, and social studies at two points in elementary schooling and at one point in secondary. Target levels of performance are set each year. Those employed at the centre have responsibilities in the associated processes in the manner outlined above. A special feature was a trial decentralization of curriculum and student services to schools, with the schools able to plan for and choose such services from whatever source they felt best provided the service, even if that source is outside the system.

In summary, then, the keys to resolving problems of role conflict, uncertainty, and ambiguity in decision-making seem to be the gaining of commitment to a shared vision, a careful specification of new roles, and making clear that responsibility in one domain is invariably replaced by responsibility in another, the adoption of a strong service orientation, an evolutionary process for the management of change, and the acquisition of the necessary knowledge and skill.

Making the Transition

In general, I believe that the shifts in the pattern of governance in public education, which have crossed national and ideological boundaries, are appropriate, given a universal concern for quality, and the need to address issues related to effectiveness, equity, excellence, efficiency, accountability, and adaptability. A substantial capacity for self-management at the school or institutional level within a centrally determined framework seems an eminently sensible pattern of governance. The central issue is the manner in which we manage the transition and resolve the tensions. What follows are some possible ways in which this can be done, with explanation and illustration drawn from the elementary and secondary sectors.

Requirements at the System Level

The most important requirements at a system level are the capacities to prepare a strategic plan, to build a framework for accountability, and to support a self-managing capacity at the school level. The first of these, the strategic plan, is now making its appearance in many school systems. Essentially, it is the outcome of an environmental scan and involves the setting of priorities for action in the short, medium, and long term, taking account of likely levels of resources and the preparation of broad plans for action. The most effective strategic plans appear to be short rather than long, and are constantly reviewed and refined in the light of the shifting priorities of governments and new threats and opportunities in the immediate environment. The strategic plan provides a framework for action for all units in the system, including schools.

As far as accountability is concerned, all units in a school system, whether at central or school levels, are expected to provide information on the extent to which goals, policies, and priorities are being addressed and intended outcomes have been achieved. Expectations must be communicated and information must be collected and analysed. Two initiatives will facilitate the process. First, at the central level, strategic plans for the system as a whole will provide a focus for the efforts of officers involved in the process. Second, at the school level, is the existence of what are being described in the New Zealand context as 'school charters': a relatively short document, agreed to by the Minister for Education and the board of trustees of a school, which sets out the mission, needs and priorities of the school as well as the broad strategies which will be employed to address centrally determined goals and priorities. The charter is the basis for allocating funds to the school. It also provides a focus for the work of review and audit teams which are part of the central framework. Charters, also proposed for higher education in New Zealand, have their counterparts in Australia with the so-called 'educational profiles' for institutions of higher education.

The key elements in what has been traditionally the inspector's role seem indispensable, no matter what structures and other organizational arrangements are put in place. The OECD report on quality of schooling (1987) sketched those major elements:

> However great the autonomy enjoyed by schools, they are still answerable to administrative authorities at local, regional and national level that have responsibility for :
> (i) Setting quality targets and providing the means of attaining them;
> (ii) Monitoring the implementation of appropriate strategies;

(iii)   Conducting regular appraisals of performance in association with the schools concerned.

(OECD, 1987, p. 89)

Perhaps the most important guidelines relate to the support of schools. Developments in other countries confirm that continued support is essential, although the organizational arrangements may differ in significant ways from those which have prevailed. Consider, for example, the experience in Edmonton, Alberta. In 1986, decisions related to the deployment of centralized curriculum and student-support services were decentralized to fourteen schools out of more than 200 schools in the system. This trial arrangement aimed to enhance efficiency and effectiveness of support services, to improve capability at the school level to determine the nature and level of support services required to meet the needs of students, and to improve the way in which support services were accessed and delivered. Schools in the project had their lump-sum allocations supplemented by amounts which reflected the historical use of support services according to type of school and level of student need. Allocations were then included in school-based budgets. Standard costs for various types of service were then determined, on a per-hour or per-incident basis, with costs charged to the school as service was requested. Schools could choose services outside those provided by the system.

It is noteworthy that the level of utilization of support declined in the first year of the trial, with schools opting in many instances to acquire other resources to solve their problems. For example, additional teachers were deployed or schools turned to other schools for expertise. A clearer definition of the requirements for a central support service also emerged (Caldwell, Smilanich and Spinks, 1988). This definition offered:

1   A vision which included the support of schools and central services as well as the opportunity to influence the setting of policies and priorities in the system and in external agencies;
2   A clarification of responsibilities between central support and schools;
3   Approaches to needs assessment which encouraged schools to plan and then allocate resources in their budgets for provision of services;
4   Service agreements with schools;
5   Enhancement of client autonomy;
6   Integrated delivery of services to schools;
7   Flexible modes of service delivery;
8   Flexible staffing patterns for those employed in central support services;
9   Development of generic knowledge, skills and attitudes as well as skills required in consultation and areas of specialization;
10 Capacity for networking;
11 Capability for research and development;
12 Capacity for monitoring the quantity and quality of service, including the opportunity to contribute to the identification of centrally determined outcomes, standards and indicators.

School-support services in New Zealand, with the exception of special education services, are to operate a quasi-free market; that is, while services will be available to schools through support centres, schools are free not to use these services, depending on their judgments about the quality of service. They may choose to secure service from any provider. The central issue is that quality of service and considerations of marketability are as relevant here as they are in the broader setting considered earlier.

Requirements at the School Level

Thus we now know the requirements at the school level and the manner in which the associated capacities can be developed. At least five key areas of knowledge and skill are required if a capacity for self-management within a centrally determined framework is to be acquired:

- School administrators will have knowledge about a wide range of approaches to learning and teaching and about the creation of appropriate environments for learning and teaching. Included here is a capacity for instructional leadership which places emphasis on the contemporary view of supervision ('working with and through others'), especially in collaborative or collegial approaches. This is the core of knowledge for administrators in the self-managing school;
- School administrators will have the capacity to work within national and state frameworks and priorities and with teachers, students, and members of the community in the design and delivery of a curriculum to meet the needs of every student. Included here is an understanding of trends in society (the 'new realities'), especially as they concern the economy and the nature of work;
- School administrators will make an ongoing and systematic approach to program evaluation a feature of the administrative process. Evaluation will be an important element in the culture of the school.
- School administrators will be able to address in practical terms the various generalizations which have emerged from recent studies of leaders and leadership, especially that on gaining commitment to a shared vision of quality;
- School administrators will be able to design and implement an ongoing, collegial, cyclical approach to goal-setting, policy-making, planning, budgeting, implementing and evaluating. Included here is a capacity for school-level strategic planning. The development of such a cycle would seem to be a prerequisite for success in self-management.

Essentially the above will ensure that schools have a capacity for what Miles (1987) called 'deep coping' in the face of continuing change. Miles and his colleagues found that the secondary schools which were most successful in effecting improvement in the United States had such a capacity, in contrast to 'shallow coping' in schools which were relatively unsuccessful. 'Deep coping' is a continuing capacity for problem-solving involving, for example, empowerment of staff, departmentally based planning groups, school-based in-service training and the acquisition and deployment of staff who were equipped to offer the necessary programs in the school. 'Shallow coping' is a general absence of these capabilities, in effect an unwillingness and incapacity to face the 'new realities' in their immediate environments.

The model for self-management which evolved from a research and development project in Tasmania has promise for guiding the efforts of schools, especially in relation to a capacity for 'deep coping' and the development of an ongoing, collegial, cyclical approach to goal-setting, policy-making, planning, budgeting, implementing and evaluating (see Caldwell and Spinks, 1988). The model has been used in several Australian states, in England and Wales, and in New Zealand. It was adopted in New Zealand as the model to guide the initial phases of training for the new patterns of school governance in that country.

Conclusion

Governments, then, are adopting a more powerful and focused role in terms of setting goals, establishing priorities, and building frameworks for accountability — all constituting a centralizing trend in the centralization–decentralization continuum — at the same time as authority and responsibility for key functions are being shifted to the school level — a decentralizing trend in the centralization–decentralization continuum.

Change, including turbulence, is now a permanent condition in education. We can gain some measure of stability as change proceeds if we can, as Drucker expressed it, 'understand, accept, and exploit the new realities'.

We now have enough experience around the world to reassure the skeptics that the various tensions can be resolved and that the transition to a new era of governance can be effectively managed.

References

BATES, R. (1988) 'The new cult of efficiency: Policy and practice in the commodification of education', Paper presented to the New Zealand Association for Researchers in Education, Massey University, December.

BESSANT, B. (1988) 'Corporate management and the institutions of higher education', *The Australian Universities' Review*, 32, 2, pp. 10–13.

CALDWELL, B.J., SMILANICH, R. and SPINKS, J.M. (1988) 'The self-managing school', *The Canadian Administrator*, 27, 8, May.

CALDWELL, B.J. and SPINKS, J.M. (1988) *The Self-Managing School*, Lewes, East Sussex, The Falmer Press.

CARNEGIE TASK FORCE ON TEACHING AS A PROFESSION (1986) *A Nation Prepared: Teachers for the 21st Century*, New York, Carnegie Forum.

CODD, J. (1988) 'Picot: A risky reform?' *PPTA Journal*, Term 3, pp. 2–5.

COLEMAN, J.S. and HOFFER, T. (1987) *Public Private Schools: The Impact of Communities*, New York, Basic Books.

DAWKINS, J. (1988) *Higher Education: A Policy Statement*, Canberra, Australian Government Publishing Service.

DEPARTMENT OF EDUCATION AND SCIENCE (1987) *The National Curriculum, 5–16 (England and Wales)*, A Consultation Paper of the Department of Education and Science.

DRUCKER, P.F. (1981) *Managing in Turbulent Times*, London, Pan.

FARRAR, E. (1987) 'Improving the urban high school: The role of leadership in the school, district and state', Paper read at a symposium of Effective Schools Programs and the Urban High School at the Annual Meeting of the American Educational Research Association, Washington, DC, April 23.

FINN, C.E. (1984) 'Toward strategic independence: Nine commandments for enhancing school effectiveness', *Phi Delta Kappan*, February, pp. 518–24.

GARMS, W.E., GUTHRIE, J.W. and PIERCE, L.C. (1978) *School Finance: The Economics and Politics of Public Education*, Englewood Cliffs, NJ, Prentice-Hall.

GRACE, G. (1988) *New Zealand Treasury, the commodification of education and the nature of educational research*, Paper presented to the New Zealand Association of Researchers in Education, Massey University, December.

LANGE, D. (1988) *Tomorrow's School*, Wellington, New Zealand Government Printer.

LANGE, D. (1989) *Learning for Life: Education and Training Beyond the Age of Fifteen*, Wellington NZ Government Printer.

MILES, M.B. (1987) '*Practical guidelines for school administrators: How to get there*', Presented at a symposium of Effective Schools Programs and the Urban High School at the Annual Meeting of the American Educational Research Association, Washington, DC, 23 April.

NATIONAL COMMISSION ON EXCELLENCE IN EDUCATION (1983) *A Nation at Risk*, Washington, DC, Government Printing Office.

NATIONAL EDUCATION ASSOCIATION — NATIONAL ASSOCIATION OF SECONDARY SCHOOL PRINCIPALS (1986) *Ventures in Good Schooling*, Washington, DC and Reston, Virginia, NEA — NASSP.

NATIONAL GOVERNORS' ASSOCIATION (1986) *Time for Results*, Washington, DC, National Governors' Association.

OECD (1987) *Quality of schooling: A clarifying report*, [Restricted Secretariat Paper ED (87)13].

O'KEEFFE, D. (1987) 'Against a national curriculum; in *A National Curriculum?*, Monograph No. 2/87 of the Institute of Economic Affairs Education Unit, London, IEA.

PURKEY, S.C. and SMITH, M.S. (1985) 'School reform: The district policy implications of the effective schools literature', *The Elementary School Journal*, 85, pp. 353–89.

PICOT, B. (1988) *Administering for Excellence*, Report of the Task Force to Review Education Administration (Brian Picot, Chairperson), Wellington, NZ Government Printer.

SHANKER, A. (1987) 'Management creates a sense of purpose', *New York Times*, 18 January.

SEXTON, S. (1987) *Response to government consultation on education*, Monograph No. 7/87 of the Institute of Economic Affairs Education Unit, London, IEA.

SEXTON, S. (1988) *A guide to the Education Reform Bill*, Monograph No. 1/88 of the Institute of Economic Affairs Education Unit, London, IEA.

WILLIAMS, B. (1988) 'The 1988 White Paper on higher education', *The Australian Universities' Review*, 32, 2, pp. 2–9.

WIRT, F.M. (1988) 'The chief education officer in comparative perspective', *Comparative Education Review*, 32, 1, pp. 39–57.

Chapter 10

On Centralization, Decentralization and School Restructuring: A Sociological Perspective

R.O. Slater

This essay on centralization and decentralization consists of two major elements, the first of which, written in an expansive mood, focuses on the language of centralization and decentralization, and tries to suggest why the two words lack the emotive tone of high politics, even though they have much to do with power. The second section attempts to make two points. One point is that school structure is not one-dimensional but multi-dimensional, and that those who would restructure schools have not just one structure to deal with but several. The discussion here is mainly about the nature of these several structures and of organizational structure in general. The other point is that the most practical question one can raise about school decentralization or restructuring has to do with their connection to school effectiveness, and where this connection is concerned organization theory, particularly contingency theory, seems especially relevant.

Why 'Centralization' and 'Decentralization' Lack the Emotive Tone of High Politics

'Centralization' and 'decentralization' are not terms that one immediately associates with the discourse of high politics. Politics are highest when they are in and around a nation's highest instruments of power, its central government and military establishment. Here, the stakes are high and the language tends to be high as well. One is more apt to encounter the likes of 'liberty' and 'equality' than 'centralization' and 'decentralization'. Centralization and decentralization lack the emotive power of 'freedom' and 'equality'. They do not stir the blood but tend to cool it; there is about them an air of rationality that simply makes them ill-suited for the high drama of high politics. Patrick Henry, for example, could never have said, 'Give me decentralization or give me death!' There are things that people are willing to die for but decentralization is not usually among them.

That centralization and decentralization lack the intrinsic excitement of the discourse of high politics might be of little interest were it not for the fact that centralization and decentralization have everything to do with power, the essential ingredient of all politics, high or low, and one of the most intrinsically exciting of all phenomena. Yet these terms, almost clinical in tone, fail to convey the emotion of their primary referent. Indeed, they almost seem to buffer power's emotive effects. Why?

Some of the confusion about the close association of centralization, decentralization, and power might come from the fact that some of those who have reviewed the centralization and decentralization literature seem themselves to be unsure of the matter. They will, for example, say things like, 'So-and-so also views centralization and decentralization within a framework of power', or 'so-and-so approaches centralization and decentralization in terms of power' or 'so-and-so uses a model of power to understand centralization and decentralization', as if there were other frameworks, approaches, and models which had nothing to do with power but which were equally useful for understanding the nature of centralization and decentralization. As anyone who takes the time to appraise the literature seriously can see, this sort of relativism is simply nonsense. The most important and significant fact about centralization and decentralization is that they are about power and its distribution.

Another factor that might confuse or obscure the close association that centralization and decentralization have with power is the desire on the part of some theorists to do away with human agency in centralization and decentralization, and to deal with them in strictly structuralist terms. Perhaps I can best clarify this statement by drawing attention to the 'alignment' component of the A.I.M. model Guthrie and Koppich (1990) use to explain education reform. This part of the model utilizes the logic of the garbage-can model of decision-making first articulated by March *et al.* (1976). One of the most striking features of the garbage-can model and the variant used by Guthrie and Koppich is the absence of human agency. 'Windows of opportunity' form mysteriously and unpredictably from a confluence of various value, problem, and solution streams. Nobody is watching over the process, orchestrating the combination of values, problems, and solutions. It is a process that occurs without human intervention and one which, by implication, structures human action, often unbeknown to the humans themselves.

Now I should point out that, in using part of the Guthrie-Koppich model to illustrate a tendency in the centralization–decentralization literature, I do not intend to say that Guthrie and Koppich leave out the human agent in their explanation of educational reform. To do so would be to ignore their notion of the 'policy entrepreneur'. In fact, a chief merit of the Guthrie-Koppich model, in my view, is the manner in which it attempts to combine both structuralist and interpretive frameworks through its use of the concepts of window of opportunity and policy entrepreneur.

But all this has been said simply to point out that some theorists attempt to understand the centralization–decentralization phenomenon with the kind of systemic thinking that underlies the garbage-can model of decision-making, the aim of which is to show how decisions can be arrived at without a decision maker, i.e., without human agency. Where there is no decision maker there is also no power to make decisions; as the maker goes, so goes the power to make. Thus, the upshot of the structuralist or garbage-can perspective in the centralization–decentralization literature is to obscure the role of power.

There is, in addition to these two factors, however, a third, and perhaps more important, explanation of why centralization and decentralization fail to convey the emotional force of the language of power: They are terms invented for the explicit purpose of obscuring the presence of power.

Centralization and decentralization belong to the technical vocabulary of organizational theory and administration, and, as is often the case with technical language, their primary function is to rationalize discourse about things not wholly rational, the things in this case being power. Centralization and decentralization are among the linguistic tools that professional administrators have at their disposal to rationalize power. They are technical devices designed, ideally, for dealing with power without suffering power's emotive effects. They are built, as Bagehot (1901) might say, not to emphasize power's dignified side but its efficient side.

This need to sanitize power, to strip it of its emotive force, grows out of the emergence of the modern democratic-liberal state. There is nothing new, of course, about the use of power to give order to society and to organize human effort. Humans have always needed a modicum of order in their societies and organization in their work, and human domination has always been a rather straightforward way to obtain both. But, at least since the 'glorious revolution' in England in 1688, the use of power as an organizing principle of society has had to rest increasingly upon reason and rationality.

The glorious revolution and the revolutions of 1776 and 1789 after it have their roots in the enlightenment which was founded upon science or reason. The glorious revolution, as Trevelyan (1974, p. 3) notes, could have also been called the sensible revolution. Reason triumphed over revelation as the source of the legitimate use of power to organize society, and out of reason's victory came, at first, liberties, and later liberty. Thus grew the commitments to rationality and liberty as twin organizing principles of society.

Equality officially joined this reason-liberty dyad in 1776; America was the first full-scale experiment with the scientific liberal-democratic state. It was to be the state in which the master organizing principles were a triad: reason (science), liberty, and equality. Adding equality, however, created a problem, a tension. Simply stated, the problem was this: How could power — the inequality of inequalities — rightfully continue as the pervasive and ubiquitous organizing principle of society if it were supposed to be subordinate to equality? Power, liberty, and reason could function without major conflict. But add equality to the mix, and a contradiction is immediately created.

The partial reconciliation of power and equality was achieved in America partly through a change in how power was conceived. In the old, British view, the Whiggish view, power has always been viewed as something rather dangerous if not downright evil. Power was not something to be trifled with. Above all, its concentration was to be avoided. If one had to live with power, it was better to have it dispersed and fragmented, where it could do less damage.

In America, around the Jacksonian period, this view of power began to change. Instead of being seen as a dangerous or bad thing which was to be kept in check as far as possible, power came to be thought of as a rather good thing, so long as it was in the hands of the people. Of course, the people in this representative democracy could only mean the President, since his was the only position subject to general election, i.e., election by all the people, all other political positions being locally elected.

By the end of the nineteenth century this tendency had grown to the point where Woodrow Wilson and others were able to argue persuasively for the concentration of power within the American presidency (Ostrom, 1976). For his model, Wilson looked to the highly rationalized French and Prussian bureaucracies. The language in which he and other centralists couched their arguments, however, was not the rhetoric of the 1780s but a new, more rational discourse of a technical and less emotive level, a scientific language, the key terms of which were centralization and decentralization. As Ostrom puts it, 'The debate which was preoccupied with the words centralization and decentralization marked the end of the era of constitutional government and the beginning of the era of presidential government' (p. 32).

So, if centralization and decentralization do not have the emotive tone typical of discourse on power, it is because they were never meant to have it. They are the tools of those who must deal with power rationally and bureaucratically. They are built to buffer power's irrational effects, and grew out of an effort to concentrate power without making the implications of this concentration apparent.

Decentralization and School Restructuring: The Meaning of 'Restructuring'

To propose to restructure the schools is to shift the focus of reform from individuals to organization. School reform in the United States began with the simple assumptions that the quality of teaching depended upon the quality of teachers, and that the quality of teachers could be legislated. Accordingly, between 1984 and 1986 alone, some 700 state statutes affecting some aspect of the teaching profession were enacted (Timar and Kirp, 1989). Much of this legislation took the carrot-stick approach to teacher improvement, offering a combination of salary incentives and performance-evaluation programs. A similar logic was also applied to learning: The quality of learning was supposed to depend upon qualities of students, important among which qualities were discipline and application. Out of this line of thinking, many school systems tightened student-discipline policies and formulated policies linking participation in extracurricular activities with academic performance. All of this was done with the belief that reforming schools meant improving teaching and learning, which meant, in turn, changing teachers and learners.

The current movement to restructure schools signals a shift in this initial focus of reform. Reformers are no longer concerned with just changing people. They are now becoming increasingly interested in changing the organizational context in which the people work. Attention, in other words, has once again turned to the school as a formal organization (Bidwell, 1965). To propose to restructure schools is to do at least two things. First, it is to call attention to the fact that a school is a complex organization — bureaucracy — and, second, it is to demand changes in the existing structure of this bureaucracy. To address this demand it is necessary to raise the following questions: How are schools currently structured? How ought they to be restructured, and why should these new structures be any more effective than the old ones?

These questions about the nature of school structure raise, in turn, more general questions of the following sort: What is organizational structure? What do we know about organizational structure and restructuring in general that might inform our efforts to understand and change school structure? It is at this point that centralization and decentralization enter the picture, for the centralization–decentralization continuum is one of what most theorists consider to be three components of organizational structure, the other two being complexity and formalization. The current movement to restructure schools is a movement to make schools less centralized, formalized, and complex.

What Is Structure?

It has already been said that centralization and decentralization are aspects of organizational structure. It may be useful to begin, therefore, by devoting a little attention to some of the most commonly held assumptions about organizational structure and structural analysis in general.

It is not essential to review the history of structuralist thought, an excellent discussion of which can be found in Bottomore and Nisbet (1978). For present purposes it is only necessary to point out that structure and structural analysis have as a basic premise the denial of human freedom or choice. From Plato to the present, structuralists and structuralism have maintained that there are forms of thought or relationships in reality that exist regardless of whether humans are aware of them or wish them to exist. There are structures in thought and the world with which humans must reckon. These structures shape and mold the action of human beings, often without their being aware of it. One of the chief aims of science in general and social science in particular is to discover these structures so that humans may control and modify them if need be or, if they cannot be changed, at least recognize their existence and compelling force.

Perhaps nowhere is this central tenet of structuralism clearer than in the French structuralism of Levi-Strauss. Levi-Straussian structuralism emerged during the 1960s and early 1970s as a reaction to existentialism and its primary imperative, human freedom. For Sartre, existentialism's chief spokesman, the source of all value in life was human freedom. Life has meaning only to the extent that a person gives it meaning, and one can give life meaning only to the degree that one is free. This was the existentialist postulate that the Levi-Straussian structuralists felt to be most problematic. As Passmore explains, 'What most repelled the existentialists, the domination of man by systems, is, from the structuralist point of view, not only inevitable but even desirable' (Passmore, 1985, p. 26).

Organizational structures, like social structures in general, function systematically to limit human choice, though in the case of organizations the structures themselves are much more likely to be a result of deliberate calculation and human intention. This is because most organizations, or at least major aspects of them, are man-made for specific purposes. They are built to get some kind of specific work done. The work to be done is usually broken down into various sub-tasks — a division of labour. From the point of view of the organization, these and only these tasks are relevant to its goals. Ideally, the more that individual behaviour is restricted to the performance of these tasks and these tasks alone, the greater the efficiency and certainty of producing the ends for which the organization was established in the first place. Organizational structure is the mechanism by which individual effort in a collective endeavour is restricted to tasks believed to be most relevant. Organizational structure, then, serves as an external control on human behaviour, control which is justified by reference to organizational effectiveness.

Of course, in every organization, including military organizations where structure is relentless, the worker is never completely controlled by structure but usually enjoys some degree of freedom or control over his or her work. In every organization, in other words, there is always a balance, however lopsided it may be, of structural control and individual autonomy. Current efforts to restructure schools may be viewed as arguments over what that balance of control and autonomy ought to be. Advocates of restructuring want new structures that are less controlling and that accordingly give more autonomy or discretion to school-site personnel, students, and parents.

Three Organizational Structures

Formalization

One of the most striking features of bureaucracy, a feature captured in the phrase 'red tape', is the manner in which they structure human behaviour through the use of rules and established procedures. Formalization refers to the degree to which organizational tasks are rule-governed. A highly formalized organization would be one in which much of what people do is stipulated by rules which are often, though not necessarily, written. A highly formalized elementary classroom, for example, might be one in which the teacher had rules for when students could talk with classmates or use the pencil sharpener, for how much paper could be used during drawing or for how much paint could be used during art. In a less formalized environment, on the other hand, these matters might be left largely up to the students.

It hardly needs pointing out that in highly formalized organizations there is little need for the direct giving of orders since rules prescribe much of behaviour. Equally obvious is that in such organizations the professional level of the workers is generally quite low since they are given little discretion, and that formalization works best when the work technology is routine. In cases where there is a great deal of uncertainty about how to do the work, mindless adherence to rules is likely to be counterproductive and there is a greater need for professionalism (Perrow, 1967).

Complexity

Complexity, a second source of structure in organizations, has three aspects. It refers to how the work is broken down and assigned to individuals within the organization, to the number of levels in the organization's hierarchy, and to the organization's degree of spatial dispersion. In general, work can either be broken down into sets of related tasks and assigned to a specialist or it can be minutely subdivided and given to non-specialists (Hall, 1987, p. 60). Hierarchical levels can be few or many, and the organization itself can be located within a relatively small space or spread out across many miles.

Centralization and Decentralization

The most direct and straightforward way to control human behaviour in general and to organize work in particular is through power; the distribution of power in an organization constitutes a third and potent structure.

The use of power, a command-obedience structure, to organize work is pervasive in modern society; it is the essence of bureaucracy, which is one reason why Max Weber referred to bureaucracies as 'systems of imperative coordination'. One or a few members of the organization imperatively coordinate or give orders to all the rest who, ideally, comply with the orders given them. In this manner, power is used to limit individual behaviour to only those tasks that bear on the ultimate outcome and, accordingly, it constitutes a structure in its own right.

In the modern democratic-liberal state, however, power cannot be used to organize work without justification. If the use of power is to be effective, those who take the orders given them must feel it right that they should do so. There must be a sense that it is appropriate for commands to be given and obeyed. Power, in other words, has to be perceived as legitimate, i.e., as authority, if its use as an organizing principle is to be effective. This idea was nicely summarized by Parsons (1989) who said that what, from the point of view of management, appears as a matter of coordination always appears, from the point of view of the worker, as a matter of cooperation.

Anyone who has taught children in the early years of schooling is well aware of this principle of legitimacy. One of the first tasks facing the kindergarten or first grade teacher is to get children to see the power structure of the school classroom as legitimate, to get them to accept, in Waller's phrase, 'the social necessity of subordination as a condition of student achievement' (Waller, 1932, p. 9)

The distribution of power in an organization constitutes a structure that more or less limits the discretion of individual members. When administrators and organization theorists talk about this power distribution and about changing it, they typically use the terms centralization and decentralization. To say that an organization is centralized or decentralized is to describe the distribution of power within it. In general, to say that an organization is centralized is to say that power is concentrated. To say that it is decentralized is to say that power is dispersed. Thus, centralization and decentralization are descriptors of the distribution of power within organizations or social systems; the function of these two terms is to give a rough picture of an organization's power distribution or structure.

The term 'rough' in the forgoing sentence deserves special emphasis, for in organizations built to get work done a number of different functions have to be carried out. Barnard (1937), for example, maintained that the functions of every executive come down to essentially three: the setting of goals, the establishment of a communication-command structure, and the recruitment of personnel. The decisions attached to each of these functions can be more or less centralized. Depending upon the complexity of the organization, the centralization of one or more of these functions may serve as 'decision premises' (Simon, 1947) for other functions. All schools, for example, require a curriculum, the hiring of teachers, and the acquisition of instructional materials and texts. Each of these functions can be more or less centralized but the centralization of one function, say, curriculum, may automatically limit decisions pertaining to another, say, the choice of what kind of teacher to hire. So, while the hiring function may be decentralized to the school level, certain decisions pertaining to it may be limited by having other functions centralized.

Thus to say that an organization is decentralized is only to give a very rough picture of its power distribution. For a more detailed picture, one would have to say which functions were decentralized, to what degree, for what purpose and to what effect on other decision-making with regard to other functions.

Organizational Structure and School Restructuring

Those who would restructure schools, then, have not only to consider changes in the distribution of power within the system but also in the degree of the system's formalization and complexity. The mix and balance of change among the three structures and across functions will determine whether or not any significant restructuring actually takes place.

If the aim is to empower teachers it will do little good to decentralize decision-making on such matters as curriculum while at the same time maintaining a high degree of formalization of curriculum. In the United States, for example, state departments of education routinely formulate policies stipulating a wide range of behaviours including how many minutes of each day each subject must be taught. It will do little good for central offices to tell teachers and school administrators that they can decide how to schedule the instructional day if these state rules or policies are kept in place. The outcome is still a centralized scheduling policy.

In general, research on organizations suggests that there is no one best way to restructure schools to achieve school effectiveness.

Decentralization, Restructuring, and School Effectiveness: The Relevance of Contingency Theory

Of course the practical administrative question that always lies behind the decision to restructure a school system is how restructuring will affect school effectiveness or those factors that the school effectiveness research suggests are correlated with effectiveness.

In a recent review of the school productivity and effectiveness literature, Geske and Teddlie (1990) note that 'while it would be foolhardy to reduce the study of school effectiveness to a simple list of basic correlates associated with student achievement, or to a five or six-step litany, it is encouraging that there is consistency in results across these studies'. Among the results they cite as being consistently related to effectiveness are those having to do with school leadership.

Geske and Teddlie cite research (Cohen, 1983; Teddlie, *et al.*, 1984) which suggests that effective principals emphasize academic goals and understate the other functions that schools perform. In down-playing non-academic activities in this manner effective principals avoid sending mixed messages about what is important. Effective principals also tend to spend more time observing classrooms, giving teachers feedback, mediating the adoption of more effective teaching practices, and guarding academic time. Finally, effective principals seem to pay more attention to how students and teachers are assigned to classrooms. These effects of leadership on school effectiveness are not, however, free of school context, and Geske and Teddlie cite further research (Hallinger and Murphy, 1986; Teddlie and Stringfield, 1985) which reported that 'effective principals in lower-SES schools were more directive and more active in instructional and curricular matters than were effective principals in upper-SES schools, who tended to be managerial, leaving academic issues up to the faculty' (1990, p. 24).

The notion that under some conditions one form of structure is more effective or efficient while under other conditions alternative forms would be more effective is what organizational theorists call the contingency approach to organizational structure (Lawrence and Lorsch, 1967). Research on organizations in general and on effective schools in particular suggests that if school policy makers and administrative personnel wish to restructure rationally, they would be advised to consider a contingency approach to restructuring.

Such an approach would require, first, that restructuring be viewed not as a single, global strategy pertaining to a monolithic school structure but as multiple strategies pertaining to several structures across several functions. Second, a contingency approach to restructuring would require that, for each restructuring strategy contemplated, they ask themselves a couple of questions: 1) How is this strategy (e.g., decentralization of curriculum) likely to interact with the social context or environment of the school(s) in question? 2) How is the result of this interaction likely to impact, say, school leadership (i.e., the principal's opportunity to observe classrooms, give feedback to teachers or guard academic time)?

Contingency theory is, of course, applicable not only to the restructuring of schools and school systems but also to the restructuring of nation-state systems as well, where the whole restructuring business can become very complicated.

To sum up, we have discussed the nature of organizational structure, and have noted that its primary function is to limit human choice in the interest of productivity. In every organization, we have noted, there are essentially three types or aspects of structure. Organizational complexity — the way work is divided and assigned, the number of levels in the hierarchy, and the spatial dispersion of offices and functions — limits the choices that people have with regard to the work they can do. On top of this complexity there are rules that further limit choices at work. Finally, in addition to these two structural constraints, there is in every organization a distribution of power which determines who can make what decisions, when, and under what circumstances. This power structure acts as a third structural constraint. Each of these three structures or structural features are associated with the organization's various functions. Each function, in other words, can be more or less decentralized, more or less formalized and more or less complex.

The decision to restructure a school or school system is really a decision to re-evaluate and change the structures of one or more of its functions. Thus, for example, the general decision to decentralize will always be followed by further decisions: Decentralize what function? How? When? For what purpose? To what effect on the organization's other functions?

References

BAGEHOT, W. (1901) *The English Constitution*, New York, M. Walter Dunne.

BARNARD, C. (1937) *Functions of the Executive*, Cambridge, MA, Harvard University Press.

BIDWELL, C.E. (1965) 'The School as a Formal Organization', in MARCH, J.G. (Ed.) *Handbook of Organizations*, Chicago, Rand MacNally, pp. 972–1022.

BOTTOMORE, T. and NISBET, R. (1978) 'Structuralism', in BOTTOMORE, T. and NISBET, R. (Eds), *A History of Sociological Analysis*, New York, Basic Books, pp. 557–98.

COHEN, M. (1983) 'Instructional Management and Social Conditions in Effective Schools', in ODDEN, A. and WEBB, L.D. (Eds) *School Finance and School Improvement; Linkages for the 1980s*, Cambridge, MA, Ballinger.

GESKE, T. and TEDDLIE, C. (1990) 'Organizational Productivity of Schools', in REYES, P. (Ed.) *Teachers and their Workplace: Commitment, Performance, and Productivity*, Newbury, CA, Sage.

HALL, R. (1987) *Organizations* (4th Ed.), Englewood Cliffs, NJ, Prentice Hall.

HALLINGER, P. and MURPHY, J. (1986) 'The Social Context of Effective Schools', in *American Journal of Education*, 94, pp. 328–55.

LAWRENCE, P. and LORSCH, J. (1967) *Organization and Environment*, Cambridge, MA, Harvard University Press.

MARCH, J.G., OLSON, J. and CHRISTENSEN, S. (1976) *Ambiguity and Choice in organizations*, Bergen, Universitlesforlaget.

OSTROM, V. (1976) 'The Contemporary Debate Over Centralization and Decentralization', in *Publicus*, 6, pp. 21–32.

PASSMORE, U. (1985) *Recent Philosophers*, London, Duckworth.

PERROW, C. (1967) 'A Framework for the Comparative Analysis of Organizations', in *American Sociological Review*, 32, pp. 194–208.

SIMON, H. (1947) *Administrative Behavior*, New York, Macmillan.

TEDDLIE, C. *et al.* (1984) *The Louisiana School Effectiveness Study; Phase Two, 1982–84*, Baton Rouge, Louisiana State Department of Education.

TEDDLIE, C. and STRINGFIELD, S. (1985) 'A Differential Analysis of Effectiveness in Middle and Lower Socioeconomic Status Schools', in *Journal of Classroom Interaction*, 20, pp. 38–44.

TIMAR, T. and KIRP, D. (1989) 'Education Reform in the 1980s: Lessons from the States', in *Phi Delta Kappan*, 70, pp. 505–11.

TREVELYAN, G.M. (1974) *Illustrated English Social History*, London, Longmans Green.

WALLER, W. (1932) *The Sociology of Teaching*, New York, John Wiley and Sons.

Chapter 11

Public Schools in Decline: Implications of the Privatization of Schools in Australia

D.S. Anderson

Introduction

More than one-quarter of Australian school children are in 'private' schools. This is the highest proportion in any Anglo-American country; furthermore, while elsewhere the private sector is either static or declining, in Australia it has been growing (UNESCO, 1989). During the 1980s the private share in Australia grew from about 20 per cent to 27 per cent, the highest since public systems were established in the late nineteenth century. By far the greater part of the private sector are the Catholic schools which educate just under 20 per cent of all school children, most, but not all, the children of Catholic parents. It is the non-Catholic component, however, that has contributed the greater part of the private growth in the 1980s. Elite schools catering for the upper part of the social order grew in numbers and size also, and a bevy of newer sorts of private school were established, ranging from those supported by ethnic and fundamentalist religious groups to schools practising various sorts of alternative education.

In this chapter we will see why there has been this unique decline in a public sector, and what the implications are of such a large private-school component for social equity and for the overall management of the educational enterprise, especially management for improved performance. First, however, some historical and political background will inform our understanding of the reasons for this large and prosperous private sector, and why the value 'alignment' (to use Guthrie and Koppich's term) remains refractory to reform.

Origins of the Dual-school System

History

The dual system of Australian schools emerged from a conflict between church and state, or more precisely, denominations and state. When the British established a colony in Australia, 200 years ago, they brought with them spiritual authority in the form of the Church of England. The church assumed responsibility for the morals and manners as well as the religious welfare of the new residents and, among other things, became involved in schooling for the young. Before too many decades had passed this monopoly over faith was challenged by representatives of the Churches of Rome and of Scotland, who claimed responsibility for the not inconsiderable numbers of Irish and Scots who had found their way to the shores of New South Wales. After decades of effort, during which denominational squabbling impaired educational progress, there remained substantial sections of the population without access to adequate schooling. Eventually civil authority intervened.

In the 1830s the colonial government established state schools at the same time as maintaining support for existing denominational schools. This created Australia's first dual system. But destructive rivalry was not eliminated, nor was effective schooling extended to all regions of the country. Towards the end of the nineteenth century, the various colonial governments (by now there were six of them), fed up with the inadequacies of the denominational system, motivated by strong democratic principles and emboldened by the Darwinian challenge to ecclesiastical authority, decided that the state had direct responsibility to see that all children received a good education. Comprehensive public-school systems were established which, in a phrase that became famous at the time, were 'free, compulsory, and secular'. Financial aid to church, or any other non-government school, ceased. Thus ended the first publicly funded dual system.

The state systems (the colonies became autonomous states in a federation in 1901) were administered by central bureaucracies under the authority of a government minister; school or regional participation in the running of schools was minimal. Devolution of authority to regions or schools was not part of the design because the sparsely settled hinterlands of the states had not developed a tradition of local government, and because the state authorities really did not trust the denominations to refrain from meddling in local school affairs. The result was a set of public school systems which provided reasonably equal, educational opportunity across a vast land.

It was against these public initiatives that the Catholic systems were built in the latter part of the nineteenth century, at enormous cost, by a church which felt itself to be a threatened and beleaguered minority in an intolerant, Protestant-dominated society. The church in Australia was encouraged by pronouncements from Rome which stimulated the development of Catholic-school systems in a number of countries at about the same time; but none of these were as successful as in Australia. Today about half of the Catholic children in Australia attend their church's schools, a fraction claimed to be higher than in any other country (Encel, 1970; Anderson, 1988).

The Protestant schools, not having the donated teaching services of the Catholic schools, had to charge substantial fees. This has restricted the social range of their clientele and many of those which survived developed into schools of social class. The Protestant churches originally played little part in the battles for the reinstatement of state aid; some even opposed the idea because it would assist their Catholic rivals. But, with the decline of sectarian feeling since World War II, elite schools have generally been more than happy to advance in the slip stream of the Catholic initiatives.

Politics

Political opposition to public funding for private schools began to collapse in the 1950s when Conservative governments saw political advantage in attracting the Catholic vote, and at the same time in assisting the elite schools with which they were not unsympathetic. Eventually the opposition Labor party, which, believing in education equality and an undivided society, had adamantly opposed state aid to any private school, now saw that it must recapture the Catholic vote if it was ever to be re-elected. Labor decided that it would fund all schools according to their need. The wealthy private schools would get nothing; impoverished Catholic schools (and most were) would get the greater part of their running costs plus some help with capital; poorer state schools would have their regular resources topped up with special grants.

There was a window for reform of schools in the 1960s and early 1970s. Education was widely seen as a means towards a more just, equal, and civilized society. It was also viewed as an end in itself, occupying a substantial portion of the life cycle, and therefore an institution which should embody the highest principles of civilized living. Astonishing reforms were achieved. An entirely new public system with participatory governance at system and school level was designed in Australia's capital territory (the founders considered, but stopped short of, associating public and private in the one administrative and planning system). Throughout the country various sorts of alternative schools were created in both the public and private sectors. Equality of educational opportunity was a slogan of the times and numerous schemes were implemented to improve the access of disadvantaged groups from pre-school to university. Resources were devoted to making educational outcomes more equal. Vast increases in public expenditure funded these new programs. In the climate of the 1980s few of these reforms would have left the drawing board.

The climate of reform infected political preferences and, after twenty-three years in opposition, Labor was elected to government in 1972, not least because of its policies for education. But, in order to get its needs legislation through a Conservative upper house of the legislature, it was forced to extend financial aid to all schools, including the wealthy elite group. Today all non-government schools are aided according to a formula which assesses their resources. The poorest (still mainly Catholic) receive over 80 per cent of their costs from state or federal government while the most well-off elite schools get about one-third. In addition there are capital grants for refurbishing or extending schools. Had it not been for the return of state aid many private schools (I will continue to use the term although clearly 'subsidized schools' would be more accurate) would have been unable to continue, and the Catholic system, desperate to replace the rapidly declining services of religious, would have collapsed. After nearly 100 years a dual system comprising public and publicly subsidized private schools has been reinstated.

Naturally public schools' interest groups resent the massive subsidies which now go to private school but their efforts have little political impact because state aid is no longer on the agenda of any significant political party. One proposal by a Labor government for a more equitable distribution of funds (mainly taking the subsidies from forty of the wealthiest schools) met with such hostility from both Catholic and Protestant school authorities that the idea was quickly dropped. The constitutional legality of state aid has been challenged in a High Court action by a public-school pressure group known as DOGS (Defence of Government Schools), which argued that aid to church schools was aid to religion. The case was lost on a majority verdict, unlike the United States where an almost identically worded constitutional provision has prevented direct, financial government aid to religious schools.

Although political support for private schools is now bipartisan the system is unstable politically in that additional aid does not reduce the leverage pressure groups can bring to bear on governments. The interest groups are not unaware of having to make a strategic judgment — the point where public funding becomes so large that unwelcome accountability requirements would be likely. Some of the large elite schools believe that point is getting close and are preparing for the contingency of financial independence. As well as being politically unstable the system is also unmanageable from a planning perspective, a point which will be elaborated later.

Conditions Favouring Privatization

On the face of things the reason for the growth of private schools in Australia is simple. It is because governments are assisting with the capital for expansion and are keeping fees low by paying a substantial part of running costs (Williams, R., 1984). Yet there are other countries where private education is not growing at the Australian rate despite the fact that, unlike the US, there is no legal impediment to direct government funding, for example Sweden, and Great Britain; and in Denmark, where government pays the greater part of private-school costs, the sector has not grown to the same extent as in Australia. A combination of several other features do, however, make Australia significantly different.

One of these is that Australia is a socially heterogeneous country. To what was a predominately Anglo-Celtic society before World War II have been added several millions of migrants, nearly half of them from continental Europe, the Middle East or Asia. Many of these wish to maintain their cultural traditions through schooling and, along with the Catholic community, are inclined to value pluralism above social cohesion.

Secondly, there is a strong egalitarian tradition within the public-school sector which has been ideologically opposed to the development of an academically selective stream, even at the price of advancing private schools. Apart from a handful of outstanding academically selective high schools in some of the capital cities, public secondary education is comprehensive. As a consequence those parents who are ambitious for their children to qualify for university entry and for the higher-status professions are liable to look for a school in the private sector.

Finally, the highly centralized systems for administering education, designed to meet the needs of a bygone era, are only now yielding to more devolved and participatory types of governance. The absence of a tradition of local control of schools and the sense of remote, anonymous, and powerful bureaucracies convey a feeling of powerlessness to some parents and community groups. Feeling that they are locked out of public schools insofar as influencing significant policy decisions is concerned, the more influential and articulate parents are liable to exit to the private option rather than give voice to their desires for reform in the public. Despite surveys showing that public-school parents are highly approving of the quality of teaching and the standards set in their own children's schools, the same surveys reveal a generalized perception of public education as a grey institution, unresponsive to needs. These images of a remote authority, insulated from any local initiatives, influence some active parents to choose private rather than public schools even though the opportunity to give effective voice is equally, if not more, remote.

In no other Anglo-American country, indeed probably in few other industrialized countries, does this combination of features pertain: legality of public funding for private schools, absence of a readily available academically selective option in the public sector, a society which is culturally mixed, and absence of participatory systems of school governance. For example, in New Zealand, which has had an education system not unlike Australia's, there is not the social diversity of Australia and in particular the Catholic proportion in the population is much smaller. There is also a long tradition of local participation in school governance. Thus in the late eighties, at the same time as Australia began to extend aid to private schools, New Zealand incorporated all but a handful of its non-government schools into the public sector.

Definitions

Values

Since substantial public funding of private schools means that fee for service is not the sharp distinguishing characteristic that it is in other countries, how do we define a private school? Espousal of a particular religious creed or cultural value is part of it. Like private schools in other countries a majority of Australian private schools is associated with main-stream religious denominations. As we have already noted there has been a rapid growth in the last decade of fundamentalist, ethnic, and alternative schools, although, as yet, these make up fewer than 2 per cent of the total.

Public schools are of course not value-free, and they are not precluded from teaching religion or morality. But they do have to respect the pluralism of religious and cultural positions in the community. As one school principal explained, 'We do not teach religion, just about it.'

An overriding value claimed by the private sector is freedom to choose. In arguing for increased funding on this ground, advocates for private schools are liable to imply that choice is not available in the public sector. This is not entirely fair in that children are generally no longer bound to their local zoned school. There may not be the diversity of value approaches in the public sector but there can be a wide range of pedagogical approaches.

Ownership and Administration

Private schools may also be distinguished from public because they are neither owned nor administered by a state authority. These days there are very few that are owned by private individuals or companies and run for profit. Apart from those owned and run by churches most are incorporated institutions with any profits accruing to the school. But even ownership and administration do not always clearly separate public from private. For example, in New Zealand all Catholic schools are in the public sector but the properties remain in the possession of the church. And in England we have the reverse case as schools which take advantage of the new provisions for opting out of control by the local government will be publicly owned but administered like 'regular' private schools.

Social Functions

It should be obvious that there is considerable diversity within both the public and private sectors and that it is therefore misleading to conduct an analysis as if public and private represented clear-cut alternatives. As well as overlaps of value and administration there are overlaps in the social functions performed by different sorts of schools.

The category of elite schools has a social significance far in excess of its share of the market. Used sociologically the term 'socially elite' school refers to those which recruit mainly from upper social strata, socializing their students for roles in the ruling class. Rarely are such schools found in the public sector although there is some overlap here with the small number of 'academically elite' public schools which tend to recruit from across the social spectrum (although generally above average), and which help upwardly mobile students into positions of power and prestige. Nevertheless elite private schools are the foremost launching pad into universities and professional occupations as may be seen in the school backgrounds of those in the population with a degree (see Figure 11.1). Over the years the rate of higher-education graduation from former private-school students has been three times that of public, with Catholic in between. In recent years, despite university expansion, private has diverged further from Catholic and public.

Schools of subcultural maintenance serve a very different social function. Their purpose is to ensure the survival, from one generation to the next, of the cultures of a particular religion or ethnic group. Although public schools are not precluded from teaching subcultural values, as is illustrated by the strenuous efforts to develop a multicultural curriculum, religious and ethnic authorities are inclined to view separate schools as a necessary condition for their culture's survival. In a famous phrase a Catholic archbishop called his schools 'the antechamber of the Church'.

A third category, viewed sociologically, are community schools or schools of social cohesion. These of course are nearly always public schools although they need not be. And, from a perspective within the Catholic Church, parochial schools are community schools.

Performance of a Dual System

With that background, plus the help of a little systems theory, we can now set about examining the Australian system as a process that is in a relatively

Figure 11.1:   School Background of Graduates

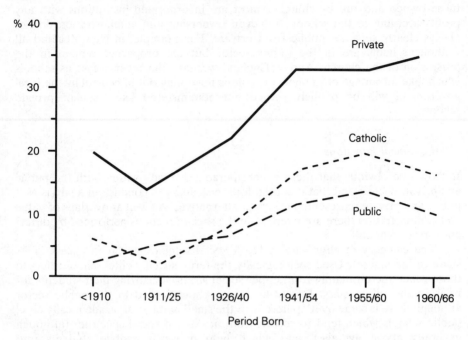

Period Born

advanced state of privatization. Our particular focus will be on the impact of a private option, which may be purchased at subsidized rates on quality in the public sector and overall.

Events in 1990 in Australia's newest and smallest education system illustrate the divisiveness of a dual system and the constraints which it imposes on planning. Hit with a major budgetary crisis the local government decided that significant economies must be made in the school sector and proposed to close or amalgamate one-quarter of all public schools. The public-school community was of course outraged at the threat to its community schools. Nevertheless the government was reluctant to reduce its capital or recurrent contributions to the private sector, judging, perhaps, that the voter backlash from that particular one-third of the citizens of Canberra would be even greater than from the public two-thirds. Catholic and yuppie are a potent political alliance.

Nor was there any suggestion from the government that Catholic schools, or other private schools, should be consolidated or closed. This is despite the fact that many were much smaller than the lower limit set for public schools. And the substantial bus subsidy so that children may travel out of their local area to private schools was regarded by the government as sacrosanct because that is essential to freedom of choice.

This particular donnybrook could be resolved, perhaps by bludgeoning the public schools parents into submission, perhaps by a change of government. The story is important, however, because it is an example of just one battle in a war that will continue until Australia's public-school systems — of extraordinarily high quality in the case of Canberra — either become residual institutions for

Figure 11.2: Public and Private Schools as a System

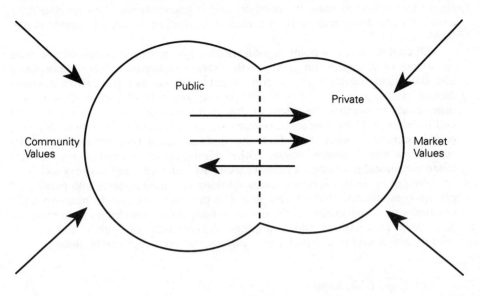

special education and welfare parents, or public and private are redesigned into some form of integrated system. At the present time the former outcome looks to be the more likely.

Public and Private as Interacting Systems

Why is the former balance unlikely to be restored? Systems theory provides a useful framework for evaluating the effect of forces from the political environment, which impinge differentially on public and private schools. Originally developed in the physical and biological sciences the ideas of equilibrium, resistance to change, and interactions between component parts have been extended to social institutions considered as dynamic systems (Emery, 1969).

Public and private schools can be thought of as two parts or subsystems of the total school system of a society (See Figure 11.2). There is a dynamic relationship between the two parts, and, as in all systems, alterations to the state of one part induces changes to the state of the remainder. Furthermore the boundary separating the two parts of this school system is permeable and actual transfers may occur across it. In the following section our particular interest is in these transfers. Before considering these, however, it is necessary to extend the theory of 'schools as a system' to include the political environment in which it exists.

Changes in its environment will cause a system to change. In a physical system alterations to temperature or pressure will lead to adjustments so as to restore equilibrium. In a biological system there may be changes in the nutrients causing an internal adaptation before homeostasis is restored. An important principle of equilibrium is that when a change is imposed on a system that is in balance, the system will adjust so as to counteract the effect of that change and return to a balanced state. In chemistry this is known as the 'Le Chatelier principle'. To top-down reformers in a human institution it may be known as pigheadedness!

Of course there is a point beyond which a system becomes unstable because the extent of change is too great for the system to accommodate. Atmospheric and ecological scientists are at present debating whether the earth's environmental system can adapt to changes in the amounts of carbon dioxide and other gases, or whether the extent of change will introduce a period of instability and turbulence. In biology some systems are symbiotic, the transactions between each component being such that the mutual advantages outweigh the disadvantages and harmony reigns. Other biological or ecological systems are inherently unstable as when a parasite feeds off and eventually destroys its host.

We can apply this sort of systems-thinking to school systems with public and private components. Our interest is in the pressures brought to bear from the environment; in particular in the different obligations, regulatory requirements, and value expectations which impinge differentially on public and private schools, which lead to unequal transactions across their common boundary.

Legal Obligations

Most countries have laws like Australia's free, compulsory, and secular legislation which require that government authorities establish and maintain an education system for all comers. Laws also oblige parents to see that their children are educated, usually in approved schools. Implicit in these arrangements is the right of every child to schooling. Indeed the right to education is regarded so highly that it is embodied in the United Nations Declaration of Human Rights. The public sector is thus characterized by a set of complementary but unequal obligations. On the one hand public schools are obliged to accept all applicants in their community whatever their ability, motivation, special needs or parents' circumstances. On the other hand parents are obliged to have their children educated, but not necessarily in the public sector. And there we have the first hint of possible instability.

Private schools are under no obligation to take any particular student. They may take all who come and pay the fees, or they may discriminate: for example according to religion, reputation, scholastic performance, athletic ability or even because father is an 'old boy'. They may expel students whom they deem to be unsatisfactory.

Intervention in the Curriculum

Governments have direct access to public-school management, but not to private. The most recent and pervasive use of public schools as an instrument of policy in Australia has been to defer the entry of teenagers to the labour market by parking them at school. A spectacular turn-around has been achieved in less than a decade: In the 1970s it was the exception to remain at school to year 12, now over two-thirds do. The majority of these often reluctant stayers are in public secondary schools where they cause enormous strains and provide yet another incentive for the conventionally ambitious parent to exit.

Schools may be used by the authorities for an economic strategy requiring particular work skills or motivation, as a means for inculcating patriotic values, or as instruments for promoting social order. In almost every case it is the public-school system, rather than the private, which governments use for these purposes, directing schools where authority is centralized, exhorting them where authority is devolved.

Even when governments bear most of the cost as in Australia, they appear loath to direct or even admonish private schools as they do public. Campaigns for better driving, or drug avoidance, or literacy, or citizenship, or national-achievement testing are targetted at the public sector. So are ideas for a national curriculum. In fact centrally designed curriculum can be of a very high quality. Unfortunately, however, intervention in curriculum by the state is often crude and offensive to some; when a church or school of privilege constructs the curriculum according to its world view that is acceptable to their clients.

Governance and Accountability

Public schools are governed, regulated and held accountable as part of the democratic political process. This may be via a minister of an elected government, who has ultimate authority even though he may delegate to regional and local officers; or it may be through a locally elected authority. In either case schools are evaluated by bureaucratic mechanisms — inspector's reports and the like — or, less frequently, by the performance of their pupils on tests or examinations. Whatever the mechanism the democratic process is remote and messages from the clients of one particular school are of little account unless the professionals in that school are listening. The idea of a market — clients evaluating schools according to their performance and sending poor performers to the wall — plays only a small part in the governance of public education.

Private schools are often governed by boards of directors, or, in the case of Catholic and other religious systems, by the church authorities. Generally the headmaster or headmistress (the terms are preferred to principal which is used in the public sector) has considerable authority over school policy. Democratic principles may operate if there is an elected governing board of client representatives but this model is not common. The market operates to the extent that parents may respond to a school's perceived reputation for efficiency, stern discipline or academic results; it is more common however for a school to be chosen because of congruence of religion or social class.

Social Values

The public school as an institution represents a valuing of social equality and justice, and of community and social cohesion. Many parents choose public schools for their children because of these values. Students from families of diverse beliefs and social origins constitute a valued part of the curriculum. Lyndsay Connors, chair of the federal government's Schools Council, argued that a loss of community representativeness threatens the core of public schooling.

'Public' refers to the people as a whole. There is something unsatisfactory, then, in the notion of a public-school system which serves only a minority, particularly an unrepresentative minority. One function of public schooling is to protect the coherence of society by transmitting and shaping the core of common principles which hold us together as a civilized society. Public schooling requires the support and protection of the majority to fulfil its true, democratic purposes. The irretrievable breakdown of marriage requires only one of the two partners involved to withdraw. The 'opting out' of public education by a sizeable section of the public can cause irretrievable breakdown of a public-school system. (Connors 1989, p. 5)

Elite private schools embody the values of freedom (to choose) and of the market. This does not mean that they are loath to maximize their reputations by recruiting students most likely to succeed. They can advertise for students, select those who will do well, and unload those who are troublesome. Connors observed that:

Instead of acting as the professional and academic leaders in their schools, we find school principals out touting for business, engaged in the futile exercise of competing with each other for a dwindling pool of students. (p. 10)

In the days of Commonwealth secondary scholarships (awarded to about 10 per cent of 14 year-olds after a national examination) winners were neatly tagged as bright prospects. Heads of elite private schools would invite parents of public-school winners in for a chat and perhaps a special reduction on tuition fees would be negotiated. In England the Thatcher government introduced something similar in the form of an 'assisted-places scheme' which pays for poor but able children to attend private schools (Edwards *et al.*, 1989). One effect of this is to make the not-so-poor parents of public-school children feel guilty and put aside money so their children too may have what the government obviously thinks is a superior education. In Australia the massive subsidies to private schools carry a similar implied message: If the government is willing to spend so much subsidizing fees, or busing children past the local public school to a distant private school, perhaps they too think that private is better.

Schools of subcultural maintenance represent a tolerance for and valuing of social pluralism. A society which supports its Catholic schools, or those of any other belief group, is respecting the right of parents to school their children according to their conscience, and of the group to transmit its culture to succeeding generations. There are delicate issues of social policy involved here: how much tolerance should be extended to groups whose values conflict with those of the dominant society? To take an extreme example, presumably a school for the children of a group of political dissidents with lessons on how to booby-trap cars would be refused a licence. But, to take two non-fictitious examples, what of a sect which taught that girls had inferior intellects to boys (Maslen, 1982); or a religious group that practised corporal punishment of children as an expression of its theological beliefs? The question posed by such examples is becoming more frequent in the private sectors of many countries. In Australia's subsidized system there is the further question of whether the state should fund these sorts of schools; and, if the decision is negative, what is the rationale for supporting the established religions or ethnic cultures?

An Unstable System

We can now put some more labels on the environments surrounding the public-private system portrayed in Figure 11.1. The value contrasts are fairly clear: choice versus equity, pluralism versus social cohesion, individual responsibility versus collective responsibility through the state. The private sector is regulated by the market, the public by bureaucratic and political accountability; at least that is the theory, and to some extent the practice. Governments are tempted to intervene in public education but not in private, even though they foot most of the bill.

These different value and regulatory pressures induce unequal transactions across the boundary separating public and private schools. We will examine in turn the movement of students, parents, teachers and power-brokers.

Students

The public system is obliged to take all who come, and, with rare exceptions, retain them until they wish to leave. There is no such obligation on private schools. Instances of expulsion are rare, but elite private schools skim the cream of able and conventionally motivated students from public schools. The effect on public schools is not just a decline in the average ability of the student body, but a loss of critical mass causing a qualitative change in academic environment and educational function. Bereft of their high-fliers public schools lose the contribution that these make to lifting the average performance of all students. And, as the number of highly able students declines, it becomes increasingly difficult for a school with a private competitor around the corner to resource more specialized academic studies.

Exceptions to the general drift from public schools may be found in areas where the elite tradition has less hold — for example in Canberra where there is a net shift from private schools to the superb public secondary colleges (senior high schools specially designed for adolescents in the last two secondary years).

Parents

Equally damaging to public schools is the exit of influential and articulate parents who, if they remained and gave voice to shortcomings, would be the chief agents for reform. Among the clients of private schools are most of the important decision makers and more powerful citizens, including, I suspect, increasing numbers of Labor politicians, many of whom were uncharacteristically coy when asked in pre-election surveys where they sent their own children to school. Less restrained are representatives of business and industry, who, in making the familiar criticisms of the educational standards of school-leavers, use the public-private division as a way of analysing the problem, public education being held responsible for their employees' shortcomings.

But there is more to it than objective assessment of quality; 'private school' has a credential value for students, irrespective of their attainments. A visiting American academic whose children attended an Australian high school in a provincial city wrote an account of how he found himself out of step socially with professional colleagues. He also reported a local informant as saying that employers 'hire the graduates of local private schools who had failed the higher school certificate exam in preference to graduates of even middle-class state schools who had passed' (Boyd, 1987).

Perhaps the most compelling evidence of public decline is where public-school teachers send their own children. Reflecting on the state of Victoria, where the hold of elite private schools is strongest, Harman says:

> I know of no other [public] high-school system in the world where so many of those who run the system, from senior officials to school principals and to classroom teachers, send their own children to non-government schools. It is no wonder that morale and aspirations in high schools are low. (quoted by Boyd, 1987, p. 186)

Boyd also cites a remark by Kenneth Davidson, the economics writer for one of Australia's leading newspapers *The Age*, that 'If present trends continue, the middle classes will cease to be represented in Australia's [public] secondary schools except in front of the blackboard'. (quoted by Boyd, p. 186)

The trend to private school from one generation to the next in an upwardly mobile group of professionals and their children has been plotted using a national longitudinal study (Anderson and Western, 1968). These professionals (engineers, lawyers, doctors, and teachers) were at school in the 1960s when non-Catholic schools accounted for about 4 per cent of the total; but more than one-third of the lawyers and medicos, and one-sixth of the engineers and teachers had been to such schools. In the mid-1980s they were asked what sort of school they had in mind for their children. As may be seen in Figure 11.3 there is a substantial shift from both public and Catholic to private school: school teachers are the only profession where a majority had both attended public school themselves and intended that their children would attend public. And even one-third of the teachers, nearly all of them teaching in the public sector, preferred private for their own children.

Teachers

The third unequal exchange, or rather it is a one-way migration, across the public-private boundary is of teachers themselves. Teachers are trained at public expense and cut their professional teeth in public schools. Private schools, able to negotiate individual contracts, can then recruit and offer packages without the constraint of industrial agreements. There are constraints however. Public-school

Figure 11.3: Type of School Attended by Professionals and their Children

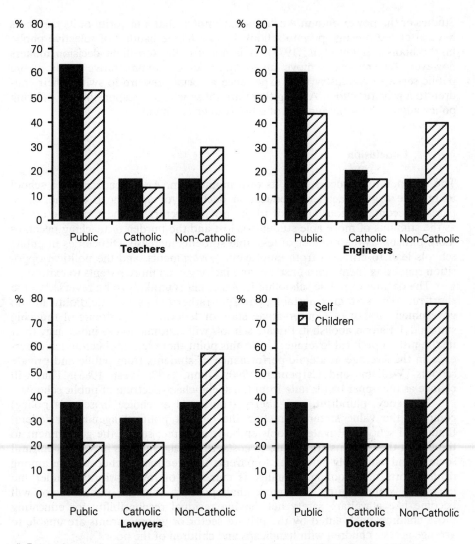

* From a longitudinal national survey commencing in the mid-1960s (See Anderson *et al.*, 1987).

systems offer a career structure and this advantage helps to retain many of the better teachers. Recently private-school teachers have become organized and even taken industrial action. In future their schools may have to offer greater career security and abide by negotiated agreements as in public schools. Public and private teacher unions have also begun to collaborate, for example in a joint approach to the industrial-relations Commission for a bench-mark salary.

Power-brokers

Studies of the power elite in Australia have noted that a majority of its members have attended prestige private schools or one of the handful of selective public high schools (Higley *et al.*, 1977). It is not just the top flight decision makers however. As employees move up to more senior administrative levels in the public service or industry they experience a social pressure to switch their children to a private school. Among them are those who are responsible for offering policy advice about the funding of schools to government.

Conclusion

The degenerative process fuels its own momentum. As the capacity of a school to provide a good academic education declines, or appears to decline, more parents become anxious and exit to the private sector. Teachers' morale erodes as the stimulus of more able students is lost and the burden of teaching becomes more difficult as the number of less able students increase. Difficulties in public schools lead to criticism from employers, governments, and the political opposition rendering them more unstable and inciting even more parents to exit.

The decline of public schooling in Australia is unlikely to be reversed in the short run. The system is unstable, parasitic rather than symbiotic. Politically no government, Labor or Conservative, state or federal, would dream of reducing state aid, let alone abolish it. Private schools will continue to use judiciously their undiminished political leverage. Up to this point there has not been much difference in the average academic performance of students from public and private schools (Williams and Carpenter, 1990; Dunn, 1982; West, 1985). That will change as the upper bands fade from the social-class spectrum of public schools.

Efficiency, pluralism, and liberty (translated as choice in schools policy) comprise the value stream directing the current political agenda for federal funding of schools. Private schools embody all three: saving the government to the extent that parents contribute to costs, reflecting interests in a multi-cultural society, and ostensibly extending to parents the freedom to choose from among diverse sorts of schooling. Equality is currently of lower priority. Under the prevailing value regime it is more than possible that the public sector will become like a welfare safety net, having residual responsibility for educating those children not wanted by the private sector or whose parents are unable to arrange access: children with handicaps and children of the poor.

Alternatively, when it becomes widely apparent that a once-strong public sector is ailing, self-correcting mechanisms may come into play. In the past there have been voices from within the private sector calling for some form of accommodation within an integrated system — a willingness to shift the value emphasis from liberty to equality. At present these voices are silent. If and when governments require private schools to be more accountable for their impact on the quality and efficiency of public schools, there may be calls from within both sectors for reforms of Australian education considered as a single system.

References

ANDERSON, D.S. (1988) 'Denomination and Type of School Attended: The Transmission of an Error', in *Journal of Australian Studies*, 22, pp. 30–9.

ANDERSON, D.S. and WESTERN, J.S. (1968) 'Notes on a Study of Professional Socialization', in *Australian and New Zealand Journal of Sociology*, 4.

BOYD, W.L. (1987) 'Balancing Public and Private Schools: The Australian Experience and American Implications', in *Educational Evaluation and Policy Analysis*, 9, 3, pp. 183–97.

CONNORS, L. (1989) 'A National Framework for Public Schooling', Address to Public Schools Night, Canberra, November.

COOKSON, P.W. Jr. and PERSELL, C.H. (1985) *Preparing for Power: America's Elite Boarding Schools*, New York, Basic Books Inc.

DUNN, T. (1982) 'Bias in HSC Examination Results', in *The Australian Journal of Education*, 26, pp. 190–203.

EDWARDS, J. and WHITTY, G. (1989) *The State and Private Education: An Evaluation of the Assisted Places Scheme*, London, The Falmer Press.

EMERY, F.E. (Ed.) (1969) *Systems Thinking*, Harmondsworth, Penguin Books Ltd.

ENCEL, S. (1970) *Equality and Authority: A Study of Class, Status and Power in Australia*, Melbourne, p. 176.

HIGLEY, J., SMART, D., PAKULSKI, J. and DEACON, D. (1977) 'The Educations of Australian Elites', in *Education Research and Perspectives*, 4, 2, pp. 52–62.

MASLEN, G. (1982) *School Ties: Private Schooling in Australia*, Sydney, Methuen.

SHERINGTON, G., PETERSEN, R.C. and BRICE, I. (1987) *Learning to Lead*, Sydney, Allen and Unwin.

UNESCO (1989) 'Development of Private Enrolment First and Second Level Education, 1975–1985', Division of Statistics on Education, Paris.

WEST, L.H.T. (1985) 'Differential Prediction of First Year University Performance for Students from Different Social Backgrounds', in *The Australian Journal of Education*, 29, pp. 175–87.

WILLIAMS, R.A. (1984) 'The Economic Determinants of Private Schooling in Australia', Department of Economics, University of Melbourne Pre-print RW-83-03.

WILLIAMS, T. and CARPENTER, P. (1990) 'Private Schooling and Public Achievement', *The Australian Journal of Education*, 34, pp. 3–24.

Chapter 12

Different Ways of Viewing School-site Councils: Whose Paradigm Is in Use Here?

H. Beare

Since the early and mid 1970s, those involved with the movement to restructure schools and school systems have had to ask how schools are to be governed, and what rationale will underlie their plans. In particular, the purpose, nature, and powers of school-site councils have featured almost universally among the agenda items for reform, especially the formal roles to be played by teachers, parents, the community, and (in the case of secondary schools) students.

This chapter considers three aspects about school-site councils. Since much of the thrust towards wider participation in the decision-making processes of schools is driven by political priorities, we need to look first at what those political imperatives are. Secondly, the vocabulary used to discuss participation in the policy arenas of schools is variously understood and therefore needs to be clarified — including terms like 'lay' and 'professional', 'involvement', 'decentralization', and 'devolution'. Finally, those involved with school-site councils bring several frames of reference to their roles which can be at times quite dissonant; we therefore consider four frameworks for thinking which are implied in the way school councils are conceived of, established, and made to operate.

The Politics of Creating School-site Councils

It sheds light on the politics of school-governance reform to consider events in Europe over recent decades. It was the *Taylor Report* (1977) in Great Britain which led to the first, recent, major reconstruction of boards of governors and boards of managers, and to an extension of their functions. Because the Taylor committee placed emphasis on creating a partnership among all those involved in the life of schools, it recommended a balance of representation in the boards' membership and deliberately avoided having voting blocs which could dominate the decision-making. Sir Keith Joseph, a Secretary of State for Education in the Thatcher government, flirted with the idea in 1984–5 of giving a voting majority to parents in the name of accountability and to force responsiveness on the teaching staff, but he was roundly criticized for the proposal, not least by the parent organizations themselves (Beare, 1985). In consequence, he withdrew the proposal in 1985. Clearly, then, there is something political, as well as educational, driving those who advocate the creation of school-site councils or their remodelling. What are likely to be the determinants of these impulses to reform, then? The European experience gives some of the clues.

Since the end to World War II, German schools, to take one example, have been required for overt political reasons to give formal powers to both parents and students. As Pritchard (1981, p. 271) puts it: 'The management of German schools is governed by an elaborate network of committees which is designed to make the system work on the lines of participatory democracy.' The scheme has an openly political purpose, for the Potsdam agreement says: 'German education shall be so controlled as completely to eliminate Nazi and militarist doctrines and to make possible the successful development of democratic ideas.' (quoted by Pritchard, op. cit.) Schools, in short, are an instrument for developing national identity and style. In an internationally competitive environment, it is unlikely that national governments will leave these matters to chance, or leave schools alone!

Nicholas Beattie has examined comparatively the 'formalized parent participation' issue in Europe which he calls 'one of the more obvious trends in western European education since the end of the Second World War' (Beattie, 1978, pp. 41–2). Indeed, he says, there has been 'remarkable unanimity' about its value, a point which aroused his scholarly curiosity. In the late 1970s, he argued that the movement appeared to grow from an underlying crisis of confidence in democratic institutions', which because of the war surfaced early in West Germany, France, and Italy but was slow to arrive in Great Britain where 'confidence in the existing political structures of British society' survived both the war and post-war periods fairly well intact. Beattie states that until the Taylor committee's report appeared in September 1977, formal parental involvement in England and Wales was almost non-existent.

An Arena for the Educated Middle Class

But education, or more precisely, being well-educated, produces its own political backlash in the form of an articulate, probing, informed middle class who make life uncomfortable for the ruling elites, be they elected or newly rich or the born-to-rule. Political dissension, then, may result from there being a significantly large proportion of well-educated, middle-class people in the community who are capable of the penetrating argumentation and lobbying on particular political issues which destabilize political boundaries, threaten the *status quo* in political parties, and produce profound insecurity in those who acquired power under the older regime. So it should not surprise us if those in power try to diminish the turbulence around them by creating formal mechanisms for participation, else where or one step removed from the main political arenas. In short, they syphon off the turbulence into village-pump politics.

The middle class are of course willing accomplices in this strategy, for it is the middle-class, educated people (and the organizations they create) who put themselves forward for election to, or as representatives on, bodies like school councils. It is in fact a constant complaint of teachers that the working class and the disadvantaged rarely serve on these committees. In one sense, then, participative decision-making is a politically diversionary tactic, a means of keeping activist people distracted by their own self-inflicted, busy work. The middle class are willing accomplices, for they think they are gaining access to the decision-making of the power structures. So Beattie argues:

> A participatory solution will be popular with individuals and groups who have lost faith in the continued appropriateness of dividing decision-making between elected representatives (whether national or local) and officials, and who see in parental participation a means of neutralizing the party-political see-saw, and establishing some sort of new 'non-political' consensus. (Beattie, 1978, p. 44)

It is clear, then, why the pressure to create participative, locally based bodies like school councils should emerge in the 1970s, for it was then two decades after the war and those who were the products both of the post-war baby boom and the enormous post-war expansion in education (secondary education for all, the democratization of access to higher education, the diversification of programs) were now *parents*, with children in primary and secondary schools.

Thus it was in the early 1970s that school councils and parent membership on them were given official sanction in Australia with the arrival of the Whitlam (Labor) government in 1972 after several decades of virtually unbroken Conservative party domination of the political arena in Australia. Indeed, the Australian Schools Commission, itself a manifestation of the same 'participatory solution', enunciated the principle of school-based decision-making in its first report (Karmel Report, 1973, ch. 2). It was during the 1970s that the Taylor committee did its influential work in the UK, leading to the rebuilding of school-site governing boards by 1980. And it was in the same decade that the US federal office attached to its categorical and school-based grants the condition that a school-site committee be set up to oversee the expenditure of the money.

It is to be expected, then, that locally based councils, including those attached to schools, would soon begin to contest the boundaries of power, and that they would soon confront the obvious tendency in those in authority of the representative body in order to produce a decision which legitimizes the wishes of the power brokers. Beattie puts it this way:

> As many educational issues can readily be defined or presented as too complex and technical for public discussion, and as the terms for public argument are usually determined either by experts or in ... party-political terms, it is also easy for governments and administrators to use parents' councils ... to legitimize their own decisions. (ibid. p. 45)

Ideas and information are the currency of commerce in these domains, of course, and they can be dangerous when in the wrong hands. Beattie observed, then, that teachers would fiercely resist parental intrusion into any jurisdiction over the curriculum and that they would try to restrict the participation of 'lay' people, including even politicians, 'to an entirely peripheral role in decisions which actually affect what children learn'. Parents would also be subject to other forms of game-playing, such as having meetings called at times inconvenient to them, or by being constricted by rules over how to get items on to the agenda. As Beattie puts it, 'leakage of information from the bureaucracy . . . is bound to occur in any participatory structure'. So parents and lay people soon discover that 'the closed professional world of education' is not based upon great erudition, noble principles, or exemplary practice as they might once have thought; 'one of the main functions of any participatory system will be to inform as many people as possible that most decisions are pragmatic and piecemeal and not determined in any simple way by large principles' (ibid.). In consequence, harmony (even if it was hoped for through participative committees) usually seems to be short-lived. Before long, the notions of consensus fade, to be replaced by hard-headed political manoeuvres; and the people who brought the participatory bodies into existence find that their creations have become trouble-some children with wills (and political agendas) of their own.

The main rationale for school-based governance during the 1970s, then, was that it empowered groups of people who were previously disenfranchised, involved the stake-holders in decisions which affected them, and sponsored equity, equality of access, social justice, and parental choice.

An Arena for the Market Economy

But in the 1980s, especially because of economic downturns and budgetary stringencies in many countries, a second persuasive rationale came into promin-ence, that of the 'market economy'. Schools should be made responsive to their client communities and held accountable for the delivery of a service which met the standards and demands of their clients. Competition for customers, the milieu of private enterprise, getting best value (the best profits, as it were) from the available resources, operational efficiency with carefully targeted objectives and measured outcomes were all market factors which school-site councils seemed designed to encourage, especially if parents and the community were given a substantial number of places on the councils and their committees.

By the 1990s, then, it was obvious that school-site councils would remain strongly in favour whether the government was conservative or left-wing. Making school governance more democratic, empowering groups which up to now have been disenfranchised, giving all classes of people access to the decision-making which in the past was confined to elites of one kind or another, and devising means whereby schools are more responsive to their clientele are likely to be priorities of left-wing, social democratic (or Labor) parties. In conse-quence, it can be predicted that Labor governments will continue to sponsor if not demand the creation of school boards.

On the other hand, conservative or right-wing governments are likely to be interested in making schools (both government and non-government) operate in an open market, surviving according to how well they satisfy their customers' wishes. Having a school board may help the particular school to achieve that market edge, but a Conservative government is more likely to leave the choice of strategies to the school in question. Thus where schools do not have in existence a body to mediate the market's views for the school, then the school may be forced to use other kinds of devices like those suggested by Toffler for the 'adaptive corporations' of the 'super-industrial' age. Toffler labels them 'early warning systems', which monitor the views of the clientele and suggest ways in which the organization should adapt to the consumer demands. He includes in the list of strategies a special committee of the governors to concern itself with corporate social responsibility; communications' councils; a 'future users' committee; a program of inviting randomly selected users to spend some hours with management; invitations to the public to telephone suggestions for improving the service; setting up a company or institutional ombudsman; creating the means of conducting referenda on major issues; or instituting an advisory board of prominent citizens (Toffler, 1985, pp. 191–204).

It seems fairly safe to conclude, then, that individual schools will be made to fend for themselves, whoever is in government, that political parties of either persuasion will not protect an individual school from a local public disenchanted by its performance. Schools — will or without councils — will be increasingly out on their own.

There is a further reason why participative machinery would be favoured in education (rather than in some other areas touched by government). It is politically prudent *not* to allow these kinds of decision-making bodies to sprout up in areas where they might damage the economy or take power away from strongly entrenched, commercial interests. So the new participative bodies tend to appear in the social welfare areas — health, education, welfare — where they will cause least damage. Beattie predicted in 1978 with wry accuracy that the Taylor Report recommendations about parent participation in the governance of education would be accepted in Great Britain, whereas the 1976 Bullock Report recommendations about worker participation in management decisions in industry would not (ibid. p. 44).

Expert Committees for Contentious Issues

A standard strategy used in political contexts to remove a contentious issue from the public agenda is to make it esoteric, to define it as 'professional', in other words to technicize it, and thereby to hide it within a closed or secret guild of *cognoscenti*. Iannaccone (1978) described this phenomenon as an 'adequate illusion'. Where an issue contains fundamentally irreconcilable challenges to the core values of society, the issue is potentially destructive to the cohesion of that society. Such issues tend to be made apolitical, he argued, or depoliticized by being defined as 'technical' and by being handed over to a body which will take the issues out of the domain of public discussion, or at least will remove the issue from the immediate environment of people like the minister. He quoted Schattschneider (1960, p. 76): 'Some controversies must be subordinated by both parties because neither side could survive the ensuing struggles.'

Not surprisingly, then, issues like public funding for private schools, which Anderson discusses in his chapter, were given in Australia to expert bodies like the Commonwealth Schools Commission and the Victorian State Board of Education. And school boards were expected to resolve, to soften or to help reconcile the growing demands both of teachers for more voice in their career decisions and of an articulate, better-educated parent group for schools more responsive to their expectations. Of course, once economic survival and especially national well-being are threatened, education has the habit of jumping out of its black box and becoming once again a topic for the public agenda. This is exactly what happened with the spate of 'expert committee' reports in the US in the early 1980s, and with the interventions of the national government through Education Minister John Dawkins in Australia in the late 1980s. It may be expedient to let others share power when the stakes are not high, but in tough times it becomes obvious again that the central controllers never really felt safe to relinquish their reserve powers.

The Literal Costs of Participation

Those with any experience of participatory management realize that it does not necessarily contribute to better decisions or to more efficient management. The Harvard urbanologist James Q. Wilson observed in the late 1960s when the strategy was beginning to be used in several new settings:

> the great theoretical importance attached to group decision-making, participative management, and power equalization in organizations ... stands in rather sharp contrast to the meagre empirically verified results of the application of such theories. Strauss (1963) and Bennis (1963), summarizing the literature on this approach, conclude that it is by no means clear how likely or under what circumstances participation will improve worker satisfaction, increase productivity, or stimulate organization innovation . . . . Shepard's evaluation of his work with the Esso Company suggests that the laboratory experience was 'slightly more helpful than useless' in changing the organization (Bennis 1963). The experiment of Morse and Reimer (1956) was one of the few done in an organization rather than in the laboratory. While the group of clerical employees subjected to participatory supervision seemed to manifest more worker satisfaction the group exposed to hierarchical supervision was the more productive. (Wilson, 1973, p. 45)

Participation may therefore simply lead to inefficiency and lower productivity. Among other things, committees are costly to service, they can waste members' time (an important consideration for public members for whom time means money), they can delay important decisions unnecessarily, and they sometimes make management lumbering and convoluted. At a time when economy, efficiency, and productivity are crucial to survival, society can literally not afford to keep ineffective committees in existence.

The second half of the 1980s therefore saw committees, commissions, and participatory machinery abolished, others remodelled (and particularly scaled down in size), and others changed in nature. Thus the Thatcher government abolished the large, unwieldy Schools Council, the New Zealand government got rid of its regional boards, and the Australian government — and a Labor administration at that! — closed down its Schools Commission and Tertiary Education Commission. Indeed, small committees with clearly defined powers, tight procedures, often with a limited life, and more closely accountable to central government have developed and there are fewer of them.

The Counterbalance of Increasing Centralization

The movement towards self-managed schools — towards decentralization and devolution — has been counterbalanced by a simultaneous and apparently contradictory movement of controls away from local or existing school systems towards higher levels of government — towards centralization, in fact. In the UK this has meant a more aggressive role for Westminster, a weakening of the power of local authorities and especially their ability to raise revenue locally, and in some cases (as with the Inner London Education Authority and some metropolitan systems) their wholesale abolition. In Australia it has seen the increasing intervention in education by the national government across the whole spectrum, child care (or pre-school) to higher education. The New Zealand regional boards were abolished following the Picot report, and there was a twin dispersion — a reworking of the powers of local schools each with its own charter and board of trustees, and the strengthening of the Wellington department as a national policy-making, policy-policing and quality-control unit.

The United States also saw a swing away from local autonomy. It occurred in California after Proposition 13 was put before the Californian state legislature in the late 1970s, moving the centre of gravity from locally elected school boards (which govern systems, not individual schools as in the UK, New Zealand, and Australia) and towards increased state controls. As another example, in 1982 the Texas legislature mandated extensive change by declaring that the State Board of Education is the 'primary policy-making body for public education and directs the public school system' (quoted in Killian, 1984, p. 193). It spelt out a state-wide curriculum, how many minutes per week were to be spent on each subject area, and a system of promotion based on 'mastery of the essential elements of the curriculum'. It codified attendance requirements, the provision of after-school tutoring programs, class sizes, and so on. In general, throughout the 1980s the state governors in the US began to show much greater interest in educational affairs.

Lawton (in Chapter 6) has alluded to the same tendency in Canada to travel in opposite directions at the same time — towards decentralization and centralization. Lawton attributes the paradox to a distrust by the central government of the intermediate (school-district) level. The same dilemma is discussed by Slater in Chapter 10.

In summary then, the creation of school boards and the way they function were bound to lay bare the conflicts which exist within any political entity. Indeed, the boards are themselves both a manifestation and an outcome of the new political sophistication, which emerged in the 1970s and the 1980s. School boards therefore have a political legitimacy which justifies their existence; and it is safer to have them than not to have them. But they need to be recognized for what they are, and they must be dealt with, serviced, advised, and participated in with shrewdness, sagacity, and political acumen, not with naivety. To use Hoyle's term, they are 'micropolitical' in nature.

The Need for Clarity over Terms

If our discussion so far has done nothing else, it should have made obvious the need for clarity about what school boards are and what they are expected to do, specially about the terms used to describe them. This definition is more than a scholar's infatuation, for terminology, like all metaphors, reveals what models of reality the chief actors are carrying in their heads. Indeed, some of the terms which appear to be used interchangeably are not synonyms but rather polar opposites. Consider the following.

Involvement and Participation

In the early 1970s, parents' organizations throughout Australia were lobbying strongly for representation in the formal decision-making of schools and school systems, using the terms 'community involvement' and 'parent participation' almost interchangeably. But the terms have important differences. 'Involvement' comes from the Latin *involvere* meaning 'to roll into', and so by extension 'to envelop, wrap up in, to surround or infold'. The implication in the word is that the person 'involved' is co-opted, brought into the act by another party. On the other hand, 'participation' is from a double-barrelled word meaning 'to have a part in' or 'to take part in'. Competitors in a race are participants; they are integral to the race; in a sense they *are* the race. Thus a participant has a right to be included, whereas someone who is involved is there by invitation. One of our bush balladists described a polo match like this:

> The game was so terrific
> That e'er half the game was done
> A spectator's leg was broken
> Just from merely looking on!

It was a case of a spectator, someone not integral to the game, becoming involved with the real participants.

The fundamental question to be asked about school governance, then, is whether the community, parents, teachers, and students are included in the decision-making process by invitation because it is convenient or useful to have them there, or whether they are there by right, so much part of the action that it is impossible to exclude them. Are they participants or merely involved? The administrative structures and processes will be different according to how that question is answered. Parents' organizations have always claimed that they are participants, whereas teachers' unions would feel more comfortable if parents were merely involved.

School and Home

One of the strongest reasons for building a partnership between school and home came from those studies in the late 1960s and early 1970s which showed how powerfully home background determined school achievement. Indeed, the research findings at the time were so devastating that many educators were unwilling to accept them. The most impressive was the American study headed by Coleman in the mid 1960s, which concluded:

Taking all these results together, one implication stands above all: That schools bring little influence to bear upon a child's achievement that is independent of his [*sic*] background and general social context. (Coleman, 1966, p. 325)

The follow-up study by Christopher Jencks reaffirmed the same result; it argued that:

the school is a much smaller part of a child's total education than most teachers and parents have assumed. The child's home and community, his [*sic*] total environment, loom larger than does the school. What the child brings to school is more important than what happens in the classroom in determining the kind of person he will become. (Kerensky, 1975, p. 44)

In consequence, it made good sense to build a coalition between the two most important educative factors in a child's life. The 1970s and 1980s saw a constructive search for models of education and of school governance which organically integrated the school and the child's home. This search implied more than merely placing parents on school governing boards. It was an attempt to get the school out of its symbolic isolation and back into the community. Sometimes this meant a physical as well as a metaphorical change of location.

Participation in Schooling: Participation in School Governance

But participating in school governance is different from participation in the education of one's own child, or of other people's children for that matter. It is quite possible for a person to take part in an educational program and yet not to participate in the governing of the school. Nor does 'parent participation' necessarily imply that a parent representative must sit on the school's governing board. Quite precisely, every parent participates in the education of his or her children, and nothing in school administration will alter that fact. But whereas changes in the administrative arrangements or in the governing machinery can and do influence the quality of the parent's contribution to the education of his or her children, putting parents on school boards is participating in school *governance*, and is one step removed from participating in the education of particular children.

Deliberative or Advisory

There can be enormous advantages to an organization if it has regular and systematic advice from its clientele. In fact, schools have for years had parents and citizens associations and parent-teacher associations which provide advice to teachers from parents. A deliberative committee, however, is much more powerful than an advisory one, for it has the legal authority to make decisions which others are bound in law to comply with. When school boards and councils were given these kinds of deliberative powers, the context changed, producing heated negotiation over the range of functions to be given to those bodies. Teachers, quite correctly, perceived that the council does not have real power unless there is some legal or quasi-legal document on which its authority depends. So school governing bodies were not seen as credible until legislation was passed formally empowering them to act. Once that legal power had been ceded, the teaching staff in particular were no longer in a position to choose what decisions of the board they would follow and what ones they would not. A deliberative body is like that; it has power to require compliance — although, in the case of schools, teachers still have the option of industrial action open to them. So a board has the potential to sour relationships and goodwill as well as to build them.

Representative or Nominated

A representative or delegate (the two terms are usually taken as synonymous) is required to present the view of the electorate which put him or her there. A representative may express a private opinion but he or she does not have discretion to let that private view intrude in formal voting. In essence, then, a representative body must be parliamentary in its nature, with each delegate exercising the right to speak and vote in conformity with his or her electorate. As such, the decision-making can be time-consuming, for a representative must be given the opportunity to go back to his or her electorate for instruction on how to vote.

Not surprisingly, then, a kind of school board was favoured in the 1970s and 1980s where the members were nominated (named) by an electorate, rather than made its formal representatives. Thus each member was expected to act as an individual and to vote according to his or her own inclinations, thereby making possible consensus decisions, discussion freed from prefabricated thinking, and (above all) speed. There were several instances in Australia in the 1970s and 1980s were a minister asked teacher unions for two or three nominees (from which he would choose one) and was presented with one name of a person whom the union wanted to make a *de facto* representative. Decision-making in a parliamentary or representative assembly (as distinct from a nominated body) is done by counting heads, and regardless of the merit of the debates within the committee, the voting is really determined by caucusing outside the committee.

Lay and Professional

At least from the late 1950s there grew up a fairly strong, united view that teaching deserved recognition as a profession. Education also acquired some of the formal characteristics of professionalism. In Australia, for example, pre-service teacher education was lengthened to at least three years, entry to training was raised to matriculation level, the single-purpose teachers colleges became multipurpose colleges of advanced education, the tertiary-level qualifications of Diploma of Teaching and Bachelor of Education were established for teachers, paraprofessional assistance was introduced, and so on.

There are good reasons why a facility responsible for delivering a professional service ought to be autonomous in some important respects. Firstly, a competent professional is in the best situation to diagnose the client's exact needs, and to prescribe what the client should have to satisfy those needs. That kind of decision ought not to be in the hands of someone remote from that particular client. Further, the professional has a direct public and private responsibility to the persons who pay for the service. The professional knows that he or she must stand or fall on an ability to deliver the quality of service which the client expects, and is willing to pay for. So a locally autonomous service enhances that professionalism.

Thus professionalism furnishes reasons why the teaching staff of a school need to exercise decision-making powers over the curriculum. During the 1970s there was strong advocacy among educators for school-based curriculum development, a term which did not imply that the teachers at each schools must literally write their own curricula (although many did, and still do); what they demanded was the power to choose which curricula were suitable for which students.

This issue of a locally decided-upon professional service raises a matter of critical importance, which was often overlooked in the 1970s and which became a source of concern in the 1980s, namely, the issue of accountability. In most locally based, autonomous clinics, the client who buys the professional service has the power to withdraw if the service is not to his or her satisfaction; and the professional requires it to be that way. The customer chooses, and the customer pays. The professional who deserves confidence survives; the one who does not satisfy does not survive. To be precise, teachers, if they are to be viewed as professional, need a local body like the school council to voice the users' concerns.

In addition, since a public agency draws its funds from the public purse, the government becomes the trustee and has an obligation to institute some accountability mechanism to ensure that the functions entrusted to it are discharged. The accountability device usually takes the form of a public or community body charged to act on behalf of the government and to be answerable to it. This is the reason why any public agency which delivers a professional service (like hospitals, community welfare agencies, and schools) usually operates under a board dominated by lay or community representatives, so that the public can be satisfied the professional services for which they are indirectly paying represent good value for money, and that the deliverers of those services are publicly accountable. And that is the way a profession would want it to be.

Not surprisingly, then, school councils provided a useful mechanism whereby the school's professional staff are held accountable for their policies and curriculum offerings. If a school staff wishes to introduce a policy, the first group whom they need to convince (apart from their working peers) are the members of the council. Take what guise it will, then, the school council provides a legal vehicle for accountability. It is interesting to note that the trend to set up school boards and councils or to change their powers coincided with the trends towards teacher professionalization and school-based curriculum development.

Decentralization and Devolution

One of the arguments for school-site councils is that they incorporate decentralization and devolution; but they are troublesome words. 'Devolution' (from the same origins as 'involve') means 'to roll down from'. It is the more technical word of the two, since with bureaucracies it has come to mean a formal handing over of power from a superior office to one lower down in the hierarchy. It implies that the power can be resumed again and that the law which placed the power in the superior officer has not been changed. Devolution is usually by regulation, by internal but official transmission of authority. The problem with the term is its implicit centralist and hierarchical assumptions. Devolution could not be conceived of except in a bureaucracy with its tiers of authority, its status hierarchy, its rules and regulations. Perhaps the converse of devolution is revolution!

Decentralization has the same problem. It means dissipating from the centre, presumably to a periphery. Again the term implies that the power to decentralize or recentralize resides at the centre, and that what happens at the periphery is of lesser importance or status than what occurs at the centre. Indeed, the term — and the thinking which usually goes with it — conveys the impression that policy can be determined at the centre and implemented at the periphery. This is of course a faulty concept, for any deliberative body, wherever located, sets policy. Policy is the decision made by whatever is defined in that arena as the 'polity', the citizenry of that small 'city-state' (or *polis*).

Were one to acknowledge all the nuances of these terms in setting up school-governing bodies, then, those councils could well take different shapes from those now in existence. But even if all these terms were clearly understood by all the participants, if each term carried a consistent meaning, there would still be conflict on school boards; we would simply have ensured that the rules of the political game would be more evenly applied. Indeed, what also emerges from these terms is that there are several models possible for school governance, and that these differences of perceived purpose and style could cause operational difficulties. What sorts of ideas *do* people have about the reasons for school boards?

A School Board Is a School Board Is a School Board

It should now be obvious from this discussion that different people could easily attribute to school boards different purposes and modes of governance, different ways of conceiving of the board. Nor is it likely that there is one best model to be universally applied, one model that will suit every circumstance. But to minimize conflict and political discord it would be wise at least to make explicit what model is being used in what particular circumstance and then to be consistent in the way one deals with it. Let us now consider four fairly conventional models; the set is not intended to be exhaustive, although it seems to include the most common versions (see Table 12.1).

Model 1: The Company of Learners

Firstly, the school can be thought of as a company of learners. If it is literally so, then those who want to learn (or their authorized agents) literally control and own the school.

Table 12.1: Conceptions of School-site Councils

If the school is conceived of as:	The council's membership will:		The council will be under the control of:	The council will:	Its resources will be derived from:
1. A company of learners	Have a voting majority of lay persons ...	Representative of the learners	Lay members (the learners who hire the teachers)	Be autonomous, since it controls the company	Client fees or member contribution
2. A professional corporation	Have a voting majority of teachers ...	Representative of the professional staff	Professionals (teachers), who own the company and provide a service for a fee	Be autonomous, since it controls the company	Client fees for services given
3. A public service	Be a board of trustees ...	Having 'personal' membership by reason of their public standing and trust	The philanthropic trust (which may be the government) providing the resources	Have powers developed from, and be advisory to, the trust providing the resources	The trust sponsoring the public service
4. A community owned enterprise	Be a 'Parliament' ...	Representative of the electorates making up the community	Lay members representing the community	Be autonomous, but answerable to the community	Voted by the community from its 'taxes'

This is the governance model which pertained in the oldest universities in the world and which is implicit now in many private schools. The model originates where a group of students — or people who want to be instructed, or who want their children to be instructed — constitute themselves as a corporate group and then hire professors or teachers to instruct them. Since it is a community of learners who hire their instructors, the governing body for such a company may be a kind of Greek assembly of the whole (as the University Convocation was originally), although it is more likely that the learners would set up an elected body to represent the interests of the whole.

In this situation, those who are learners or who pay money into the company or who have money paid in on their behalf would be eligible to sit on the governing board. The instructors, as employees, would usually not sit on the board (since that could represent a conflict of interest), or if they did they would certainly not be in a voting majority. However, it seems likely that such a board would appoint someone skilled in administering and in educating (who may or may not be a teacher) both to advise the governors and to manage the enterprise.

In this model the governing board is a lay body, with the instructors employees of that board. The management team, acting on behalf of the governing body, would have delegated power (of hiring and firing, of directing and financing) over the instructors. It also seems likely that the instructors themselves would form their own teams, management arrangements, and committee structures, to ensure that they can discharge their instructional tasks adequately. The corporation could thereby have a bicameral administration.

It is clear that many parents associated with schools hold to this model of school governance. It is the model which seems to prevail in many private schools, but it is also implicit in much of the rhetoric of the parent bodies associated with public education.

Model 2: The Company of Teachers

Secondly, the school can be conceived of as a group of teachers who have come together to 'sell' their skill and knowledge to the public. This second model has also pertained in some of the world's oldest universities. In this case, the company is a community of scholars and they control, indeed own, the organization. In this governance model the scholars themselves may meet as an assembly (it is called such in some universities) or as an academic board; or there may be a smaller body (or bodies) set up to manage the company's business.

The company would need someone to lead its executive and to handle its management. He or she could be a head teacher, someone elected or appointed to lead the instructional team, a kind of *primus inter pares*. There could also be some kind of internal hierarchy or set of offices whereby to regulate the activities of the body corporate. The company itself could hire or set up managers or administrators to run the company's business while the instructors themselves carry on with the enterprise's main task of teaching. The important point about the model is that the management is beholden to the instructors, and a board of scholars or teachers is the supreme council. It would not contain lay or managerial members except in a minor or advisory capacity. In such a model it may be convenient or prudent to set up advisory councils of the users, or of the community at large, but these bodies would not govern, outvote or outrank the bodies containing the instructors themselves.

This might be considered the classic professional model, which assumes that only the scholar-instructors themselves comprehend well enough the body of knowledge and skills being taught to know how to govern the enterprise. This is the model of school governance which many teachers and teacher unions appear to carry in their heads. Those states, provinces, or countries where no school boards or councils exist have effectively opted for this model: The school is run by teachers from resources voted to it by legislatures or raised by some other activity.

Model 3: The Board of Trustees

A third way is to conceive of the school as a charitable or philanthropic agency provided to give a needed service to the community. This model assumes that there is some altruistic body (it may be private donors or it may be the government) which has donated resources in trust for the purpose of providing education.

The organization is therefore run by a board of trustees who understand the intentions of the donors, who are trusted by the donors, and who administer the funds in conformity with the philanthropist's stated purposes. In this context, then, the purposes of the school would be defined in some legal way for the trustees; indeed, the Education Act, its regulations, and the papers of transmission of authority have usually done this where the government is the supplier of resources.

The trustees of the company are likely to be persons who are well-reputed, respected in the community, 'people who can be trusted'. It is likely that they will be nominated rather than elected, chosen by the donors for their personal standing and integrity as citizens. It is possible, too, that some of them could be instructors, either from the school or elsewhere, just as it is possible that some could be from among the parents and the learners. But they are appointed because of their personal status, because they command the confidence of the donors of the resources. In short, the board of trustees is not a representative body.

The model does not dictate the way the school is internally organized and run; the board would need to satisfy itself that the school is fulfilling the purposes for which it was set up. Just as in the first model, though, it seems likely that the instructors themselves would form their own academic councils and working parties, that there would be a head teacher or chief executive among them, and that the trustees will also be concerned that there are suitable management arrangements. But the trustees ultimately operate on behalf of the donors and in them resides from the donors the ultimate responsibility for the well-being of the school.

This is the model which appeared to operate in Great Britain before the Taylor report, and which explains why the terms 'board of governors' and 'board of managers' were in use. It is also the model implicit in many statements made about school boards in Australia by politicians and business people, and in public commentaries.

A problem in this model is the degree to which the board of trustees have power to take independent action. It was mainly this question which caused much of the early uneasiness with the Australian Capital Territory Schools Authority, whose members assumed they had more power than the minister seemed willing to grant them and especially in the period when the national minister (to which the authority was answerable) and the authority's chairperson were members of opposing political parties.

The 'board of trustees' model is strongly implicit in systems which have operated as centralized bureaucracies. In these contexts, the school and any governing body set up within the system are considered to be units within a larger corporation which holds centrally the ultimate power of sanction. Degrees of local self-determination can be accommodated within the 'board of trustees' model. Indeed, of the four models, this is the one which most easily fits the fairly simple notions of decentralization and devolution.

Model 4: The Parliamentary Body

A fourth model is to see the school as belonging to its local community; in fact, many parents and members of the public in particular seem to act as though the community owns the school, even when it does not necessarily pay much towards its recurrent and capital budget. The school itself can also be conceived of as some kind of city-state consisting of several definable electorates. Thus the teachers constitute one electorate, the parents another, the local community another, the government another, and even the larger school system as another. On the other hand, the electorates may be purely political, as is the case with local authorities in the United Kingdom and with school boards in the United States.

This *polis* or city-state, for its good governance, needs a representative assembly, a Parliament to which members are elected from each of the defined electorates. In this context, then, the governing board is clearly a representative, not a nominated, body and its members are chosen and must vote as delegates. In consequence, the governing body acts like a miniature legislature and probably needs the panoply of institutional supports which keep a Parliament effective — such as subsidiary officers, formal debating and legislative procedures, and a research staff to provide it with policy documentation of one kind or another. Such a Parliament derives its power from some kind of constitution, which may (and usually is) decided upon in another place, such as in a state law. In such a local Parliament a conventional political environment would be expected, with decisions made as the result of coalitions of interests.

The resources for such a Parliament could come from several sources, of course, and obtaining the desired level of those resources would be handled in the way any Parliament does, by negotiation, lobbying, politicking. Then allocation of the budget among competing priorities would involve a typical parliamentary political process.

Which Model to Favour?

Each of these four models has an internal logic of its own, and constitutes the role of teachers, parents, students, and the government in quite different ways:

sometimes as participants, sometimes as the involved; sometimes as representatives, sometimes as holding personal membership; sometimes as controllers, sometimes as paid providers, or helpers; sometimes as employers, sometimes as the employed. Much of the conflict, apprehensiveness or unease about school-governing boards derives from the fact that in some critical areas the models are incompatible with each other. So problems are sure to arise when contestants on any one policy issue judge the context from quite different conceptual frameworks. At the least, what model is in operation in any one context should be defined explicitly. All four models could operate for government as well as non-government schools.

Conclusion

In this chapter, I have argued that school-site councils are micropolitical contexts, and that they have been brought into existence as much by political imperatives as by educational ones. In consequence, it is prudent to be clear what is meant by the terminology used to describe these councils and their work. Above all, there are several ways of explaining what the board or council is, and one needs to be aware that turbulence will result from the fact that each has its own internal logic, but constitute the organizational world in quite different frameworks. It would reduce unnecessary tensions if the model in operation were chosen deliberately and then made explicit.

Such a deliberate choice is important, for as schools are restructured, they will need to be capable of acting quickly as independent entities. Alvin Toffler (1985) has argued in *The Adaptive Corporation* that the organizational structures which served well from 1955 to 1970 are no longer appropriate for the fluid environment of the future, which he describes as 'unstable, accelerative, and revolutionary. Instead of constructing permanent edifices', he argues, 'today's executives may have to de-construct their companies to maximize manoeuvreability. They must be experts not in bureaucracy but in the coordination of adhocracy' (Toffler, 1985, pp. 1–2). In that kind of world, school administrators, no less than managers in any other field, will need to know exactly what authority and legislative powers they have at their school's disposal, and what the political environment will permit them to do.

Note

This chapter is derived from Beare, H. (1988) 'Conflicts in School Governance', in Randell, S. (Ed.) *Turbulence and Change in the Administrator's World*, Armidale, New South Wales, Department of Administrative and Higher Education Studies, University of New England, and is used have with permission.

References

Act Schools Authority (Interim) (1974–5) 'Guidelines for school education', in Lovegrove, T. and Tronc, K. (Eds) *Open education and the secondary school: A book of readings*, Adelaide, Education Department of South Australia.

BEARE, H. (1984) 'Community/parent involvement and participation in education', *The educational magazine*, 1, 2.

BEARE, H. (1985) 'Parents on school councils and the principle of partnership', *The educational magazine*, 42, 3.

BEATTIE, N. (1978) 'Formalized parental participation in education: A comparative perspective (France, German Federal Republic, England and Wales)', *Comparative education* 14, 1, March.

BEATTIE, N. (1985) *Professional parents*, London, The Falmer Press.

COLEMAN, J.S. *et al.* (1966) *Equality of educational opportunity*, Washington, DC, US Department of Health, Education and Welfare.

DAVIS, J. (1987) 'The control of education', in ANDERSON, J. (Ed.) *Shaping education*, Carlton, Australian College of Education, 1987.

ERIC CLEARINGHOUSE ON EDUCATIONAL MANAGEMENT (1977) *Participative decision-making*, Research Action Brief 2, Eugene, Oregon.

IANNACCONE, L. (1978) 'Measurement in education for the 1980s: a politics of education', Unpublished paper, University of California at Santa Barbara.

KARMEL, P.H. (1973) *Schools in Australia*, Report of the Interim Committee for the Australian Schools Commission (Chair: P.H. Karmel), Canberra, AGPS.

KERENSKY, V.M. (1975) 'The educative community', *National elementary principal*, 54, 3, January–February.

KILLIAN, M.G. (1984) 'Local control — the vanishing myth in Texas', *Phi Delta Kappan*, 66, 3, November.

MORRIS, J.E. (1971) 'Accountability: watchword for the 70s', *The clearing house* 45, 6, February.

PRITCHARD, R.M.O. (1981) 'Pupil and parent representation in Ireland and Germany', *Comparative education*, 17, 3.

SALLIS, J. (1988) *Schools, Parents and Governors: A New Approach to Accountability*, London, Routledge.

SCHATTSCHNEIDER, E.E. (1960) *The semisovereign people*, New York, Holt, Rinehart and Winston.

TAYLOR, T. (1977) *A new partnership for our schools*, Report of the Committee of Enquiry into the Management and Government of Schools (Chair: T. Taylor), London, HMSO.

TOFFLER, A. (1985) *The Adaptive Corporation*, London, Pan Books.

WILSON, J.Q. (1973) 'Innovation in organization: notes towards a theory', in ROWE, L.A. and BOISE, W.B. (Eds) (1973) *Organizational and managerial innovation: A reader*, Pacific Palisades, California, Goodyear.

Chapter 13

A Framework for Allocating Authority in a System of Schools

A.D. Swanson

Many western nations are experiencing harsh, internal criticisms of their educational systems. Responding to that criticism, governments, educators, and policy analysts are carefully (but perhaps not systematically) evaluating existing practice and structures against desired outcomes. The purpose of this chapter is to develop a basis for analysing and evaluating formal governing structures for education and strategies for allocating ultimate authority over decisions about education. It is assumed that current 'convoluted and fragmented' efforts (Hancock, Kirst, and Grossman, 1983) can only aggravate the situation and that no less than a total assessment and redesign of the control and operational structures of education can produce the kind of services required for a new era.

This chapter provides a framework for conceptualizing the allocation of authority for making decisions about education among interested parties. The framework augments Easton's simplified model of a political system with a decision matrix which arrays types of decisions (who gets what, when, and how) with decision makers (society/government, the teaching profession, and the family). The conceptualization is useful in highlighting relationships between characteristics of governance framework for allocating authority structures, the nature of decisions made, and the likely success in implementing decisions made through alternative structures under varying value priorities. Events in the United States, England and Australia are discussed within the context of the model. Twelve propositions derived from the discussion are presented which need to be studied over the next several years.

Background Ideas

The forces leading to educational reform reflect worldwide changes in social, economic, political, and technological relationships. These have been dubbed by Toffler (1980) as 'the third wave', by Naisbitt (1982), and by Naisbitt and Aburdene (1990) as 'megatrends'. Others have referred to their amalgam as both 'the post-industrial society'. and 'the information society'. Whatever it is called, the present age is considerably different from that which preceded it. The magnitude of the shift has been likened to that from feudalism to capitalism or from an agriculturally based economy to industrialization. All social institutions are being called upon to make appropriate adjustments; educational institutions are not being exempted.

Industrialization brought with it a high degree of centralization and bureaucratization. Marion Joseph Levy (1966, p. 55), in his epic study of *Modernization and the Structure of Societies*, concluded that, 'the degree of centralization always increases with modernization ... and continues to increase with further modernization.' Levy also directly links the level of modernization with the level of bureaucratization and increases in the importance of government as the main focus of that centralization. Levy recognized certain dangers in centralization and bureaucratization when he admonished those who believe in democracy and the sacredness of the individual to organize bureaucracies so that impersonality, which is one of bureaucracy's special virtues, does not result in undesired consequences.

Levy noted further that less coordination and control than the minimum needed to provide social stability is neither feasible for, nor popular among, modern societies. On the other hand, he raised the question of how much coordination and control there can be without overloading the cognitive capacities of the individuals who must plan and direct operations, or without the structures becoming so brittle that any small change within the society will fracture the whole system.

In trying to apply Levy's ideas to the contemporary context, one cannot help wondering if technological and sociological developments have negated the relationships between centralization and modernization, or if our bureaucracies have exceeded their capacity for coordination and control (Murphy, 1983). The answer to both questions is probably yes.

One of the characteristics of the information society is a trend toward decentralization. Naisbitt (1982, p. 98) observes that, 'The growth of decentralization parallels the decline of industry ... Agricultural and information societies are decentralized societies.'

Toffler (1980) identified six guiding principles of both the capitalist and socialist wings of industrial society: standardization, specialization, synchronization, concentration, maximization, and centralization.

> These principles in turn, each reinforcing the other, led relentlessly to the rise of bureaucracy. They produced some of the biggest, most rigid, most powerful bureaucratic organizations the world had ever seen, leaving the individual to wander in a Kafka-like world of looming mega-organizations ... Today, every one of these fundamental principles is under attack by forces of the Third Wave [the information society]. (Toffler, 1980, pp. 59–60)

Peters and Waterman (1982), in studying what they considered to be America's best-run companies, noted that widely held ideas about efficiency and economies of scale have led to the building of big bureaucracies which cannot act. They argue that conventional estimates of scale economies vastly underestimate transaction costs, i.e., the cost of communication, coordination, and deciding. Their 'excellent companies', however, recognize that beyond a surprisingly small size, diseconomies of scale seem to set in with vengeance. These companies have found numerous ways to break things up in order to make their organizations fluid and to put the right resources against problems. They call the process 'chunking'. Peters (1988) questions if 'big' has ever been more efficient or innovative.

Turning to education specifically, structuring the decision-making process is particularly complex because education is both a public and a private good. Procuring educational services incurs costs and produces benefits which accrue to individuals independently (producers and consumers alike), and at the same time incurs social costs and produces benefits which accrue to society collectively. Downs (1957, p. 282) identifies government as that agency in the division of labour which has as its proper function the maximization of social welfare. When results generated by free markets are ethically or economically unsatisfactory, government can be used as a tool of intervention to set things right. Levin (1987) comments:

> Public education stands at the intersection of two legitimate rights: the right of a democratic society to assure its reproduction and continuous democratic functioning through providing a common set of values and knowledge and the right of families to decide the ways in which their children will be molded and the types of influences to which their children will be exposed. To the degree that families have different political, social, and religious beliefs and values, there may be a basic incompatibility between their private concerns and the public functions of schooling. (Levin, 1987, p. 629)

Levin concludes, 'That Schools are expected to provide both public and private benefits raises a potential dilemma.'

Thus, in decisions about education, natural tensions exist between individuals, members of the teaching profession, and society. To the extent that decisions are made in the private sector, individuals can maximize their personal aspirations within the limits of their economic resources and according to individual value preferences. Professionals are free to provide or withhold services and to determine the nature of those services. But when decisions are made through the political process, individuals and groups of varying value orientations must negotiate a single solution and their value preferences may be compromised in the process.

In Chapter 2, Guthrie and Koppich identify and define three strongly preferred values in most cultures that significantly influence public policy: equality, efficiency, and liberty. Because of the conceptual inconsistencies among these objects of policy, it is not possible to emphasize all at the same time in public policy, or in individual lives, as desirable as each may be. Priorities must be established among them by individuals and by society. This is a dynamic process in that priorities of individuals change with circumstances and when there has been a sufficient shift among individuals, shifts in public priorities follow (Ravitch, 1985, chap. 5). Agreement upon priorities is not necessary for private or market-sector decisions beyond the aggregation of the family. In the public sector, however, a singular decision is required involving negotiation and compromise among interested partisans, generating significant social stress in the process. The higher the level of aggregation, the more difficult agreement becomes because of the greater amount of heterogeneity introduced (Friedman, 1962).

With respect to education, driven by a priority concern for equity, the trend over the past several decades has been toward centralizing decisions at the state and federal levels. The current level of criticism of public education suggests that we may have passed the optimal point of centralization; at the very least, the possibility should be studied. Some decisions may be made best by central authorities, but others may best be left to those with professional expertise at the school level or to those having a personal stake in the happiness and welfare of a specific child, the family. There is growing evidence that this is the case (Chubb and Moe, 1985; Coleman and Hoffer, 1987; Coons and Sugarman, 1978; Cremin, 1976; Elmore and McLaughlin, 1988; McNeil, 1986; Wise, 1979, 1988).

A Framework for Allocating Authority in a System of Schools

The pattern of allocation of authority for making policy decisions among interested parties appears to shape the nature of the decisions made and the effectiveness with which they are implemented. Determining a satisfactory pattern is a continuing problem changing along with priorities placed on fundamental social values.

Figure 13.1 depicts the policy-making process based on Easton's (1965) simplified model of a political system. The political-economic system is shown as a decision matrix whose vertical dimension represents types of issues needing to be addressed by the system and whose horizontal dimension represents potential decision makers, i.e., families (or individuals), the teaching profession, and society (through government).

The five types of educational policy issues included in the matrix are:

1 Setting goals and objectives for the educational enterprise;
2 Allocating resources to and among educational services;
3 Determining the means by which educational services are provided;
4 Determining for whom educational services are provided;
5 Determining the level of investment in population quality to promote economic growth.

These issues are an elaboration of what Guthrie and Koppich referred to in Chapter 2 as 'who gets what, when, and under what circumstances'.

The potential concern of each set of decision makers extends to each of the issues although the actual level of interest and expertise will vary from issue to issue. Societal concerns become paramount over those issues in education where there is significant spillover of benefits and where there are redistributive and intergenerational considerations. The teaching profession holds the technical expertise of schooling. Parents are the guardians of interests and needs of individual children. The family holds the most intimate knowledge about, and caring concern for, a child. It is through the family that a child's voice is heard (Bridge, 1976; Coons and Sugarman, 1978).

'Demand' inputs to the policy-making process include values and goals (liberty, equality, and efficiency), existing knowledge, and requirements for a qualified workforce. The latter requirement is, at the same time, a 'support' input in that trained personnel are required to implement any policies which are made,

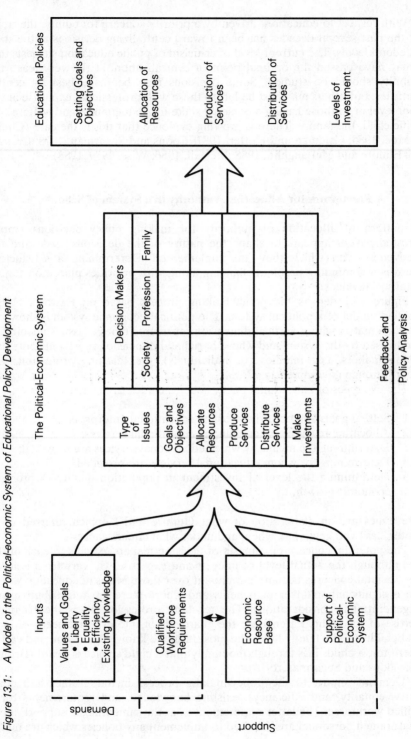

Figure 13.1: A Model of the Political-economic System of Educational Policy Development

and indeed, the qualifications of available labour will strongly influence which policy alternatives are feasible and which are not. Other supportive inputs are the economic base from which resources must be drawn to finance implementation and the behaviour of citizens in general which sustain the political-economic system through obeying laws, paying taxes, and accepting outcomes of elections. The outputs of the process are educational policies, categorized in the figure according to the five types of issues which must be addressed. The policies are derived through aggregative processes involving society collectively, the profession, and the family.

Within any given context, significantly different patterns of allocation of authority can be structured depending upon the relative priorities given to policy objectives (Kirst, 1988). The extreme centralization of authority is characterized by making all decisions collectively and administering them through public institutions. This approximates the current arrangement in the United States, tempered modestly by placing the locus of decision-making at the state level (rather than federal), devolving some authority to school districts, and permitting unsubsidized private schools to function. This arrangement allows the family to make only one basic decision: whether to participate in 'free' public schools or to opt for private schools and substantial tuition fees. If the decision is to go with public schools, there is a related family decision which can be made by those who can afford it, the purchase of a home or renting of an apartment in a school district of choice. Centralization of authority has been motivated largely to promote equality, but judging from the flood of national criticism, liberty and efficiency have suffered.

The extreme decentralization of authority is characterized by having no public schools and no subsidies, leaving the production and distribution of educational services entirely to market mechanisms. This position enhances efficiency and some definitions of liberty, but has substantial negative effects on equality. Equality concerns could be accommodated by maintaining public financing through a regulated voucher system, leaving the production of services to the private and/or public sectors (Center for the Study of Public Policy, 1970; Wise and Darling-Hammond, 1984). To meet societal concerns fully, some curricular regulations would be needed also.

To promote liberty and efficiency while retaining considerable control over equality, some districts have moved toward open enrolment and magnet-school policies (Raywid, 1985). Raising student academic standards and standards for entering the teaching profession, improving working conditions, providing differentiated career ladders, school-site decision-making, and teacher empowerment have all been proposed in the interest of improving efficiency. Some of these proposed reforms would further centralize authority, strengthening the influence of society, while others would decentralize authority, strengthening the influence of the profession and families.

McGinn and Street (1986) characterize centralization and decentralization as a dyad:

> Decentralization is not primarily an issue of control by government of individual citizens. Instead it is a question of the distribution of power among various groups in society. A highly participatory society — one in which all citizens actually do participate — is likely to require a

competent and powerful state that actively and continuously seeks to redistribute power among groups and individuals in the society. The location of authority in local government does not protect the local citizen from tyranny, and the redistribution of power through the market mechanism in a society that currently is highly inequitable is a guarantee that inequities will persist and worsen. On the other hand, competition and markets can contribute to social justice in circumstances where there is a relatively equitable balance of powers among the participants in the competition or market ... A strong state must first achieve some minimal degree of social equity so that decentralization can lead to genuine participation. (McGinn and Street, 1986, pp. 489–90)

Whether authority over education is to be centralized or decentralized is not the issue. Centralization and decentralization of authority are means toward desired ends, not ends in themselves (Hanson, 1986). Using the framework presented in Figure 13.1 as a basis for analysis, the following section examines the historical development of educational governance in the United States and the current situations in England and Australia.

Discussion of the Framework

The United States

During the industrial age, the organization of schooling in the United States followed the same centralizing tendencies as did industry and other services of government. Schooling is now facing a restructuring similar to other institutions to make it compatible with the conditions of an information society. The common-school concept emerged when the United States was still primarily in an agrarian age. The common school was 'public', but the formal governance structure was similar to the town meeting and the communities served were typically very small. Even in the few small cities of that period, school governance was at the ward level. School consolidation started in those cities with the establishment of the city school district. From there the school district grew along with the city and the bureaucracy which managed it. Then centralization of rural schools began. Tyack (1974) reports it this way:

This movement to take control of the rural common school away from the local community and to turn it over to the professionals was part of a more general organizational revolution in American education in which laymen lost much of their direct control over the schools. In the cities schoolmen pioneered new bureaucratic patterns of educational organization. They sought to 'free education from politics'. (Tyack, 1974, p. 25)

Using Figure 13.1 as a point of reference, control lay largely in the hands of families through the town-meeting format at the origin of public education in the United States. The teaching profession was weak and the larger society as represented by the state was relatively inactive other than to provide enabling legislation. The principles of liberty and equality of educational opportunity within the community (among socio-economic classes but not races) were dominant. Efficiency was not yet a concern of the schools.

With the growing sophistication of the teaching profession, especially its administrators, professional control and bureaucratization took over — a shift of authority to the left in Figure 13.1 (Callahan, 1962). States became more involved by enacting compulsory attendance laws, setting certain basic standards as for teacher certification, consolidating rural schools, and providing some financing including equalization aid. The federal government entered the scene by providing aid for vocational education. Liberty was less a concern than before; efficiency considerations came into play for the first time; and equality concerns began to take on a statewide dimension.

Following World War II there was a rapid expansion of suburbs and suburban school districts. Municipalities and school districts became quite homogeneous in socio-economic status and ethnicity with the white middle class being concentrated in the suburbs. A decline in the quality of educational services provided in urban centres followed. During the 1950s and through the 1970s, civil rights suits were successfully pursued in federal courts to correct the inequities which resulted (Levin, 1987). Litigation was followed by state and federal legislation which had the effect of making specific court decisions universal. Local decisions about the nature and distribution of educational services were constrained by national and state guidelines and mandates concerning pupil assignment, employment, discipline, and curriculum.

Also in the 1970s, society's influence was enlarged with respect to the allocation of resources, again through litigation followed by legislation (Berne and Stiefel, 1983; Guthrie *et al.*, 1988, chap. 8). States increased their participation in financing school operations, school buildings, and transportation. The federal role in school finance became a significant factor for the first time, coming in the form of categorical aid (Chapter 1) and bilingual education grants, and focused on poor or handicapped children within urban centres. State-education departments grew in size and influence. Student achievement declined, and along with it the credibility of the teaching profession. The principle of equality was the dominant concern during this period and was defined in racial and ethnic as well as socio-economic terms. Liberty and efficiency suffered as the constraints placed on local-school districts by state and federal governments grew. The dominant decision makers had become the state and federal governments representing society in the figure (Guthrie, 1980; Ravitch, 1983).

Deterioration in the quality of student achievement during the 1970s became a national concern early in the 1980s with the publication of numerous reports on the state of education. The current educational-reform movement followed. To arrest the decline in standards most states intervened with mandated curricula, competency examinations for both students and teachers, and stiffer requirements for teacher certification and student diplomas. This initial phase of the reform movement severely constrained what remained of the discretionary authority of educational officials at the school-district level creating for many individuals and communities a substantial mismatch between aspirations for schools and the reality of those schools. The locus of authority had completed its movement from the family and the profession to society.

But legislating higher standards did not necessarily produce higher standards (Iannaccone, 1985) and state governors, among others, were quick to notice. From the mid-1960s through the early 1980s efficiency and equality had been pursued through centralized authority. Policy implementation studies of that period (Chubb and Moe, 1985; Coleman and Hoffer, 1987; Coons and Sugarman, 1978; Elmore and McLaughlin, 1988; Farrar, DeSanctis, and Cohen, 1980; McNeil, 1986; Wise, 1979, 1988) showed that federal and state governments are particularly effective in dealing with issues of equality and access; but such governments appear to be less effective in dealing with matters of efficiency and 'production', i.e., how a school is organized and operated. Learning from experience, there is a renewed appreciation of the concept of liberty in the United States and a tendency to pursue efficiency through decentralized authority and equity through centralized authority.

Liberty and efficiency are back as policy concerns (Iannaccone, 1985). School-based decision-making and family choice of schooling represent important tactics in an overall strategy of decentralization. These tactics return some decision-making authority to parents and teachers in order to induce market-like forces into the public-school sector for the purpose of increasing the efficiency of that sector. There is a strong desire to retain equality as a guiding principle, but considerable doubt as to the probability of doing so in the presence of the current priority given to liberty and efficiency.

England

England offers a particularly interesting case. Centralization and decentralization forces are at work simultaneously. England has had traditionally one of the world's most decentralized educational systems. Its Department of Education and Science (1978) described the system as a national system, locally administered. While there are Local Education Authorities (LEAs) which, with the national government, set financial constraints, most pedagogical decisions, including curriculum, were made at the school-building level with the headmaster or headmistress being the key decision maker. This led to markedly dissimilar educational programs even within the same LEA.

In the 1987 general election all of the major political parties advocated a national curriculum for schools. The Thatcher government moved decisively in that direction by legislating The Education Reform Act (1988). The Act provided for a nationally mandated core curriculum and the preparation of study guides for each core subject which define minimum content and competencies. A national system of assessment is being established to measure pupil performance in core subjects at ages 7, 11, 14 and 16.

While the Act expanded the national government's authority over curriculum, it left to schools complete discretion over the implementation of the curriculum and for determining offerings beyond the core. In other areas, the scope of schools' authority, through their boards of governors, was increased by granting boards control over admissions, budget allocations, and appointment and dismissal of teaching and non-teaching staffs. Schools are funded by a direct appropriation from their LEAs through pupil-driven formulas. These funds can be dispersed by school-building authorities as they feel appropriate to implement their program philosophy, stripping LEAs of their former allocative powers. This funding scheme, coupled with parental choice of schooling, generated market-like incentives for schools. Fewer pupils served means less money for a school; more pupils served means more money. Under this arrangement schools can become financially as well as educationally bankrupt.

LEAs have been the big losers in the power shuffle. They had previously been able to establish enrolment ceilings for schools and to control budget allocations. Another reduction of their former powers was the granting to schools with more than 300 registered pupils the authority to withdraw from the LEA to which they belong and to apply directly to the national government for financial maintenance grants.

In studying the implications of these reforms, Thomas and Ranson (1988) observe:

> The Education Reform Bill is a centerpiece in the constituting of a new moral and political order of individual rights and private choice, where the public accountability of government is to the private individual as consumer not citizen ... The idea that general well-being of society is best served when private individuals are allowed to pursue their self-interest leads to a rejection of any kind of organic theory of the state which superimposes higher values on those individuals ... The model of humanity upon which rests the postulate of self-interest ignores the moral issues which necessarily arise from the context of people as social animals. As a result, the analysis fails to take account of the contribution of social decisions to efficiency and welfare. (Thomas and Ranson, 1988, pp. 16–19)

Supporters of the new policy argue that the 'higher values' of the state will be superimposed on individuals through mandating a core curriculum and providing relative uniformity in financial-support levels. Such a position views the Act as a compromise permitting the exercise of both social and individual interests (Morris, 1986).

In reference to Figure 13.1, society in England strengthened its control over the setting of goals and objectives through mandating a core curriculum, the allocation of resources in terms of expenditure per pupil, and the production of services in terms of prescribing and monitoring the core curriculum. On the other hand, the family voice in decisions about the distribution of services (the selection of schools) was enhanced, indirectly strengthening its influence on all other decisions. The profession, while losing much discretion over curriculum, still maintained strong influence over the implementation of the curriculum. In other respects, the influence of professionals was strengthened by shifting to the school-level decisions about allocation of resources to the instructional process.

Australia

Similar tensions were experienced by several Australian states and territories in the 1980s. Traditionally, Australian schools have been operated as highly centralized state systems (Butts, 1955; Hancock, Kirst and Grossmam, 1983;

Partridge, 1968). There were no local education authorities, and teachers and administrators were selected, employed, and assigned by the respective state bureaucracies. The curriculum was also prescribed by the states.

In the 1960s, public funding was extended to private schools, primarily to save the Roman Catholic schools from collapse at a time when public schools were finding it difficult to accommodate their own burgeoning rolls. The intent was equalitarian: to upgrade the quality of education in the underfinanced private sector (Hogan, 1984). For the most part, Roman Catholic parochial schools serve a non-elitist working-class constituency while Protestant and independent schools cater for business and professional classes. Today, the publicly subsidized private schools provide an alternative to the public schools. Overall, about a third of all school-aged children attend private schools. The proportion is over half at the upper-secondary grades. Private schools, regardless of affiliation, now provide the standard of excellence (Boyd, 1987).

In essence, Australia has two publicly financed systems of education: one highly centralized, the other highly decentralized. Ironically, non-government schools (the decentralized system) have come to serve as models for the reform of government schools (the centralized system). Reformers charge that extreme centralization has resulted in government schools which are impersonal, uncaring, and institutional in character. They claim that teachers and principals in government schools identify with 'the teaching service' (the state bureaus for employing teachers) rather than with the schools and communities to which they are assigned. Transfers have been frequent with assignment based on formula and longevity, not on local conditions or merit (Swanson, 1986).

In reference to Figure 13.1, state governments (society) make decisions for public schools concerning the setting of goals and objectives, allocation of resources and production of services. For private schools, state governments strongly influence the amount spent per pupil (except for the elite private schools), but the way the money is spent is determined by school trustees in consultation with their professional employees. Decisions about production of services are left largely to the discretion of those employees within constraints of the school's goals and objectives, which are set by the school's trustees and the school budget. The family has choice of a public school (in some places, public schools) and of many private schools, most of which charge low tuition making them affordable to most families.

During the 1980s, many government and educational leaders worked to improve the efficiency of state schools by redefining the bureaucratic incentives which govern them. Progress in this direction occurred in Victoria (Chapman and Boyd, 1986; Frazer, Dunstan and Creed, 1985; Harman, 1987; Victorian Ministry of Education, 1986), South Australia (Jones, 1970), Western Australia (Western Australia Ministry of Education, 1987; Australian Capital Territory (Schools Authority, 1986; Hughes and Mulford, 1978). The goal was to improve the efficiency of public schools by implanting in them an incentive structure similar to that governing private schools, while protecting the public interest in equality of educational opportunities. To do this, the reformers sought to move to the schools much of the authority vested in state ministries of education, including power over the budget, curriculum, and personnel.

These reforms were initiated by Labour governments in Australia in contrast to a Conservative government in England. The Australian proposals went beyond the English proposals for devolution by also placing major responsibility for curriculum development with the schools (Australian Capital Territory Schools Authority, 1985; Commonwealth Schools Commission, 1985). But, not unexpectedly, the opposition was very strong in Australia, especially from bureaucrats unwilling to share their power and from teachers' unions who found it strategically preferable to bargain with one agency rather than with hundreds (Baron, 1981; Blackmore and Spaull, 1987).

Summary and Conclusion

The issue of allocating authority to make decisions about education is not solely a matter of centralization or decentralization. Nor is it solely a matter of state power, teacher power, or people power. There are legitimate concerns about education at all levels of the socio-political hierarchy; the critical issue is achieving the best balance among legitimate interests. The best balance will vary from society to society and over time within a society as contexts, value definitions, and priorities change (Wirt, 1986). The framework for allocating authority in a system of schools presented in Figure 13.1 provides a useful lens through which to observe and evaluate events within a society and across societies.

In this section, the experiences of the United States, England, and Australia are discussed in juxtaposition according to the elements and relationships suggested by the model. The section concludes with the presentation of twelve propositions derived from the discussion which need to be studied over the next few years.

The United States developed a highly decentralized system of public schooling a century and a half ago to further the objectives of equality in a sparsely populated agrarian society. As the nation grew in population, industrialized, and urbanized, a relatively equitable rural system evolved into a highly inequitable and divisive urban system. Efforts to restore equality brought oppressiveness, impersonality, and inefficiency. The rising demands for high levels of human competence in the workforce and the increasing competitiveness of international markets have raised concern over the ability of the American school system to educate the nation's youth to a level sufficient to enable them to meet the challenges.

In many respects, Australia and the United States are moving in opposite directions (Murphy, 1983); but, having started at opposite ends of the spectrum, they are moving toward each other (Hughes, 1987). In the search for equality and efficiency, Australia developed a highly centralized system of public schooling. Also in the name of equality, Australia extended extensive financial assistance to mostly underfinanced private schools, a move which had the unintended consequence of enhancing aspects of liberty. While the government and non-elite private schools now operate at about the same expenditure levels per pupil in Australia, the non-government schools are setting the standards of excellence and efficiency. In seeking to bring efficiency to government schools, some states have moved to trim down the central educational bureaucracies and to divest authority to schools. To restore some of the social control over equality lost in the public financing of private schools, there is a movement toward greater public regulation of private schools. Public schools are becoming more like private schools and private schools are becoming more like public schools.

The pattern in England is the clearest, perhaps because it is a single system, though highly devolved. The reallocation of power is apparent. As McGinn and Street (1986) suggest, it is not government versus citizens but a redressing of the balance of power among government and citizens to improve efficiency and liberty. The pattern struck by the English Education Reform Act could well be a prototype of the educational structure toward which Australia and the United States are groping. The Committee for Economic Development (1985), for example, has recommended that each state in the United States promulgate a core curriculum. Doyle (1988) predicted that the United States will back into a national curriculum.

A primary area of research and scholarship during the decade of the 1990s needs to be the relationships between educational governance structures, the nature of policy decisions generated, and the effectiveness of their implementation within the context of fundamental value preferences. In the analysis of the situations in England, Australia, and the United States with the aid of the framework presented in Figure 13.1, a number of propositions are suggested for investigation.

1   The optimal provision of educational services for a society requires the *distribution* of authority among government, teaching profession, and families;

2   Consensus on what is an optimal provision of educational services is dynamic, shifting over time in response to changes in social, economic, political, and ideological contexts;

3   The family holds the most intimate knowledge about and caring concern for the child and is the preferred spokesperson for the welfare of the child;

4   Societal concerns are paramount where there are significant spillover benefits from education and where there are redistributive and inter-generational considerations;

5   The teaching profession holds the technical expertise of schooling and is most qualified to make decisions concerning the organization and administration of educational services;

6   Centralization of authority over education-policy decisions reduces the realization of individual interests, increases social stress and makes decision-making and implementation more difficult.

7   Decentralization of authority over education policy increases inequity in the allocation of human and economic resources to the provision of educational services;

8   Decentralization of authority over education policy increases heterogeneity and reduces social integration;

9   Policies promoting equality have their greatest impact when made at a high level of social aggregation;

10 The policy objective of equality requires the involvement of government in decisions related to the allocation of resources and curriculum definition;

11 The policy objectives of liberty and efficiency can best be realized through market mechanisms;

12 Realization of the policy objective of efficiency requires that the teaching profession play a dominant role in making decisions about how educational services will be produced.

A better understanding of the accuracy and implications of the propositions is essential to the development of informed policy with respect to education. Careful analysis and evaluation of the many 'natural experiments' which have taken place and will take place constitute an important part of the research. Since most developed western nations face similar social and economic pressures, yet hold differing policy priorities, important insights into relationships between governance structures and policy outputs should be gained through cross-country comparisons. Educational researchers should also continue to be alert to, and guided by, the experiences of other information-age organizations in the public and private sectors.

This chapter has suggested reasons for the current turbulence over issues of educational governance. Agreeing on acceptable allocation patterns of authority is a dynamic process, varying over time and among cultures according to priorities given to fundamental social and personal values. A framework for allocating authority in a system of schools has been presented as a vehicle for evaluating alternative patterns. The model depicts the political-economic structure as a grid of decisions (who gets what, when, and how) and decision makers (society/government, the teaching profession, and the family). The model shifts the focus of the governance debate from a simplistic discussion of the relative virtues of centralized and decentralized power placement to the identification of the optimal distribution of authority in the provision of educational services given certain fundamental values and policy objectives. The model has been applied succinctly to the historical development of educational governance in the United States and to the current situations in England and Australia. Our analysis has suggested a number of propositions as guides to research concerning the design of formal structures for the making of decisions about education and the allocation of ultimate authority among decision makers within the structures. And for the 1990s, models like these which address the complexities of the education reform movement are likely to become more needed.

References

AUSTRALIAN CAPITAL TERRITORY SCHOOLS AUTHORITY (1985) *Choice of schools in the ACT: Parents have their say*, Canberra, Australia.

AUSTRALIAN CAPITAL TERRITORY SCHOOLS AUTHORITY (1986) *School boards: Partnership and participation*, Canberra, Australia.

BARON, G. (1981) *The politics of school government*, Oxford, England, Pergamon Press.

BERNE, R. and STIEFEL, L.L. (1983) 'Changes in school finance equity: A national perspective', *Journal of Education Finance*, 8, pp. 419–35.

BLACKMORE, J. and SPAULL, A. (1987) 'Australian teacher unionism: New directions', in BOYD, W.L and SMART, D. (Eds), *Educational Policy in Australia and America: Comparative Perspectives*, New York, The Falmer Press, pp. 195–232.

BOYD, W.L. (1987) 'Balancing public and private schools: The Australian experience and American implications', in BOYD, W.L. and SMART, D. (Eds) *Educational*

Policy in Australia and America: Comparative Perspectives, New York, The Falmer Press, pp. 163–83.

BRIDGE, R.G. (1976) 'Parent participation in school innovations', *Teachers College Record*, 77, pp. 366–84.

BUTTS, R.F. (1955) *Assumptions underlying Australian education*, Melbourne, Australia, Australian Council for Educational Research.

CALLAHAN, R.E. (1962) *Education and the cult of efficiency: A study of the social forces that have shaped the administration of the public schools*, Chicago, The University of Chicago Press.

CENTER FOR THE STUDY OF PUBLIC POLICY (1970) *Education vouchers: A report on financing elementary education by grants to parents*, Cambridge, MA.

CHAPMAN, J. and BOYD, W.L. (1986) 'Decentralization, devolution and the school principal: Australian lessons on statewide educational reform', *Educational Administration Quarterly*, 22, 4, pp. 28–58.

CHUBB, J.E. and MOE, T.M. (1985) *Politics, markets, and the organization of schools* (Project Report 85-A15), Stanford, CA, Stanford University School of Education, Institute for Research on Educational Finance and Governance.

COLEMAN, J.S. and HOFFER, T. (1987) *Public and private high schools: The impact of communities*, New York, Basic Books.

COMMITTEE FOR ECONOMIC DEVELOPMENT (1985) *Investing in our children: Business and the public schools*, New York.

COMMONWEALTH SCHOOLS COMMISSION (1985) *Choice and diversity in government schooling*, Canberra, Australia.

COONS, J.E. and SUGARMAN, S.D. (1978) *Education by choice: The case for family control*, Berkeley, CA, University of California Press.

CREMIN, L.A. (1976) *Public education*, New York, Basic Books.

DEPARTMENT OF EDUCATION AND SCIENCE (1978) *The Department of Education and Science — a brief guide*, London, HMSO.

DOWNS, A. (1957) *An economic theory of democracy*, New York, Harper and Row.

DOYLE, D.P. (1988) 'The excellence movement, academic standards, a core curriculum and choice: How do they connect?', in BOYD, W.L. and KERCHNER, C.T. (Eds) *The Politics of Excellence and Choice in Education*, New York, The Falmer Press, pp. 13–23.

EASTON, D.A. (1965) *A framework for political analysis*, Englewood Cliffs, NJ, Prentice Hall.

ELMORE, R.F. and McLAUGHLIN, M.W. (1988) *Steady work: Policy, practice, and the reform of American education*, (Report R-3574–NIE/RC), Santa Monica, CA, The Rand Corporation.

FARRAR, E., DESANCTIS, J.E. and COHEN, D.K. (1980) 'Views from below: Implementation research in education', *Teachers College Record*, Fall, pp. 77–100.

FRAZER, M., DUNSTAN, J. and CREED, P. (Eds) (1985) *Perspectives on organizational change: Lessons from education*, Melbourne, Australia, Longman.

FRIEDMAN, M. (1962) *Capitalism and Freedom*, Chicago, University of Chicago Press.

GUTHRIE, J.W. (Ed.) (1980) *School finance policies and practices: The 1980s a decade of conflict*, Cambridge, MA, Ballinger.

GUTHRIE, J.W., GARMS, W.I. and PIERCE, L.C. (1988) *School finance and education policy: Enhancing educational efficiency, equality and choice*, Englewood Cliffs, NJ, Prentice Hall.

HANCOCK, G., KIRST, M.W. and GROSSMAN, D.L. (Eds) (1983) *Contemporary issues in educational policy: Perspectives from Australia and USA*, Canberra, Australia, Australian Capital Territory Schools Authority.

HANSON, E.M. (1986) *Educational reform and administrative development: The cases of Colombia and Venezuela*, Stanford, CA, Hoover Institution Press.

HARMAN, G. (1987) 'Statewide arrangements for organizing Australian education', in BOYD, W.L. and SMART, D. (Eds) *Educational Policy in Australia and America: Comparative Perspectives*, New York, The Falmer Press, pp. 283–94.

HOGAN, M. (1984) *Public vs. private schools: funding and direction in Australia.* Ringwood, Victoria, Australia, Penguin Books.

HUGHES, P. (1987) 'Reorganization in education in a climate of changing social expectations: A commentary', in BOYD, W.L. and SMART, D. (Eds) *Educational Policy in Australia and America: Comparative Perspectives*, New York, The Falmer Press, pp. 295–309.

HUGHES, P. and MULFORD, W. (Eds) (1978) *The development of an independent education authority: Retrospect and prospect in the Australian Capital Territory*, Melbourne, Australian Council for Educational Research.

IANNACCONE, L. (1985) 'Excellence: An emergent educational issue', *Politics of Education Bulletin*, 12, pp. 1, 3–8.

JONES, A.W. (1970) *The freedom and authority memorandum*, Adelaide, Australia, Education Department of South Australia.

KIRST, M.W. (1988) 'Recent educational reform in the United States: Looking backward and forward', *Educational Administration Quarterly*, 24, pp. 319–28.

LEVIN, B. (1987) 'The courts as educational policy makers in the USA', in BOYD, W.L. and SMART, D. (Eds) *Educational Policy in Australia and America: Comparative Perspectives*, New York, The Falmer Press, pp. 100–28.

LEVIN, H.M. (1987) 'Education as a public and private good', *Journal of Policy Analysis and Management*, 6, pp. 628–41.

LEVY, M.J. (1966) *Modernization and the Structure of Societies* Princeton, NJ, Princeton University Press.

MCGINN, N. and STREET, S. (1986) 'Educational decentralization: Weak State or Strong State?' *Comparative Education Review*, 30, pp. 471–90.

NCNEIL, L.M. (1986) *Contradictions of control: School structure and school knowledge*, New York, Routledge, Chapman and Hall.

MORRIS, G. (1986) 'The county LEA', in RANSOM, S. and TOMLINSON, J. (Eds) *The changing government of education*, London, Allen and Unwin.

MURPHY, J.T. (1983) 'School administrators besieged: A look at Australian and American education', in HANCOCK, G., KIRST, W. and GROSSMAN, D.L. (Eds) *Contemporary issues in educational policy: perspectives from Australia and USA*, Canberra, Australia, Australian Capital Territory schools Authority and Curriculum Development Centre, pp. 77–96.

NAISBITT, J. (1982) *Megatrends: Ten new directions transforming our lives*, New York, Warner Books.

NAISBITT, J. and ABURDENE, P. (1990) *Megatrends, 2000: Ten new directions for the 1990s*, New York, Morrow.

PARTRIDGE, P.H. (1968) *Society, schools and progress in Australia*, Oxford, England, Pergamon Press.

PETERS, T. (1988) *Thriving on chaos: Handbook for a management revolution*, New York, Knopf.

PETERS, T.J. and WATERMAN, R.H. Jr. (1982) *In search of excellence: Lessons from America's best-run companies*, New York, Warner Books Inc.

RAVITCH, D. (1983) *The trouble crusade: American education 1945–1980*, New York, Basic Books.

RAVITCH, D. (1985) *The schools we deserve: Reflections on the educational crises of our times*, New York, Basic Books.

RAWID, M.A. (1985) 'Family choice arrangements in public schools: A review of the literature', *Review of Educational Research*, 55, pp. 435–67.

SWANSON, A.D. (1986) 'Centralization and decentralization of School governance: An American views the conflict in Australia', Unpublished manuscript, State

A.D. Swanson

University of New York at Buffalo, Department of Education Organization, Administration and Policy.

THOMAS, H. and RANSON, S. (1988) *Education reform: The national initiative in Britain*, Paper presented at the annual meeting of the American Educational Research Association, April, New Orleans, LA.

TOFFLER, A. (1980) *The third wave*, New York, Bantam Books.

TYACK, D.B. (1974) *The one best system: A history of American urban education*, Cambridge, MA, Harvard University Press.

VICTORIAN MINISTRY OF EDUCATION MINISTRY STRUCTURES TEAM (1986) *Taking the schools into the 1990s*, Melbourne, Australia, Victoria Ministry of Education.

WESTERN AUSTRALIA MINISTRY OF EDUCATION (1987) *Better schools in Western Australia: A programme for improvement*, Perth, Australia.

WIRT, F.M. (1986) *Multiple paths for understanding the role of values in state policy*, Paper presented at the Annual Meeting of the American Education Research Association, San Francisco, CA. (ERIC Document Reproduction Service ED278086).

WISE, A.E. (1979) *Legislated learning: The bureaucratization of the American classroom*, Berkeley, CA, University of California Press.

WISE, A.E. (1988) 'Two conflicting trends in school reform: Legislated learning revisited', *Phi Delta Kappan*, 69, pp. 328–32.

WISE, A.E. and DARLING-HAMMOND, L. (1984) 'Education by vouchers: Private choice and public interest', *Educational Theory*, 34, pp. 29–47.

Notes on Contributors

Don S. Anderson
Research School of Social Sciences, The Australian National University, Canberra, Australia.

Hedley Beare
Institute of Education, University of Melbourne, Australia.

Ron K. Browne
Former Secretary, Australian Education Council, Melbourne, Australia.

Brian J. Caldwell
Institute of Education, University of Melbourne, Australia.

James W. Guthrie
Graduate School of Education, University of California at Berkeley, United States of America.

Julia E. Koppich
Graduate School of Education, University of California at Berkeley, United States of America.

Stephen B. Lawton
The Ontario Institute for Studies in Education, Toronto, Canada.

William Lowe Boyd
College of Education, The Pennsylvania State University, University Park, Pennsylvania, United States of America.

R.J.S. (Mac) Macpherson
School of Teacher Education, University of Tasmania (Newnham Campus), Launceston, Tasmania, Australia.

Takeshi Sasamori
Faculty of Education, Aoyama Gakuin University, Tokyo, Japan.

Notes on Contributors

Robert O. Slater
Administrative and Foundational Services, Louisiana State University, United States of America.

Austin D. Swanson
Department of Educational Organization, Administration, and Policy, State University of New York at Buffalo, United States of America.

Hywel Thomas
School of Education, University of Birmingham, United Kingdom.

L. Warren Louden
Former Chief Executive Officer, Western Australian Ministry of Education, Perth, Australia.

Index